MICKEY COHEN

Robert Christiansen Jr.
TRUE CRIME

Mickey Cohen

THE LIFE AND CRIMES
OF L.A.'S NOTORIOUS MOBSTER

TERE TEREBA

ECW PRESS

Copyright © Tere Tereba, 2012

Published by ECW Press
2120 Queen Street East, Suite 200, Toronto, Ontario, Canada M4E 1E2
416-694-3348 / info@ecwpress.com

Library and Archives Canada Cataloguing in Publication

Tereba, Tere
Mickey Cohen : the life and crimes of L.A.'s notorious mobster / Tere Tereba.

1. Cohen, Mickey, 1914–1976. 2. Criminals—California—Los Angeles—Biography.
3. Gangsters—California—Los Angeles—Biography. 4. Organized crime—California—Los Angeles—History. 5. Hollywood (Los Angeles, Calif.)—History. I. Title.

HV6248.C64T47 2012   364.1092   C2011-906974-1

ISBN: 978-1-77041-000-8 (cloth); 978-1-77041-063-3 (paper)
also issued as:
978-1-77090-202-2 (PDF); 978-1-77090-203-9 (EPUB)

Interior design: Ingrid Paulson
Cover photos: "Mickey Cohen (leaving courtroom), 1951" and "Mickey Cohen (in handcuffs) at Federal Building, 1958," courtesy of University of Southern California, on behalf of the USC Special Collections; "blank newspaper" © spxChrome / iStockphoto
Author photo: Leonardo DeVega
Printing: Edwards Brothers Malloy   5   4   3   2   1

Printed and bound in the United States

For the incomparable Jerry Leiber

CONTENTS

Prologue: A Dangerous Place

Sherry's
9039 Sunset Boulevard
Los Angeles County, California
July 20, 1949

It was well after midnight and twenty-one-year-old Shirley Temple had just spent another late night at Sherry's, the after-hours nightspot on the Sunset Strip. When the attendant delivered her navy blue Cadillac, the beautiful former child star slipped behind the wheel and drove west on Sunset Boulevard, toward her home in Brentwood. She had driven several miles before she observed a man's fedora on the seat beside her.

"Pulling to the curb, I inspected the hat carefully, found no identification, then noticed the car upholstery was not mine," she explained. "On the floor in the back lay a long, locked, black leather case, soft to the touch but with something hard inside . . . When I returned to the nightclub, the valet tumbled over himself with gratitude. What he had delivered was Mickey Cohen's look-alike Cadillac."

Two years earlier, in 1947, Mickey Cohen had become Los Angeles's most prominent underworld figure. Standing five-foot-five in his custom-made elevator shoes, the pudgy, squat-legged former prizefighter was now as much a part of the local color as movie stars, palm trees, and smog. Having grown into a figure of immense fascination to the public, his exploits were

1

constant headline-makers. L.A.'s Capone — he seemed able to get away with murder. Many assassinations were ascribed to him, and in the past year alone, there had been multiple heavily publicized attempts on his life. Cunning, ruthless, and flamboyant, at thirty-five, Mickey Cohen was at the center of an ongoing underworld war and major political upheaval.

Police, political figures, and members of the underworld had all heard the story: Cohen was again slated for assassination. The local Mafia wanted him dead, while another rival offered an apartment house as compensation for accomplishing the deed. A cadre of rogue cops had vowed to kill him, and members of his own gang were eager to displace him. Threatening to end the careers of an array of LAPD brass and prominent officials, he was scheduled to appear before a grand jury investigating police corruption.

After dining with a lobbyist considered to be California's political kingmaker, Mickey turned up at Sherry's. It was common knowledge the no-frills, smoke-filled restaurant was his favorite last-round hangout. Resplendent in an impeccably tailored pigeon gray suit, he settled into his regular spot, booth #12. Back to the wall, he sat surrounded by members of the press. The journalists he entertained were following him, anticipating high drama. While satisfying his addiction to chocolate ice cream, Mickey held court, kibitzing with them in his unique patois of fractured grammar and four-syllable words. Florabel Muir, the veteran newswoman who had become his covert advocate, asked him if it was dangerous to be clubbing.

"Not as long as you people are around," the mobster told her. "Even a crazy man wouldn't take a chance shooting where a reporter might get hit." Knocking wood, he added, "You're too hot."

It was nearing 4 a.m. when plans for his exit began. Flanking the exit were plainclothes police, a sergeant from LAPD's Gangster Squad, and Special Agent Harry Cooper, the high-ranking state officer who, in a stunning move, had recently been assigned — by California's attorney general — as Cohen's bodyguard. Seeing the lawmen at the door, journalist Muir jokingly said to them, "What are you standing out here for? Trying to get yourself shot?"

Given an all-clear signal, Cohen and his party, accompanied by a phalanx of bodyguards from both sides of the law, moved onto the neon-lit Strip. Muir lagged behind, stopping to buy the morning edition of the

Examiner. As she picked up the paper, the journalist heard a volley, then another. Looking out the door, what she saw unfolded like a movie.

A few feet away, a screaming man and young woman lay sprawled on the sidewalk. As the fusillade continued, she watched Cohen, blood darkening the shoulder of his jacket, shout commands. Then the state officer was hit. Clutching his stomach, Special Agent Cooper was still gripping his revolver as Cohen's men struggled to pull him into a car. The wounded mob boss took charge, hoisting the hulking cop into the back seat as the big sedan roared into the night.

This was the sixth of eleven attempts on the Hollywood mobster's charmed and violent life. Nearly thirty years later, at the end of nearly sixty years of crime, Mickey Cohen would die peacefully in his sleep, outliving many formidable assassins and all his prominent enemies, as well as his legendary sponsors, Bugsy Siegel, Frank Costello, and Lucky Luciano, as the most brazen and colorful gangster of them all.

ACT I

THE
CALIFORNIA
WILDCAT

1

BOYLE HEIGHTS BOYCHIK

"If anyone called someone a kike, spic, or wop in
our neighborhood, we would beat his head in."
MICKEY COHEN

A mong waves of Jewish immigrants escaping the poverty and anti-Semitism experienced in czarist Russia, Mickey Cohen's parents, Max and Fanny, made their way to the United States in the first years of the twentieth century. Indigent, uneducated, and unable to speak the language, the couple settled into the ghetto neighborhood of Brownsville, Brooklyn.

Max Cohen "was in some kind of import business with Jewish fishes," as Mickey would later describe his father's occupation. There were already five children in the household, three older boys and two small daughters, when Meyer Harris — called Mickey — arrived on September 4, 1913. Max died two months later. His youngest child had no memory of him. Told his father had been a good provider who adapted quickly in America, Mickey Cohen later portrayed his father as a man of religion and integrity. "According to the rest of the family," he said, "he was orthodox in his faith and very orthodox in his attitude toward the sanctity of the family and home."

Left with six children, and little else, in 1915 Fanny boldly embarked to Los Angeles, America's newest city. Leaving the older children with relatives, Mickey, barely two, and Lillian, his four-year-old sister, accompanied her.

By then, Los Angeles had already tasted boom times. Founded in 1781 by Spanish missionaries, the region was controlled by Mexico beginning in 1821, until it became a territory of the United States after the Mexican-American War of 1846. Dramatic change would not happen until decades later, when in 1876 the Southern Pacific Railroad transformed the geographically isolated cow town. With the opening of the railroad, commerce began to flourish, making Los Angeles a viable destination for tourists and settlers. Then oil was discovered. With people flooding the area, real estate development and speculation took off.

Located eight miles west of downtown, Hollywood was one of scores of new hamlets that sprang up in the patchwork of empty land, orange groves, and oil and bean fields that defined the sprawling, yet sparsely populated, city of Los Angeles. Using his political clout, William H. Workman, who later became mayor of the city, proposed a development for the white-collared middle classes two miles east of downtown. After a bridge linking the area to the central city was built across the Los Angeles River, ground was broken in 1875. Situated on a bluff, with commanding views of downtown to the west, the community of Boyle Heights was born.

Boyle Heights was Fanny Cohen's destination. By the time she arrived, due to discriminatory residential laws and escalating prices in other areas, the neighborhood had devolved into the city's melting pot. Populated by immigrants, mainly Eastern European Jews and also Mexicans, Italians, Russians, Japanese, and Chinese, the narrow streets were dotted with tiny one-story houses. The run-down frame cottages were no different from those in the oldest sections of Hollywood or the shotgun shacks of Venice-at-the-Sea, the beachside village at the end of the Pacific Electric's Red Car line. But culturally Boyle Heights developed a much different tone.

Los Angeles was home to the largest Jewish population west of Chicago, and Boyle Heights had grown into a sun-drenched variation of Manhattan's Lower East Side. Yiddish was spoken in homes and on the streets, and all types of establishments catered to the needs of the residents. Brooklyn Avenue, the neighborhood's main thoroughfare, was lined with tiny shops and signage in Yiddish: religious bookstores; kosher butchers and bakeries; delicatessens and groceries stores, pickle barrels outside the doors. Observant Jews, dressed traditionally — men in long black coats, yarmulkes covering their heads, full beards, and curling sideburns — walked the heat-baked streets to the Breed Street Shul, looking as they had in centuries past. Filled with the sights, sounds, smells, and flavors of the old country, Boyle Heights was a suburban shtetl inside the boundaries of the country's fastest growing city.

The established gentry of Los Angeles were strictly WASP — and highly prejudiced — even when it came to the extraordinarily wealthy Jews of Hollywood's burgeoning movie colony. Boyle Heights was considered the city's Jewish slum.

A tiny woman who spoke little English, Fanny Cohen was accustomed to a harsh existence and adversity. She had experienced the dangerous odyssey from her native Kiev to New York, her young husband's death, and the difficult journey across America to the Pacific coast. Mickey remembered his widowed mother as a "tremendous woman." Settling into rented rooms in a two-story stucco building at 131 North Breed Street, she opened a mom-and-pop grocery. After establishing herself, she sent for her older children. Mickey's earliest memory was stacking cans in his mother's shop: "I can still remember wiping the dust from the canned goods. We always had food on the table and Ma always managed to keep us in good clothes, but it was real tough." With keen survival instincts, during Prohibition Fanny looked the other way when her older boys put a still in the small drugstore they had opened with a licensed pharmacist.

Without the influence of a father and with his hard-working mother constantly occupied, Fanny's youngest child had little supervision. Living within walking distance of the downtown business district, Bunker Hill, Chinatown, Little Italy, and Russian Hill, Mickey began exploring the streets of L.A.

Each day his brothers would drop him off at the corner of Brooklyn and Soto, at the center of Boyle Heights' block-long commercial district. Instructed not to speak, the tiny boy sat on a stack of newspapers, legs dangling. Not yet six, he hawked the Los Angeles Record. Mickey remembered himself as quiet and bashful: "My job was to sit there on the papers, and somebody would come by and take a paper and drop the money in my hand. I graduated to do business with a delicatessen man who used to trade me hot dogs for a paper. I was really looking to make a buck at a very early age."

Mickey Cohen began his formal education as a social outcast. Eleven years his senior, his brother Harry was a surrogate father and corrupting influence. He had already exposed his youngest sibling to gambling, boot-legging, and assorted chicanery by the time Mickey was enrolled at Cornwell (now Sheridan) Elementary School. Harry took the child with him on all-night gambling forays, telling him to stay in the car and sleep. He taught him how to make gin in the drugstore.

Rarely in class, Mickey described his education: "Although I entered the first grade in September 1918, my frequent absences from school caused by my desire to hustle an extra buck for my family, kept me in the first grade for a year-and-a-half. In June of 1922, I was still in B-3."

Failing to learn the basics, Mickey couldn't read, write, or count beyond five until he was nearly thirty. Like a Dickensian street urchin transported to sunlit California, when he wasn't peddling papers he hung out at the neighborhood pool hall. Racking balls for pool hustlers, he worked passing bets and bootleg liquor. Sampling tobacco and alcohol, he would never be tempted by these vices. He didn't enjoy the taste.

His first legal run-in happened at age eight. Caught by Prohibition officers at the gin mill behind his brothers' drugstore, he dropped a plate of hot food on the officers as they bent over to inspect the still. Taken to juvenile hall, he was booked for bootlegging. He would later boast his debut offense was fixed by his brother Louis's political connection.

His brother Sam was a devout Jew and the family's disciplinarian; to straighten out his troubled young sibling, Sam enrolled him in an Orthodox Jewish Hebrew school. A half-hour into his first day there, Mickey disrupted an assembly by turning the lights on and off, and he smacked another student in the mouth. The rabbi sent him home. He called the family, tell-ing them that Mickey had been expelled and could not return.

Soon thereafter he was caught with a crate of peanut candy he had stolen from a factory that was located near the family drugstore. As punish-ment, juvenile authorities sent him to Alvarado Special. The reform school was located next to a junior high, where a chain-link fence separated the school yards. There the law-abiding boys and the juvenile delinquents would face off, exchanging taunts.

Armed with a baseball bat, he was apprehended after attempting to hold up the box office of the Columbia, a downtown theater. Mickey was then sent to an even tougher reform school, located in an old redwood building atop Fort Hill, high above downtown. He would later remember the syllabus was nothing but woodshop and baseball. Severe beatings with a bicycle tire, "for any old thing," were a common practice. He spent seven months of his tenth year incarcerated there.

Mickey then began selling papers in the heart of downtown Los Angeles, where his growing capacity to fight became an asset. He later boasted, "I hung around the Newsboys Club at Spring and Court Streets and became rather adept at whipping other newsboys who challenged my rights to profitable corners." Streetwise vendors, who paid high premiums for coveted corners, began hiring Mickey Cohen as protection.

Spending day and night downtown, in the shadow of the tall buildings that lined the ten-square blocks of Los Angeles's vibrant central business district, at Seventh and Broadway, and Eighth and Hill, Mickey peddled a Hearst tabloid, the *Los Angeles Examiner*. The more sensational the headline, the better the small black-haired boy liked it. "Ex-tra, Ex-tra, Get Your Red-Hot Ex-Trah!" he'd shout. Major stories — the dramatic story surrounding the death of President Warren G. Harding, the thrilling Dempsey-Firpo fight, and the Teapot Dome scandal, which involved local oil-magnate Edward Doheny and Washington politicos — were memorable headlines. The double-extras carried premium value; guaranteed to sell out, they commanded a greater price. Mickey often slept in the men's room at the *Examiner's* headquarters, waiting for the first sheets to roll off the press.

He was allowed this privilege because of a relationship he developed with James H. Richardson, the *Examiner's* city editor. A man who would later play a key role in Mickey Cohen's life, during the 1920s Jim Richardson was in the throes of alcoholism. In exchange for the early editions, Mickey aided the newsman, sometimes helping him to sober up, sometimes delivering bootleg booze to him. It became known that little Mickey Cohen, who by then had two other Jewish kids and a Mexican boy working for him, had first access to the papers.

With a natural sense of humor and a warm and generous streak, Mickey was well liked by many in the close-knit environment of Boyle Heights. The kids in the neighborhood — Jewish, Mexican, and Italian — got along well. It wasn't until later, at the Los Angeles Coliseum and the Olympic Auditorium, that Mickey first heard racial slurs. "If anyone called someone a kike, spic, or wop in our neighborhood, we would beat his head in," he explained.

*Teenage boxer Mickey Cohen
proudly wearing, like the great
Jewish champions of the era,
blue satin trunks emblazoned
with a Star of David and his
monogram. Circa 1930.*

After his legal run-ins Mickey was put on probation. His brother Sam got him a job at a dress-manufacturing firm, Hunt, Broughton, and Hunt. Mickey's main duty was running errands for Mrs. Hunt. Mickey remembered the Hunts as kindly "elite people," who had warm feelings for him, the illiterate kid from the ghetto. Boxing referee Abe Roth, a well-regarded figure in the local sports scene, volunteered as his mentor in the Big Brother program. Lunching with him on Saturdays, Roth trained the street-brawler in the sport of boxing, giving the fatherless boy pointers on technique and introducing him to Queensberry's rules.

When he was eleven Mickey began boxing in three-round amateur fights all over L.A. He fought in Compton, Watts, and East Los Angeles. Fighting to protect downtown corners by day, he had bouts nearly every night. Losing very few matches, the boy grew confident of his boxing skills.

At thirteen, Mickey easily won the city flyweight title at the American Legion Newsboy's Championship and saw his name in print for the first time. Occasionally, the Hunts would drive him to his matches in their big Cadillac sedan. He fondly remembered them betting on him and how they showed him off. The boxers he idolized were Mushy Callahan, Bud Taylor, and Jackie Fields, Boyle Heights's 1924 Olympic gold medalist, who was born Jakob Finkelstein.

Mickey loved boxing, but he loved "hustling" more. From selling papers downtown and candy and sodas at the Olympic to scalping tickets, he hustled constantly. The hustling brought him what he wanted most: money. Penny by penny, nickel by nickel, dime by dime, dollar by dollar, money bought him things his mother could never afford. He began outfitting himself. His first purchase was a pair of socks from a department store. He treated girls to ice cream, and eventually he managed to acquire a jalopy before he was old enough to drive. Money meant everything to him: material possessions, respect, and attention. Mickey dreamed of more.

Hidden from his mother, his money, mainly dollars, was kept in a bankroll. When Mickey was twelve, Fanny accidentally found a roll of nearly two hundred dollars. Thinking he "must have robbed a bank," she called her son Sam to discipline the wayward boy. The strait-laced older sibling thrashed Mickey.

By fourteen, Mickey began taking over key corners he once protected. If the vendors didn't capitulate to his demands — and work for *him* — he would beat them. If there was a way to steal money, he was happy to do that, too.

Young Mickey Cohen's credo was simple and never changed: "Anything to make a buck."

2

SCHOOL OF HARD KNOCKS

*"He liked to dress well and would spend his last
twenty dollars on a hat."*
FIGHT MANAGER EDDIE BORDEN,
SPEAKING OF MICKEY COHEN

Now fifteen, Mickey's world began rapidly shifting. His family life
changed abruptly with his mother's remarriage. Mickey decided to
become a professional prizefighter and his brother Harry volunteered as
his manager.

On July 1, 1928, the *Los Angeles Times* ran an article on the sports page
about an upcoming professional fight at the Olympic Auditorium. Entitled
"Denver Boxer in Local Debut," the piece was about Mickey Cohen, purportedly eighteen, who had an extensive professional record. In fact, the
boxer fighting at the Coliseum *was* a seasoned young pro from Colorado,
named David Cohen, who also used the nickname Mickey. The confusion
surrounding the fight caused truant authorities to begin looking for the
underage boxer from Boyle Heights.

Perhaps as a response to the confluence of events and to join Harry
who had moved back East, Mickey packed his belongings, telling his mother
he was going to the beach. Instead, he ran away from home. He hitchhiked
and rode the rails across the country with hobos. Traveling to Pittsburgh
and Detroit, he finally joined Harry, who was living in Cleveland. While

Mickey was on his journey, the stock market crashed — driving the country into the Great Depression.

The Cleveland in which Mickey arrived was not the city we know today. Cleveland was then the nation's fifth-largest city. Located in northeastern Ohio, on the southern shore of Lake Erie, the city was a manufacturing giant. Rich, dynamic, and gray, the steel town had experienced decades of tremendous prosperity. During the 1920s, Cleveland's unique location fostered a booming parallel economy.

Prohibition was a federal law in America. Canada faced certain Prohibition bans, but the law was decided locally. Across Lake Erie, in Canada, the manufacturing and selling of alcohol for export was completely legal. The U.S.-Canadian border sliced across the middle of the long, narrow lake, and the close proximity made Cleveland a major repository of high-grade Canadian spirits. Smuggling became big business. The money and power at stake became so immense that by the late 1920s and into the early 1930s there was gang war over territory and spoils in Cleveland.

By this time four equal partners, Morris "Moe" Dalitz, Louis Rothkopf, Morris Kleinman, and Samuel Tucker, controlled the sale of illicit liquor and gambling in the region. Smooth, cunning, and flush with cash, they were well protected by local authorities and diversified in many legitimate businesses. The Italian element of what authorities referred to as "one big ring stretching from Detroit to Niagara Falls" was known as the Mayfield Road Gang, or the Hill Mob. Anthony Milano; his brother, Frank; and Alfred Polizzi led it. Over the years these mobsters would move from their Prohibition beginnings to silently become among the nation's wealthiest and most influential men. An inside look at the enormous profits the Cleveland mobsters were making during Prohibition was revealed when taxmen claimed that Morris Kleinman hadn't filed returns for 1929–30, while banking an astonishing $1,674,571.24 (more than $21 million today) in eight accounts held by his Liberty Poultry Corporation.

Cleveland's gang leaders were part of the newly organized underworld syndicate of young and forward-thinking Jews and Italians who chose cooperation over competition. The multi-ethnic assemblage, called the Combination, started with New York's Broadway Mob of Lucky Luciano, Meyer Lansky, Frank Costello, and Bugsy Siegel and expanded during the early 1930s across the country. Al Capone had a similar arrangement in

Chicago. Former NYPD organized crime specialist Ralph F. Salerno explained, "There is a happy marriage of convenience between Jewish and Italian gangsters. It [the Combination] represents the three Ms: Money, Muscle, and Moxie. The Jews supply the moxie. The Italians take care of the muscle. And they split the money between them."

Fifteen-year-old Mickey Cohen immediately became immersed in Cleveland's boxing world. While hanging around the city's gyms, Mickey made friends with local boys and met leaders of the underworld. He soon learned the fight game and the racket world were "one and the same." Morris Kleinman, once a boxer who held Cleveland's lightweight title, kept his hand in the game as a promoter and manager. All the influential racketeers were involved in the sport.

Mickey observed the mob leaders, realizing they had "money, clothes, and class" — things he envisioned for himself. They noticed his skills and found the young flyweight impressive enough to be trained and mentored in New York. Top fight managers signed him up. At sixteen, he arrived in Manhattan and was boarded at the Abbey Hotel, at Fifty-First near Broadway.

Privileged survivors of the market crash continued to live extravagantly in the intoxicating night world of Depression-era Manhattan. Cash-rich gangsters and brassy showgirls mixed with adventurous members of the social register in the mob-owned cabarets and speakeasies that dotted Broadway.

As unemployment reached unprecedented heights, life became grim for the vast majority of people. For many it consisted of breadlines and soup kitchens. For teenaged Mickey Cohen, the Manhattan experience was a focused and disciplined life at Stillman's Gym, roadwork in Central Park, and boxing matches.

Located up a flight of narrow stairs at 919 W. Fifty-Fourth Street, near Eighth Avenue, Stillman's was the center of the boxing universe — and the Combination. Lou Stillman, a former detective who always had a loaded .38 poking out of his jacket, ran the place with an iron fist. Two bouncers manned the thick metal door at the gym's entrance. Noisy, smoke filled, and crowded, the gym exuded the smell of liniment and cigars. The main room featured two rings. As champion fighters sparred, members of the

Broadway Mob sat ringside on folding chairs, studying scratch sheets and quietly talking business. And they were all there: the bosses, the hangers-on, and the bums. Journalists, among them Damon Runyon, and showbiz stars, like Al Jolson, the Broadway legend then enjoying unparalleled success with the first talking movie, *The Jazz Singer*, loved the action.

It was a dream come true for the young boxer from Boyle Heights.

Mickey's managers got him noticed. Introducing him to prominent figures around Madison Square Garden and publicizing him, they billed him as the "California Wildcat" and the "Featherweight with the Dempsey Punch." Good matches were made. Like the great Jewish champions of the era, he proudly wore blue satin trunks trimmed in white, a bold Star of David embroidered on the left leg, which was monogrammed with his initials. He fought some contenders and entered the ring on the under-bill of a bout at the Garden. He would later describe himself as "a snippy kid who thought he could box."

Ultimately the teenage boxer became disillusioned about his abilities in the ring. Lonely, Mickey missed his Italian friends in Cleveland and his brother. After a year and a half in Manhattan, he returned to Cleveland. But the experience had heightened his awareness of other possibilities: "I had gotten a taste from New York of what the racket world was — the glamour, the way they dressed, the way they always had a pocket full of money . . . The top ones . . . always carried themselves as gentlemen."

The Great Depression continued to hold the country in its grip. For 25 cents, gangster pictures, platinum blonde Jean Harlow, and *Dracula* provided the masses a few hours of escape in the gilded movie palaces of the era. But like everywhere else, times were bleak in Cleveland. Given pocket money and meager expenses by his managers, Mickey Cohen continued to box.

Living in the homes of his friends' parents on the Hill, Cleveland's Little Italy, Mickey often slept by day and played pinochle all night. Introduced to guns, he learned to fire them. A fascination developed; he loved to examine different models, noting their unique attributes. A hardened armed robber got him a revolver, customizing it with a special pearl handle.

For Mickey Cohen, the gun became the great equalizer. Charged with adrenalin, he was overtaken by feelings of power and grandiosity whenever he held a gun in his hand. He later described his feelings in a moment of candor: "I felt like king of the world . . . when I whipped out that big .38, it made me as big as a guy six-foot-ten."

Then the young boxer "sought a new means of livelihood." He began what the underworld calls "rooting," armed robberies. Two or three times a week he robbed with two older men who were ex-convicts and professional bandits. The rush from the heists, as much as the money, excited Mickey Cohen. Not receiving a fair share for his efforts, he recruited three Italian friends to join him in a robbery ring. He explained with pride years later, "I was the youngest, but I was sort of looked upon as the leader of our outfit."

Assembled in a hotel room before a job, each man in the gang would empty his pockets. "The two biggest sins among heist men," Mickey observed, "are when you drop something while doin' the work and leave identification. No wrist watches on. Nothin' that could come off." The second infraction: "If someone holds back with intentions of keeping it for himself, instead of dividing . . . that calls for the death penalty. I was in charge of dividing up the score, but I was handicapped by not being able to add or subtract. So I made the boys divide everything into equal piles and that was my substitute for arithmetic."

He later recalled the weaponry used in his new occupation: "Every kind, pistols, shotguns, tommy guns. Whatever was handy." The modus operandi: "We specialized in gambling joints, cafés, and whorehouses. In one bookie joint, I raised [lined victims against the wall, their arms in the air] two hundred people." He took any fight offered him and any heist, too. His band carelessly robbed several operations protected by the underworld. "At that time I never had a thorough understanding of what the syndicate meant. I took it all as a joke," he said.

His imprudent choices proved to have severe ramifications. He confided years later, "I was informed I would have my lights put out if I tampered any further with their territory. I paid no attention to their statements and kept on heistin' wherever I wanted."

One member of his gang was the nephew of the Mafia don of Buffalo. After much persuasion, Mickey agreed to drive with his friends to Buffalo to meet the mafioso.

He remembered the underworld leader as "an old immigrant Italian, who took quite a liking to me. He refused to believe I was a Jew, as I had so many Italian ways about me from being connected with Italian people. The owner of a fine, large Italian restaurant . . . the uncle kidded with me, 'You gotta too much guts for-a your own good.'"

The Buffalo boss called the Cleveland leaders, making arrangements so that no harm would come to his nephew or the other Italian boys. Mickey said the mafioso asked for consideration and cooperation for him, as well. Standing near the phone, he overheard the one-sided conversation: "'I also wanta-to make-a sure the Jew is in good shape . . . will be looked after.' He kept repeating, 'The Jew, he-sa good boy, he-sa more like-a Italian than a Jew.'"

Told to return to Cleveland, on the drive back his friends "kept drilling into me what I couldn't seem to grasp . . . that the Mafia and the syndicate was no organization to fool with and must be given complete respect, especially from now on."

The three Italian boys were called into a meeting by the Cleveland bosses and were quickly dismissed. Then the Jewish kid was called in. Standing before the Mafia leaders, soft-spoken immigrants approaching middle-age, Mickey observed the mahoffs, a term he often used for gang-land bosses, and would later describe the meeting as follows: "These men . . . looked upon as really gods . . . they were very stern, but kind, and belittled our way of thinking." Recognizing that his violent and fearless nature was an attribute they could exploit, after telling the teenage boxer to stay away from their businesses, the bosses offered Cohen a proposal: "They . . . paid me the compliment of being the head and brains of the little outfit . . . and said they thought I should lend my talents and guts to going along with them."

Mickey agreed to respect the syndicate's wishes and was placed under the jurisdiction of Anthony Milano. At nineteen, the "Jew Boy," as Mickey was called by the Italians on the Hill, was put on the payroll as an enforcer. An agreement was made that jobs he perpetrated on his own remained his personal business, as long as they didn't interfere with Combination activities.

His life took a turn. Anthony Milano, FBI #433240, Cleveland PD #11100, became a father figure. Born Antonino Milano on December 5,

1888, in Milanesi, Reggio Calabria, Italy, his police record dated back to 1912 and included arrests for "suspicious person, 'black hand' suspect, and counterfeiting." Among his criminal associates was the underworld's most important leader, Lucky Luciano. Mickey found "Mr. Milano" to be a gentleman, a family man devoted to his wife and four small sons, as well as a highly regarded mob leader.

"Pleasure lay only in a grin of approval from *the people*," the eminent writer Ben Hecht would observe of Cohen. "*The people*, synonym for the underworld's leaders, is a significant word . . . The real gangster offers it almost mystic allegiance."

Milano was one of the underworld's most dominant *people*. Young Mickey learned to respect him — and the allegiance would last throughout his life.

His association with the underworld had begun, but he didn't abandon the fight game. "I fought with the best of them, including Baby Arizmendi," he later commented. "I wasn't the worst; neither was I the best."

After fighting featherweight titleholder Tommy Paul at Cleveland in 1931, he began to genuinely question his future in the ring. Knocked senseless and bleeding badly in the opening seconds of the match, it was the first time he was seriously injured during a bout. Mickey was photographed on the sports page of the *Los Angeles Times* the next year, and he was matched with world champion Chalky Wright at L.A.'s Olympic Auditorium. The fight ended in defeat for him. At Tijuana in May 1933, featherweight star Baby Arizmendi KO'd him in the third.

"I must have been a real crazy punk," he admitted to Ben Hecht years later. "I'm fighting a pretty good man named Carpenter, and the fight is on the belly [the bout wasn't fixed]. It's a very important fight for me because a lot of *the people* are at the ringside." Eager to impress the underworld bosses, in the first three rounds he tore his opponent apart. But the man wouldn't go down. Mickey finally floored him, but he got up again. Five times, six times, the same thing happened.

"I finally got so upset by his not stayin' down that I jump in and start biting his ear off. So help me, I got it nearly bitten off before the referee can pry us apart," he confessed. "My opponent runs around hollerin' with

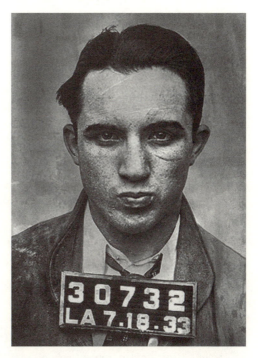

Cohen's mugshot, 1933,
from his first adult arrest.

a glove over his bloody ear. The referee hangs on to me. 'You got him dead! What do you want to do — eat him?'"

After more than one hundred armed robberies without incident, his first adult arrest: Los Angeles, July 18, 1933. The city cops pinched him on suspicion of robbery. His mug shot showed an insolent nineteen-year-old with a glaring stare, defiant scowl, and patent leather hair. He wore a number, #30732. By this time a soldier on Anthony Milano's payroll, he was released the next day, and no case was filed.

And a life-altering disease afflicted Mickey Cohen during this period. The malady — never before revealed — was dropped among thousands of facts in the 1,755-page FBI file on Meyer Harris Cohen, #755912. A 1961 document titled "Physical Description" asserted that he had normal vision and hearing; five missing teeth; blood pressure of 120/84; an intelligence quotient of "98, average intelligence group"; and a "broken leg at age 8, according to relatives interviewed, not confirmed." Under the category "Previous Illness," the document states "Gonorrhea, 1932." Before antibiotics were introduced in the 1940s, the social disease was impossible to cure and difficult to remedy. At the time he contracted the disease, the most popular treatment was Protargol, colloidal silver marketed by Bayer. Still in his teens when he contracted gonorrhea, the disease ravished Mickey's body and scarred his psyche for life.

Other physical problems affected his performance in the ring. His left eye had been badly cut and opened easily, and he fought to maintain his weight. Matches became scarce and third-rate. After seventy-nine professional fights, he was finished as a boxer. He'd grown up in the blinding light of the boxing game, attended by trainers and cut-men, cajoled by managers, crowds roaring in his ears. All the years of attention and dreams of glory had come to an end. At twenty, Mickey Cohen was just another punk.

"He had a fighting heart and would tackle anybody. He wouldn't listen to me, and I quit managing him when he wanted to go up against anybody just for the purse," fight manager Eddie Borden told journalist Florabel Muir. "He never had any idea of the value of money. He liked to dress well and would spend his last twenty dollars on a hat."

Self-conscious and insecure, Mickey's entire existence had been spent on street corners and in reform schools, freight cars, and sweaty locker rooms. Taking great pride in his personal tidiness, he shaved his heavy beard often, his nails were always clean and clipped, and his hair was neatly trimmed and slicked back, shining with Brilliantine. He loved to dress luxuriously and drench his body in fine cologne. The costly clothing looked and felt good, and it impressed others. But even in an expensive fedora, tailor-made suit, and camel-hair coat, he looked like the fifth banana in a B-fight picture: tawny face bristled with purple five o'clock shadow, his nose pummeled into a tiny pug, thick black brows hooded dark expressionless eyes, and across his left cheekbone, a scar swirled under his eye. His short legs, round cheeks, and pouting mouth evoked a dark cupid.

But his damaged face, diminutive stature, and lack of education no longer seemed a hindrance to him. He was now part of a violent and alien world that functioned outside of society and the law — Mickey Cohen had found his true vocation.

★ ★ ★

In Cleveland, two events altered his course. Given a highly important and treacherous assignment, he was ordered to beat an encroaching gangland

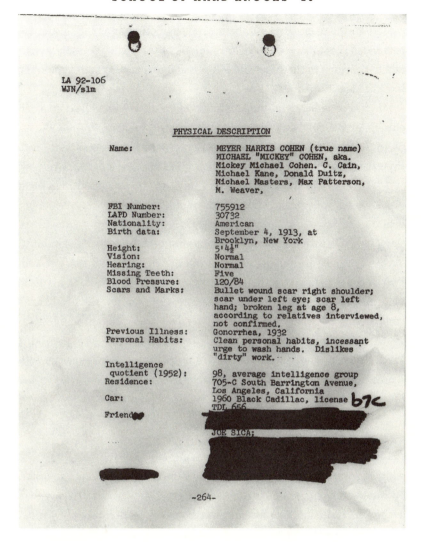

LA 92-106
WJN/slm

PHYSICAL DESCRIPTION

Name:	MEYER HARRIS COHEN (true name) MICHAEL "MICKEY" COHEN, aka. Mickey Michael Cohen. C. Cain, Michael Kane, Donald Duitz, Michael Masters, Max Patterson, M. Weaver,
FBI Number:	755912
LAPD Number:	30732
Nationality:	American
Birth data:	September 4, 1913, at Brooklyn, New York
Height:	5'4½"
Vision:	Normal
Hearing:	Normal
Missing Teeth:	Five
Blood Pressure:	120/84
Scars and Marks:	Bullet wound scar right shoulder; scar under left eye; scar left hand; broken leg at age 8, according to relatives interviewed, not confirmed.
Previous Illness:	Gonorrhea, 1932
Personal Habits:	Clean personal habits, incessant urge to wash hands. Dislikes "dirty" work.
Intelligence quotient (1952):	98, average intelligence group
Residence:	705-C South Barrington Avenue, Los Angeles, California
Car:	1960 Black Cadillac, license b7c TDL 656
Friends	

JOE SICA;

-264-

Revealed here for the first time, a life-shaping biographical detail that appears only in this FBI file: Mickey Cohen contracted gonorrhea as a teenager, before the disease was curable by antibiotics. The disease is an obvious factor in his boundless obsession with cleanliness.

competitor. Needing someone to identify the victim, Mickey recalled, "The tipster pointed out the wrong guy. This man was walking down the street with his wife. I jumped him and she yelled, 'You got the wrong guy!' I paid no attention and finished the work." Aggravated that the "finger man" had caused an innocent person to be hurt, Mickey then beat the tipster. He recalled, "This tipster was a relative of one of the higher echelon, a man much respected in the syndicate. This man didn't look so kindly upon the Jew kid's hot-headedness."

In a second incident, freelancing Mickey and his band held up a cafeteria. After a shoot-out, his partner, Frank Niccoli, alias Frankie Burns, was immediately apprehended. Convicted, Niccoli was sent to prison. Eventually identified by a witness, Mickey was arrested for armed robbery.

"The case was pushed around for months," he explained. "Finally it was lowered from robbery to embezzlement, through a fix. And finally I beat the rap.

"There was such difficulty straightening out the matter, including a stream of front page publicity, that it was decided I get out of Cleveland. Part of the situation was that one of my boys had been killed on a heist with me. The cops were worked up by the press to find the dead man's companions. So all the heat was considerable, from different sources."

After these flagrant misdeeds, Mickey was pleased *the people* "didn't kiss me off." Instead, they transferred him to Chicago. He was placed with Joe Barron, an important Jewish gambler who ran a large casino on the upper North Side.

Al Capone had ruled Chicago since the mid-1920s. "The Big Fella," Capone's gangland moniker, was America's most famous and infamous gangster. Rising quickly from the bottom, by the time Capone was twenty-five, authorities estimated that his outfit was squeezing $100 million a year out of Prohibition-era Chicago.

Capone was king. At a Cubs game, sitting President Hoover was roundly booed, while the crowd wildly cheered the murderous mobster. They blamed Hoover for the Great Depression, while Capone, in a sly promotional ploy, polished his image by establishing a fine soup kitchen. When gang wars raged, Capone held press conferences. His huge organization was matched by political favor: "I own the police," Big Al crowed — and Mayor Bill Thompson, too.

Since his early days in New York, the vicious Capone had been closely connected to the Luciano-Lansky-Siegel-Costello mob. The association began in 1919, with a show of camaraderie by a reckless thirteen-year-old, who would later become notorious as Bugsy Siegel. Meyer Lansky revealed to Israeli journalists years later, "It was Bugsy Siegel who knew him well when Capone lived and worked on the Lower East Side. He found himself in great difficulty when the police got out a warrant for him on a murder charge — he had beat up a Brooklyn bartender so badly he died. Bugsy Siegel was a close enough friend of Capone's to hide him out with one of his aunts, somewhere on East Fourteenth Street."

On the run, twenty-year-old Capone left for Chicago. There he was mentored by Johnny "The Fox" Torrio, one of the sharpest gangsters to ever come out of New York's Five Points. Prohibition had begun, and over a brief span "the outfit," as the Capone mob was called, grew into a multi-ethnic powerhouse.

Mickey Cohen idolized Capone, fourteen years his senior. He said with great admiration, "Capone was the only man in any of the syndicates who could make a decision without a round table. He decided by himself on all money matters and all penalties."

The young *shtarker*, Yiddish for tough guy, was greatly flattered when friends noted a physical resemblance to Big Al. Mickey emulated the expensively dressed Capone in every way he could, and he loved to sport wide "gangster hats" in his trademark style. Until the end of his life, he would make fantastic, fanciful claims of having met Capone.

But when Mickey Cohen turned up in Chicago in 1934, it was no longer Alphonse Capone's dominion. His legendary outfit was now a legacy, run by relatives, captains, and accountants. Ravaged by syphilis, contracted in his early years as a pimp, Capone was incarcerated in Alcatraz, serving an eleven-year federal sentence for income tax evasion.

Working as protection for Barron's casino and bookmaking operation, Mickey described his new arrangement, "He . . . gave me a little 'louse book' to operate inside of his big book. A louse book is for those able . . . to bet only dimes, quarters, and half-dollars. Besides the louse book, he gave me the poker concession at night."

A man came to Barron's casino bragging that he had been paid twenty dollars to extort the operation. Mickey recalled a confrontation, "I don't ask who engaged him but I said, 'I'm going to give you a chance to prove you're a tough guy.' And I pulled a gun. In that time I would've felt undressed if I wasn't carrying a gun. The tough guy ran behind a door and I blasted him through the door which is the last I saw of him."

Jailed for homicide at the precinct house, Mickey watched as Barron's friend, an old-school Irish boss from St. Louis's Egan Rats gang, smoothly pled his case. The fix was impressive: no court date, no record.

He admitted years later, "[At the time] I would have taken on Jack Dempsey — that's how crazy I was about myself. The truth was that a lot of Chicago guys resented a thin little Jew kid having so much guts."

Capone captains held court in the cafés, gyms, and gambling halls he frequented. Having survived the gang wars of the 1920s, many had multiple murders credited to them. Mickey became acquainted with Dago Lawrence Mangano and Ralph and Mattie Capone, the bosses' brothers. Other key players noticed him, including Capone's favorite assassin, "Machine Gun" Jack McGurn. Born Vicenzo Gibaldi, McGurn was young, good-looking, and as dapper as Astaire. A former boxer, he was suspected of major involvement in the St. Valentine's Day Massacre and had notoriously slashed comic Joe E. Lewis's face, after the performer left his Green Mill cabaret to work at a rival nightclub. McGurn would be assassinated in the early hours of February 15, 1936.

With the approval of the outfit, Mickey opened a poker game in the Loop, Chicago's business district. Mickey recalled the Clark Street operation: "This was during the real Depression days. I had accumulated quite an organization around me, six or seven guys who had need for food and sleeping quarters, so as the months went by our meager bankroll dwindled."

He also had a girlfriend. During much of his time in Cleveland and Chicago, Cohen lived with Georgia, a lovely Irish redhead. "A wonderful girl," he said. Georgia cooked and took care of him, not caring if he was flush or "lookin' at a last sawbuck." After five years together, she met a man who wanted to marry her. Innately shy around females, it was apparent Mickey's bout with gonorrhea, as well as his criminal lifestyle, initiated his deeply circumspect feelings about women, and particularly marriage. He admitted that he took her for granted, and they parted amicably.

Unable to survive with the poker concession, he returned to the ring for a handful of fights. Mickey and his boys robbed small businesses, sometimes three a day, for eating money. But the paltry income couldn't sustain the band, or Mickey's shopping sprees. "It was suggested to me . . . that we open up with craps . . . as it seemed the only way to see daylight and restore the bankroll in full," he said.

Converting a poker table into a homemade crap table, the "half-baked" enterprise was financed with a borrowed bankroll that had to be returned, in full, each night. A "bust-out" game, anyone who played would lose. He bought a cop and hired cabbies as steerers to bring gamblers to the game. Top mechanics — skilled cardsharps who utilized loaded and shaved dice — were brought in. Mickey recalled, "[Mechanics learned] that this was a helluva spot to stop . . . they could . . . pick up a good score because the mechanic would get half."

Craps was forbidden in the Loop. Other forms of gambling were easily controlled, but the dice game, where losses mounted quickly, was notorious as an unpredictable and dangerous endeavor. To prevent bloodshed, the outfit and the police had a pact to keep the game out of the crowded business district.

Capone's financial wizard, pudgy middle-aged Jack Guzik, called Greasy Thumb for the deliberate finger motion he used when lubricating authorities with cash, was now the titular boss of the outfit. When word reached the meek-looking former pimp that dice had returned to the Loop, Guzik came up from balmy Florida. Again at the center of upheaval, Mickey remembered, "I was summoned to a round table on the second floor of an Italian restaurant. Guzik acted as spokesman." Mickey was issued an ultimatum: the crap game must close.

He refused to listen.

A few nights later, the rebellious Angeleno was standing on Clark Street, nearby his game. A long black car drove slowly by, tommy gun blasting. Falling into a snow bank, Mickey was not hit.

The Capones were accustomed to fiery hoods. Mickey later divulged that the shooting was a reprimand, intended to frighten, not kill him. By this time Mickey Cohen had earned a reputation — in the city that prided itself on being a tough town — as a valuable enforcer. He recalled being well liked by the bosses: "there was a lot of different tricks I was called on to do for them which I done."

On Randolph Street, in the heart of the busy Loop, a man with a personal grudge pulled a gun on Mickey. Years later he related the event with great detail: "After he stuck the pistol in me he put it in his coat pocket and kept it there. I wheeled around and grabbed him and I got my hand into the coat pocket with his, and my finger on the trigger." Passing a beat cop who was on his payroll, Mickey continued walking then forced his foe into a crowded drugstore: "I was trying to talk him out of it, trying to save the joint, too, and my life. He's getting more belligerent all the time."

Mickey grabbed a sugar dispenser and slammed him in the head. Women screamed and patrons scurried for safety as the man's head exploded like a melon, spewing blood and tissue everywhere. Mickey was later circumspect, admitting, "I was a wild kid at the time and hot as a pistol . . . peeved."

Charges were filed against him for assault. The Capone fixer requested a postponement after, with proper underworld etiquette, Mickey had refused to cooperate with police, even to make a case for self-defense.

The bosses from Cleveland — both the Jews and the Italians — remained in his corner. He was instructed to go home. To L.A.

A plan was in place. It involved Bugsy Siegel.

3

THE COASTERS

"Work . . . that's what being with Benny
[Bugsy Siegel] would be like."
MICKEY COHEN

Mickey returned to the city of his childhood in 1937. The once troubled newsboy was now hardened, volatile, and remained illiterate. He found Los Angeles to still be a big small town. The underworld setup, the twenty-three-year-old learned, was not the eastern system. In his hometown, "gambling and everything . . . was completely run by cops and stool pigeons," he recalled.

Mickey soon came to understand that a small group of middle-aged "businessmen" had controlled the lucrative L.A. rackets since the time he was selling papers in the downtown streets. Completely entrenched in the political system, they were not considered gangsters. "On Spring [Street] are the two financial centers — one legitimate stock exchange and the other the gamble and bootleg exchange where 'big shots' control the rum and roulette trade of Los Angeles," observed author Basil Woon. Hearst editor James H. Richardson recalled the absolute power of Los Angeles's white-shoe racketeers: "A syndicate of gamblers and vice-mongers had the city in its grip. The syndicate owned the police department. They had it so well organized that when Scarface Al Capone came out from Chicago . . . with the thought of taking charge himself, he was rousted . . . and put on

"Politician" Charlie Crawford, L.A.'s racket king of the Roaring Twenties, colluded with city hall and law enforcement. Circa 1930.

a train back to Chicago. And the boys who did the rousting . . . were cops owned body and soul by the syndicate."

During the Roaring Twenties, Charles Herbert Crawford was the unrivaled boss of L.A.'s rackets. Thirty-four when he moved to Los Angeles in 1913, he was called the Gray Wolf for his pewter-color hair and crafty nature. He first rose to prominence as a young man, allied with Seattle politicians during the boom days of the Klondike gold rush. Good-time Charlie's gambling halls and brothels ran wide open there for years. Tellingly, when he tried to expand with a five-hundred-room brothel on land that carried a city lease, Seattle's municipal government fell due to the scandal.

In downtown L.A., at Maple and Fifth, at the heart of Mickey Cohen's childhood meanderings, the Gray Wolf established a large, beautiful saloon with a casino and prostitutes on the second floor. At the Maple Bar, Charlie Crawford, big, red-faced, and full of personality, entertained the police brass and ward-healers who would facilitate his rise to the top. With the election of Mayor George Cryer in 1921, Crawford's cabal was given the exclusive franchise on all vice activities in the city.

A rare photo of Guy McAfee, LAPD captain turned under-world kingpin, living it up. After Charlie Crawford was assassinated in 1931, he became L.A.'s number one racket figure. Circa 1936.

Crawford's former close associate was alleged to be behind his 1931 murder. The rival, Guy McAfee, forty-three, once captain of the LAPD vice squad — and the template for the corrupt L.A. cop — replaced Crawford as the region's most important racketeer.

As Mickey's star rose, he would become familiar with all the city's old-line racketeers — and their businesses.

In 1933, Frank L. Shaw, a backslapping former wholesale grocery sales-man, was elected mayor of Los Angeles. He immediately took corruption to unprecedented levels. His brother, Joe, a retired navy lieutenant, handled the fraud. Everything was for sale at Joe the Sailor's office in city hall — from vice monopolies and no-bid city contracts to high-placed civil service positions. There was even a macabre scheme, alleged to run out of the coroner's office, where cash and valuables from homes of the recently departed were kicked back to city hall.

LAPD Chief James E. Davis was in collusion with the Shaws. Immaculate and stocky, Two-Gun Jim was quite the showman. He loved to boisterously rail at reporters about Commies and crooks while shooting the dangling ash from a cigarette that was clenched between the teeth of

Top independent L.A. gangster Tony Cornero exits jail after a raid on his gambling ship, The Lux. *1946.*

a submissive rookie. When not posing for press photographers with beauty queens, he sanctioned illegal wiretaps, entrapped enemies, and established the notorious "bum brigade," where illegal Mexicans and penniless Okies escaping the Dust Bowl were arrested as they crossed the city line.

Guy McAfee, tall and lanky with a shock of wavy hair and jug-ears, and Farmer Page, his partner and a former Los Angeles newsboy a generation before Mickey Cohen, held sway with the profoundly avaricious Joe Shaw. Their syndicate's exclusive control of the territory's 600 brothels, 300 gambling houses, 1,800 bookie joints, and 23,000 legal slot machines continued unabated.

Independent L.A. gangster Tony Cornero was a major rumrunner during Prohibition. A millionaire by the time he was thirty, the former taxi driver warred with Farmer Page over bootlegging spoils, and Page's syndicate barred Cornero from gambling operations. Inventively, Cornero took his shop offshore, into international waters. He docked an ancient trawler, refitted as a luxury casino, just beyond the three-mile limit, and the legendary era of Los Angeles's fabulous gambling ships began. The *Monte Carlo, Monfalcone, Rose Isle,* and *Johanna Smith,* sailing under the flag of Cornero rivals Guy McAfee and Farmer Page, were soon launched in Santa Monica Bay. Daily, thousands of affluent gamblers left Prohibition, the Depression, and their inhibitions onshore.

On the sidelines was mafioso Jack Dragna — a man destined to become one of Mickey Cohen's greatest enemies. Born Ignaucio Rizzotti in 1891, he arrived in California around 1910. A native of Corleone, Sicily, he had the right pedigree and was seeped in the traditions of the old country. Although lacking the success and flair of unaffiliated Cornero, among his countrymen Dragna was a feared man of power and respect. By the mid-1920s, he was considered the unofficial mayor of the Italian ghetto that had cropped up in the first decade of the century, near Boyle Heights. As president of the Italian Protective League (IPL), Dragna claimed to be the defender of the immigrant community. But according to a police report his organization was "strictly a muscle outfit" with "fingers in gambling, boot-legging, and smuggling, and was suspected of many Black Hand killings."

A relative of Tommy Lucchese, boss of one of New York's five crime families instituted by Lucky Luciano in 1931, Dragna's blood ties assured him a prime spot in the new underworld order. With Johnny Rosselli, a smooth friend representing the Chicago outfit, he began his move beyond the Italian community during the era of Mayor Shaw.

In 1935, while Mickey was still in the East, the complacent politicians, police, and underworld establishment of the lush L.A. region learned that revolution was in the air. For the first time, the Angelenos had a *real* gangster in their midst. Bugsy Siegel and Hollywood — perfect casting.

Born Berish Siegel in 1906, at 88 Cannon Street on the Lower East Side of Manhattan, Bugsy was seven years older than Mickey Cohen. Involved in criminal activities from the time he was ten, he grew up in the streets of New York, loving guns and girls. He had been partnered with Meyer Lansky, Lucky Luciano, and Frank Costello since his adolescence. By the early 1930s, these men had become the dominant leaders of nationally organized crime.

In Hollywood, Siegel's true identity as gangland's consummate executioner was whispered about, but that was all. In the land of stardust and

The Most Wanted Man in Hollywood: the handsome and dashing Mr.
Benjamin Siegel. Circa 1942.

reinvention, the notorious Bugsy Siegel was known simply as Ben, millionaire playboy and sportsman. According to Mickey, when Benjamin Siegel relocated to California he was given carte blanche by his partners: "Siegel . . . part and parcel of the top — one of the six tops — was right up

Published for the first time here: from the borough of Manhattan, the original birth certificate of Benjamin "Bugsy" Siegel showing his birth name, Berish Siegel, and his Cannon Street birthplace.

with Capone so far as making a single decision. His own round table."

The prospect of taking over the juicy L.A. rackets looked like child's play to him.

★ ★ ★

Ordered by Cleveland to contact Siegel immediately upon arriving in L.A., Mickey ignored the command. Returning to his wayward ways, with Joe Gentile, a gray-haired man in his sixties, and Joe Sica, a tough contemporary from New Jersey, Mickey began a wild rooting spree. Another father figure to Cohen, Gentile assumed the role of tipster for the band and cooked Mickey spaghetti. "Joe Sica was close to me in my work on heists and other action," Cohen said. "His brother Fred was just a kid but . . . a great car thief . . . I'd say, 'Fred, go pick up a car.' He'd be back in ten minutes with any type we wanted." The Sicas would remain his lifelong partners.

Mickey rented an apartment in Hadden Hall, on Eighth Street at Fedora, in the mid-Wilshire district. He took his share from the armed robberies and spent it. Buying clothes at the town's most extravagant venues, Bullock's Wilshire and Alexander and Oviatt's haberdashery, Mickey partied at every nightclub in town. Bugsy Siegel didn't fit into his plans. "Work . . . that's what being with Benny would be like," Mickey concluded. The mob legend would be forced to make the first move.

After receiving a hot tip, Mickey carefully cased a large bookmaking establishment on Franklin Avenue in Hollywood. Told that it was run by gambler Morrie Orloff, "I knocked at the door at 9 a.m.," Mickey said. "The joint worked with a peephole. The doorman is an ex-copper. I says . . . 'Is Morrie in?'" Informed that he didn't arrive until ten or later, Mickey said that he had a delivery and had been instructed to make a pickup. "Put it through the peephole," the guard ordered.

Mickey continued the con, saying the package was large. "He made the mistake of opening the door." Mickey made his move. "I put a .45 in his belly. Only three guys are in the joint besides the copper."

Once in, his boys followed. A shotgun held on the bookies, they waited for Morrie Orloff. "Morrie was the big money," Mickey had been told. "As each . . . bookmaker comes in, we take his money and send him to face the wall."

Little Davie Schneiderman, partner of top mafioso Johnny Rosselli, was one of the men who arrived. Mickey couldn't believe his good fortune when he saw the man's giant bankroll: "He had just got through pickin' up $23,000 [$345,000 today] for Jack Dragna, who is head guy with *the people*. . . . We heist him, takin' his rings also," Mickey added. "Dago Louie, who is another head guy with *the people*, is by the wall. He says to me, 'You gotta alla da money. Whya you wanna stay around here?'"

Mickey threatened the older Italian, "Mind your own business or I'll put a phone through your head. I'm stayin' for Morrie Orloff if I gotta stay 'til tomorrow."

A man spoke up, saying he was Orloff and proving his identity with a monogrammed ring. After relieving him of his cash and jewelry, the bandits left.

It was soon apparent the tip was bum. One of the largest bookmaking operations in the city, it was run by Rosselli and Dragna for the eastern organization. "Combination people and all," Mickey confirmed. "A fellow who knew me as a kid fighter comes to me . . . Little Davie, who I clipped for $23,000, had reported the matter."

Once again, Mickey Cohen learned his lessons the hard way: Dragna and Rosselli had accepted an alliance decreed by Lucky Luciano for his Jewish partner to take control of the territory for the eastern syndicate when Siegel moved to Los Angeles.

Soon Mickey was directed to appear at the Hollywood YMCA, where Ben Siegel sparred, played handball, and held meetings. Informed he would finally meet "Mr. Siegel," as Bugsy was deferentially called by anyone who wasn't an intimate, Mickey was ordered to stand at attention in front of him.

Ushered into the steam room, Mickey recalled his first sighting of the tall, tanned, and flawlessly built young mob boss: "He comes out naked with a big towel around him and a smile on his face." Mickey remembered that at first Siegel "was nice, saying that he'd wanted to meet me." But he quickly got to the point: "That piece of work . . . was . . . pretty good, but I want you to do me a favor . . . kick back the $23,000 and a certain piece of jewelry."

Indignant, Mickey snarled that he wouldn't kick back to his mother. For an instant, a look of confusion flashed across Siegel's handsome face: no one talked back to him. "Them eastern guys are used to giving an order only once," Mickey disclosed. "He looks at me cold and says, 'You heard what I said.'"

Hotheaded Mickey ranted back, "Go take a fuck for yourself!" Moving as quickly as his stumpy legs would propel him, Mickey remembered running "out of that steam room, before I started melting." Chasing after him, his handler couldn't believe what had happened. He notified Mickey that he had just signed his own death warrant.

Immediately shown who was boss, Mickey recalled what his outburst had wrought, "I'm picked up and held in a cell for eight days without bail." Released on the ninth day, he was ordered downtown to the law office of Jerry Giesler. Sitting there calmly staring at him were Bugsy Siegel and Johnny Rosselli. The Bug again demanded that Mickey return the score: it was made clear that the $23,000 was Combination money; Dragna and Rosselli were in business *with him*.

"Siegel's second in command was Jack Dragna . . . a quiet guy until he got excited," Mickey said. Dragna was "related to Three-Finger Brown [Tommy Lucchese] in the east, one of the important syndicate figures."

Finally returning the booty, Mickey was advised that "Mr. Siegel thinks you belong in a mental institution."

But Benjamin Siegel recognized that the crazy young mutt could be useful to him. "'You little son of a bitch,'" Mickey remembered him saying with a grin. "'You reflect my younger days.'"

4

FIELDS OF MANNA

"Cohen's debut in California was in the capacity of a pimp."

INFORMATION CONCERNING

MEYER HARRIS COHEN, FBI MEMO

B y 1938, the Great Depression had begun to ease, and Hollywood was booming as never before. Movies were the fifth-largest industry in the country, and it was a banner year for film attendance. Landmark Technicolor productions *The Wizard of Oz* and *Gone With the Wind* were in development, while Walt Disney had already achieved great success with *Snow White*, the first Technicolor animated feature. On a mission to gain control of the richest, most hedonistic territory in the land, Bugsy Siegel put Mickey Cohen to work. Using his fists and guns, the fiery young Angeleno began raiding the protected gambling clubs and brothels controlled by local racketeers.

Lee Francis had reigned as the most elite madam in Los Angeles for nearly two decades. Tall, attractive, and dark haired, she had business acumen. Sponsored by, and the mistress of, L.A. racket boss Charlie Crawford, she catered to the wealthiest, most powerful men of film, industry, politics, and international society — and the occasional woman like Metro's thrill-seeking bombshell Jean Harlow, who was interested in male companionship. Recounting details of her business, Lee Francis recalled, "I paid very high protection money — as much as 50% of the gross . . . It was all very dramatic even to my leaving the money each week in a tin can in the backyard so that a city hall messenger could pick it up." Always seeking exotic techniques and exciting new women to intrigue her demanding and jaded clientele, Lee Francis explored sex venues from Paris and Madrid to Kashmir and the Canary Islands. Offering a full complement of the world's most beautiful females, she arranged spectacular orgies and satisfied even the most bizarre indulgences.

Madam Francis's luxurious parlors were also a civilized meeting ground for both sexes. Slinky, expensively clad prostitutes mingled among playboys, politicos, wealthy Pasadena matrons, and filmland's most prestigious personages. Enigmatic Greta Garbo; MGM producer Irving Thalberg; and matinee idols Clark Gable, Errol Flynn, and John Barrymore played cards, sipped champagne, and sampled caviar while a hot black jazz band played. Guests were entertained by louche cinematic fare like *The Casting Couch*, a short film described by the madam as a "very frank story of a casting director at a mythical studio and detailing what a girl had to do to get a job from him."

Mickey Cohen remembered raiding Madam Francis's bordello: "This joint was the top call joint in town . . . [T]here were some pretty good looking broads. I was a neat looking . . . kid, and always dressed fairly nice . . . I had this big goddamn gun on them to make me all powerful. So a couple of the broads . . . talked up to me. One of them gave me her phone number . . . I did call her."

That call would dramatically change his personal destiny.

LAPD Captain Jack Arthur Donahoe swore that Mickey was "strictly on the heist" when he first returned to L.A. Informants claimed Mickey had expanded his activities and moved into prostitution:

According to a 1949 FBI recap from the Meyer Harris Cohen file:

COHEN's debut in California was in the capacity of a pimp. However, he had ambitions to become a major hoodlum and by 1938 informant [name redacted] advised that he was running a bookmaking establishment in fashionable Westwood. By 1938 COHEN was also baiting hoodlum "big

shots" from the East by making guns and transportation available when
they arrived in Los Angeles for visits or enforced vacations . . . COHEN's
prestige in underworld circles was rapidly mounting even while he was
in Cleveland. He carried out muscle jobs with dispatch and showed no
qualms or compunctions against killing. COHEN's reputation followed
him to California.

Writer Budd Schulberg was a contemporary of Mickey's who had grown
up in Los Angeles and loved boxing. But the similarities ended there. His
father, B.P. Schulberg, was the former head of Paramount Pictures and had
held the exclusive contract of quixotic flapper Clara Bow, one of the most
popular stars of silent films. As a fair-haired prince of Hollywood, Budd
Schulberg had been surrounded by cinematic luminaries, Wall Street finan-
ciers, and visiting dignitaries his entire life. The Schulbergs were enormous
boxing fans and every Wednesday and Friday night the family attended
prizefights at the Hollywood Legion Stadium, where they watched the
bouts from press seats. Budd Schulberg fondly remembered, "I must confess
we had a special kvell [Yiddish for joyous feeling] for the exploits of our
Jewish boxers."

In 1938, Budd Schulberg was a fledgling writer living at his family's
Green Gate Cottage in the isolated and exclusive Malibu Colony. There
he was developing his iconic Hollywood character, Sammy Glick, a rapa-
cious, soulless figure who would stop at nothing to get to the top. At the
undeveloped Colony, Budd and his sister, Sonya, a shy young woman who
wrote poetry, became acquainted with Mickey Cohen. Most likely installed
at a beach hideout by Siegel's minions, he presented himself to the
Schulbergs as a prizefighter. "I liked him," Budd Schulberg said of Cohen.
"He was like a little merchant or agent. He was affable. Warm and cordial.
We would talk boxing, and my sister, Sonya, would take walks along the
beach with him."

Cohen was distantly exposed to a wildly exotic world of unimaginable
opulence through Siegel. Although married to Esther Krakower, his childhood sweetheart, and the doting father of two young daughters, the New
York mobster was a chronic womanizer. Under the auspices of one lover,
his life would take an extraordinary turn. Bugsy Siegel became a socialite.

Movie idol Cary Grant accompanies Siegel's much older lover and mentor, international society figure Countess Dorothy di Frasso. Circa 1938.

This lover was the Countess di Frasso. An American, born Dorothy Caldwell Taylor in 1888, her family was fantastically wealthy and blue-chip illustrious. One of the brightest lights of high society, she garnered her title by marrying a distinguished member of the Roman aristocracy. Leading separate lives, the madcap heiress traveled the world while her elderly husband stayed in Rome.

When she began a romance with handsome young film star Gary Cooper in the early 1930s, she bought a mansion at 913 North Bedford Drive in Beverly Hills. Chauffeured around in a customized Rolls-Royce town car, with an Afghan hound by her side, Dottie di Frasso began showing the provincial movie folk what living was about.

After her affair with Cooper ended, she moved on to Clark Gable, the screen's leading male star. But by 1937, the year Mickey Cohen returned to Los Angeles, she was nearing fifty and on the prowl for an exciting new man. When a prominent hotelier invited dashing Bugsy Siegel to her box at Santa Anita racetrack, the countess was electrified by his mega-watt smile, movie-star looks, and diamond-in-the-rough charm. An affair ensued. Benjamin Siegel became the love of her life.

Having spent his thirty years with eyes cast toward the main chance, Siegel didn't let an eighteen-year age gap stop his social climb. When talking to his peers, mob mastermind and financier Meyer Lansky recalled Siegel proudly referred to Countess di Frasso as "my fancy lady." Gossip columnist Hedda Hopper revealed, "Bugsy had a list of important people to meet, and Dorothy di Frasso was the front for this campaign. She conned some of the biggest names in our town to take this hoodlum into their homes."

A special function introduced her new lover, and Siegel provided the entertainment. Beginning with a simulated brawl in the checkerboard marble entrance hall of the countess's home, the evening ended with boxing bouts in a ring that had been installed on the verdant grounds of the estate. The Hollywood royals were all there — Marlene Dietrich, Loretta Young, Merle Oberon, Fred Astaire, Dolores Del Rio, Cary Grant, and Clark Gable — and they wildly cheered as the boxers battered each other for their amusement. One could bet Mickey Cohen was put to work that evening, lurking in the shadow of privilege.

The Jewish mob boss began to act as host at the countess's frequent, and wildly sought-after, social gatherings. Attending the countess's soirees were the screen's most glamorous talent, their bosses, and people like William Randolph Hearst and his movie star mistress, Marion Davies; Orson Welles, the town's new "boy genius"; Barbara Hutton, "the world's richest girl"; the society decorator Lady Mendl, famously known as Elsie de Wolfe; as well as a large assortment of European aristocrats and the countess's brother's fabulously wealthy Wall Street associates.

Living like a member of the leisure set, Siegel enjoyed English-style riding and golf at Hillcrest, the exclusive Jewish country club, where two Hollywood moguls sponsored his membership. Along with the cinematic elite, he was invited to attend a seemingly unending stream of premieres and parties. At Santa Anita, he passed out winning tips like candy.

The studio heads received him. Hollywood's handful of moguls traded in power and intimidation, just like gangsters. Each with their own fief that included political contacts and private police forces, they controlled every aspect of their businesses, including their contract employees' lives. Like Siegel, they put on white tie and tails and learned refinements, but they never lost their hard edges or ruthless behavior. Gamblers to the man, at life and at the tables, the studio heads eagerly embraced the charismatic gangster.

For Siegel it was a pleasure, and good for business, to be sought after by the rich, the powerful, and the beautiful. Bugsy Siegel, debonair underworld boss and executioner, thrived on the Hollywood lifestyle.

"Ben — no one called him 'Bugsy' — was an extraordinary organizer, a brilliant businessman. Ben had magnetic charm, enormous blue eyes. Physically he was irresistible. Only, he had bad diction — he spoke like a gangster," Hollywood insider Richard Gully confided to writer Amy Fine Collins.

Mickey observed Siegel. The crude bandit coveted the life of his elegantly dressed boss. He carefully observed Siegel's "smooth and rough" technique and was determined to emulate him. He said, "I found Benny to be a person with brilliant intelligence — he would look right through you. He commanded 1,000 percent respect and got it. Also, he was tough. He came out the hard way — been through it all — muscle work, heists, killings."

While playing consort to the countess, Siegel worked obsessively at building his own three-acre showplace at 250 Delfern Drive in Holmby Hills, L.A.'s wealthiest and most exclusive enclave. There he plotted to obliterate the underworld competition.

Dragna and Rosselli were on board. Tony Cornero went along with the new order; Siegel invested in his latest gambling ship, the *Rex*. Control of the dog track in Culver City and the horse tracks, Santa Anita, Hollywood Park, and Del Mar, down to Agua Caliente in Mexico, were part of his plan of conquest. Siegel demanded his share of the illicit spoils of all existing bookmaking operations, illegal gambling clubs, and brothels. But there was much resistance from the downtown syndicate.

L.A. racket boss Farmer Page's niece, Patricia A. Nealis, revealed,

"Lucky Luciano tried in 1935 to buy into a casino. But, surprise, surprise . . . all gambling joints were off-limits to him on orders of the LAPD. They did not want the New York mob operating in Los Angeles."

Fortuitously for Siegel, the entire political landscape of the city of Los Angeles shifted abruptly in 1938. The event that upset the status quo was the near-fatal car bombing of a private investigator in the employ of prominent cafeteria owner Clifford Clinton, a vocal reformer who was challenging corrupt Mayor Frank Shaw's administration.

The bombing was the handiwork of LAPD Chief James E. Davis's "intelligence" squad. The ensuing investigation generated headline news and revealed a political conspiracy that tied corrupt cops directly to the mayor. The scandal forced Chief Davis's retirement and set into motion an unprecedented mayoral recall election. Reformer Fletcher E. Bowron, a former newsman and superior court judge, easily defeated now disgraced Mayor Shaw.

Another event made it clear that the terrain was drastically changing. Les Bruneman, a prominent member of the local syndicate, refused to join Siegel's plan. After clashing with Johnny Rosselli, Bruneman was shot three times by a Dragna gunman. Miraculously he survived. Stubbornly, Bruneman still refused to comply. The second time he wasn't so fortunate. In a wild shootout at the Roost Café on Temple Street, Bruneman wielded two pistols, but five assailants felled their prey.

While the Bruneman assassination sent a clear message to the local racketeers, an unusual event sealed their fate. In a highly unorthodox move brokered by Hearst editor Jim Richardson, newly elected Mayor Bowron held a secret meeting with independent gangster and gambling ship owner Tony Cornero. From Cornero the mayor received the names of twenty-six high-ranking LAPD officers owned by the underworld establishment. Their dismissals decimated the ranks of the LAPD and dismantled the protection enjoyed by their patrons — virtually ending the heyday of the existing racketeers in the city of Los Angeles.

With associates, and many of the disgraced cops, racket boss Guy McAfee and his partner, Farmer Page, fled to Las Vegas, a tiny, undeveloped desert outpost in Nevada, where gambling was legal.

The shift in the power balance set Siegel's play for dominance into action.

★ ★ ★

Control of illicit activity in the region proved to be about location. And for the underworld it was the tale of the two L.A.s — city and county. The city police, the LAPD, held no authority in the sheriff's county land: if they saw illegal pursuits occurring across the street — but in county territory — they were powerless to act. Los Angeles County Sheriff Biscailuz and his deputies held the jurisdiction.

After the scandal decimated the LAPD, the city of Los Angeles was closed to underworld activity. But Los Angeles County remained wide open. Sheriff Eugene Biscailuz's mighty domain stretched from Lancaster in the north to Catalina Island, twenty-six miles off the coast, south to Orange County, and east to San Bernadino County — from the desert to the mountains to the sea. Geographically the largest county in the country, at more than four thousand square miles, it was bigger than many eastern states and made up forty-three percent of the state's population.

The sheriff held immense power, overseeing thousands of deputies, the California Highway Patrol, and the independent police forces of forty-six large municipalities. He had his own air force, yet there were only twelve remote sheriff's stations in the massive territory.

Under the sheriff's sole jurisdiction were countless islands of county land scattered throughout the vast city of Los Angeles. County territory inside the city included many of the region's wealthiest and most treasured properties: Beverly Hills, Culver City (home to the Tiffany of studios, MGM), Santa Monica, and a scantily developed 1.7-mile stretch of Sunset Boulevard, between Hollywood and Beverly Hills, that would become legendary as the Sunset Strip.

Biscailuz became an iconic figure in Southern California, and truth and fiction blended in Raymond Chandler's *The Long Goodbye*. In the Los Angeles–based crime novel, the author knowingly describes a colorful sheriff. Vain and inscrutable, the lawman is a publicity-conscious figure who relishes leading important parades dressed in ranchero gear astride a massive silver-bridled stallion. Chandler's sheriff is a ringer for Eugene Biscailuz:

> The Sheriff had a good act . . . his hair was dark and his skin was brown and he had the impassive poise of a cigar store Indian and about the

same kind of brains. But nobody had ever called him a crook. There had been crooks in his department and they had fooled him as well as they had fooled the public, but none of the crookedness rubbed off.

In 1938, the only fix that mattered was Los Angeles County, long notorious as a haven for illegal activities. Captain George "Ironman" Contreras, onetime chief detective for the L.A. County DA's office, was alleged to be directly in charge of corrupt operations at the sheriff's department. In the heavily publicized cleanup of the city, the well-entrenched local racketeers may have decamped for Las Vegas, but they continued to control lucrative and well-established businesses in the sheriff's territory, through fronts.

Starting in the mid-1930s and operating in the county territory of the sparsely developed Sunset Strip, the Clover Club was the height of exclusivity. Small and blood red, the dry-martini-and-diamond operation was unlike other Hollywood establishments; photographers were never allowed past the armed bouncers. Beyond the celebrity-packed supper club and dance floor, and behind crimson-lacquered doors, secret panels, and one-way mirrors, was the heart of the operation: the illegal casino. At the crowded backroom gaming tables, gambling-addicted movie tycoons, like David O. Selznick and B.P. Schulberg, lost immense fortunes nightly.

A flashy young gambler named Eddie Nealis operated the Clover, and reputedly Guy McAfee's and Farmer Page's remaining operations. Page's brother-in-law, Nealis was a handsome Mexican "half-breed." Cohen recalled, "Nealis was hooked up in every type of operation. He was handling ten million dollars a year." According to Mickey, Curly Robinson, a diminutive figure Cohen described as a "bald-headed businessman-type," was Nealis's partner. Freelancing bulls from the sheriff's department and Irish Jimmy Fox, a fierce old-timer with a daunting reputation, were the enforcers.

Mickey confirmed that "Siegel was starting to get entrenched. . . . [G]oing to set things up eastern style — everything of consequence would go through his organization. He would be in sole charge of paying out the dough."

Siegel talked with Nealis, who refused to give the eastern mobster any of the spoils. Mickey recalled that Nealis was "a right-as-day-was-long sort of guy, but he had California ways, couldn't feature having to cut in with anybody else." Cohen's assignment was to destroy his operations. He dutifully wrecked five establishments. Mickey disclosed years later, "Siegel was fixed on bringing Nealis to his knees. Nealis started playing a Los Angeles con with Siegel — sporting talk. 'That Mexican son of a bitch thinks he's coming in with me,' said Siegel. 'Keep on him!'"

Mickey affirmed, "Jimmy Fox was the tough guy in Los Angeles. He was Nealis's muscle. Siegel gave me $5,000 [approximately $75,000 today] to get rid of Fox. He recently beat a rap for killing three guys in a hotel." In the home of a pair of high-powered bookies, Mickey shot Fox and left him for dead. He lived — but was never a threat to Mickey Cohen again. "He pulled a gun — I hit him first," Mickey chillingly confirmed later. "They didn't hold me."

The violence ratcheted higher. Mickey piously revealed, "Cops took a stand for Nealis. Nealis had one cop who had killed eleven people in cold blood." In a confrontation with this deputy, Cohen gave fair warning: "To me you're no cop. Being you're no cop I gotta right to kill you. So come prepared. The next time I see you I'm going to hit you between the eyes." Cohen noted with satisfaction that the murderous deputy "felt I was sincere."

To protect the underworld establishment, corrupt county law enforcers "put on [a] campaign of rousting and harassment on me that was in a class by itself," Mickey later confirmed. He recalled powerful Captain Contreras "pinched me . . . and told me that if he ever saw me on the Sunset Strip that he would personally shoot me in the head."

Mickey didn't relent: "I gave Nealis a rough time. I whacked him across the mouth . . . 'Let's see what you can do with your cop friends about this.'"

With Siegel's approval, Mickey began dealing exclusively with the "little gentleman," Curly Robinson. Faithful to Nealis, Robinson tried to bring the two together. But after a run-in, Cohen decided to kill Nealis. He acquired the key to one of Nealis's apartments and waited for him to enter. Nealis inserted the key into the lock then pulled it out and fled. "I laid a perfect trap for him, but either fate was with him or a sixth sense," Mickey smugly recalled. Terrified by the situation, Nealis retreated to Mexico City.

In a move that proved to assure the rise of Mickey Cohen, "seeing the handwriting on the wall," according to the mobster, Curly Robinson relented and went into business with *him*. With this move, the eastern syndicate finally shook the once absolute power of the local leaders.

The rough road smoothly paved, Siegel took over. The strategically located Sunset Strip magically blossomed into a unique playground for hedonistic movie elite, international society, and top eastern mobsters. There was no place like it on earth. The nightclubs, restaurants, hotels, and shops were intimate and exclusive: Ciro's, the Clover Club, the Trocadero, Mocambo, the Chateau Marmont, the Sunset Tower, the Players Club, the Garden of Allah, Club Gala, La Rue's. The star power, talent, and wealth of the patrons — immense. All about money, glamour, and excess, the Sunset Strip became known as the place where the best of everything could be bought — for the right price. And by his mid-thirties, Bugsy Siegel controlled it all.

Industrial shakedowns were a lucrative racket the Angelenos had never exploited. Willie Bioff, a former pimp from Chicago, was brought to the coast to take control of the International Alliance of Theatrical Stage Employees (IATSE), the studio crafts labor union. Following the lead of industrial racketeer Lepke Buchalter, a New York partner, Ben Siegel took a slice of the movie labor action.

Nobody liked union troubles. The film moguls had no choice but to go along with the underworld's program. A crowd scene scheduled for the morning? Threats of a walkout by hundreds of extras? A call to Ben Siegel would smooth things over: everyone knew he was the power behind central casting.

By the end of the 1930s, the view from the top of the Hollywood Hills seemed unlimited. As conceived by Benjamin Siegel, and executed by Mickey Cohen, a new vision for Los Angeles was beginning to unfold.

While Mickey battled for total control of the territory, Siegel cast his attention to an assortment of new endeavors. Always looking for a good front or another big score, Siegel and the countess occupied themselves with wild schemes and high adventure: a soybean-canning factory; a mysterious hunt for buried treasure off the coast of South America; a European grand tour during which the couple socialized with royalty and visited the palace-like casinos at Monte Carlo and Cannes; and a bomb for Mussolini.

Although regarded by Siegel as just a capable thug, Mickey Cohen was getting ahead. His bankroll, wardrobe, and reputation were rapidly expanding. And he'd found Miss Right.

5

YOUNG BLOOD

"He was surrounded by Bugsy's leftovers . . .
the ones coming in and the ones going out."
A MICKEY COHEN LAWYER

Mickey had gone from Boyle Heights to the fringes of the big leagues. And just like Budd Schulberg's fictional character, Sammy Glick, he could not run fast enough. Constrained by no moral code or the law, Cohen would do anything for money and to gain influential connections.

Siegel's enforcer spent his evenings in the city's decadent nightclubs, encircled by beautiful girls who flocked to Hollywood, eager to break into the movies. Hospitable, amusing, and with movie-extra jobs to offer, Mickey Cohen could have as much female companionship as he wanted. A Cohen lawyer confided to this author, "He was surrounded by Bugsy's leftovers . . . the ones coming in and the ones going out." But he was no tomcat like Siegel.

He was looking for someone special. Later he claimed to be introduced to her at Billy Gray's Band Box, a popular cabaret on North Fairfax. Twenty-one to Mickey's twenty-five, LaVonne Norma Weaver was tiny, with shining auburn hair, fine symmetrical features, large brown eyes, a pert nose, and a slim frame. A wholesomely beautiful shiksa from Los Angeles, according to Mickey she had worked at the studios as a dance instructor and modeled teen fashions. Journalist Florabel Muir would later note that she "looked and acted like a debutante." Future press clippings would trumpet that in the era of celebrated aviatrix Amelia Earhart, LaVonne had learned to fly a plane and dreamed of becoming a commercial pilot.

Mickey said she "intrigued" him. And he said LaVonne seemed willing not to ask questions about his lifestyle, accepting that he was "in the boxing game." Mickey bragged to a lawyer, "She can cook in three languages."

But, so the story goes, their first date began unusually. Scheduled to call on her at seven, she was dressed in her finest and still waiting — at eleven. Rather than Mickey, a strange man came to pick her up. Explaining that Mickey was busy, he drove LaVonne to her date's apartment, where she continued to wait in a smoke-filled room full of men. By the time Mickey finished dressing it was midnight. He escorted the patient young woman to an exclusive cabaret. He was courteous, engaging, and made no physical demands: a complete gentleman. LaVonne also claimed to be "intrigued."

"I'd never seen anyone quite like him," Lavonne later told a reporter.

"Not since," Mickey chimed in.

"You can say that again," she retorted. "We started going around together and it wasn't until Jack Donahoe, a captain in the Los Angeles police, told me all about Mickey that I really knew who he was. But by that time it was too late. I was in love."

Mickey claimed years later that LaVonne was "sweet and pretty — a virtuous girl. I fell in love, but . . . I felt all the time I was abusing the privilege by misleading her. I would . . . leave her sitting with [Joe] Gentile while I went out on a heist that was planned, she would get suspicious and look at me!"

But LaVonne's true background would prove to be well hidden. Her wholesome public persona was a cleverly fabricated piece of fiction invented by Mickey Cohen.

★ ★ ★

Less than three months after Hitler's panzers rolled into Poland on September 1, 1939, setting off World War II, a blow devastated Ben Siegel's carefully crafted world. Just as he decided to become a movie star himself, one of his former soldiers arrived, uninvited, in Hollywood. Harry "Big Greenie" Greenberg knew all of Siegel's and Lepke's black secrets and the inner workings of their Brooklyn assassination ring, dubbed Murder Inc. by the press. Broke, and on the run from immigration authorities, Greenberg

threatened to turn informant. In New York, the hierarchy of the organization sanctioned his assassination.

Siegel was to arrange the execution, but because of his elevated position, he was not to be directly involved. The "work" was to be left to his
close associate Frankie Carbo, a prominent boxing manager and reputed
assassin. But Siegel was unable to delegate this scenario, and the "Bugsy"
side of his psyche took control. On Thanksgiving eve 1939, authorities
claimed that Carbo and Siegel shot and killed Harry Greenberg on a bleak
Hollywood street. It was the first execution of an eastern hoodlum in Los
Angeles history. Informants in New York soon began implicating Siegel in
the Big Greenie execution.

For the first time in his life, Bugsy Siegel was in serious trouble.
Indicted for the murder of Greenberg, he would spend much of the next
two years fighting to stay out of the gas chamber.

During 1940, and the next year, most of Siegel's men were under indictment or being closely scrutinized. Fresh blood was needed to keep the
businesses afloat. Mickey and his obscure gang began to move beyond
muscle work. Mickey recalled a meeting with Siegel. "He . . . says to me,
'You're a gutty kid, but you need some finesse and polish or you're going to
wind up being on the heavy . . . the rest of your life. You got ability that if
used in the proper way would put you in a different scale.'" Taking up slack
and new responsibilities, Mickey began learning bookmaking and the fine
points of the gambling business.

He confided to writer Ben Hecht years later, "I didn't have no wish to
be a ruler. In fact that was actually contrary to my nature at that time. I
just wanted to be myself — Mickey. I was just an egotistical punk. Winning
a street fight, knockin' over a score, having money to buy the best hats — I
lived for them moments." As Hecht described him, "Young Cohen was
gangster from his toes up. No glimmering of other codes disturbed him."

Mickey met the legendary gambler Nick the Greek. Born in Crete in
1883, Nicolas Dandolas was from an affluent family and had studied
philosophy. With a stipend from his grandfather, he came to the U.S. at
eighteen. He quickly became a gambler fabled for the immense fortunes
he won — and lost. The legend of the man and the tales Dandolas spun

Frankie Carbo, a boxing czar, was Siegel's close friend who was tried and finally acquitted as a co-conspirator in the first eastern syndicate murder to take place in Los Angeles. 1938.

for Mickey, like the one about an Indian sect where members achieved extraordinarily longevity due to a diet of special bread and breathing techniques, fascinated the young hoodlum. The Greek, he remembered warmly, took "a fatherly interest in me and took me to the [Santa Anita] race track for the first time."

At the beautiful track in suburban Arcadia, Mickey Cohen became a racetrack bookie. Taking bets a few feet away from the Pinkerton detectives, he professed naïveté about the legality of bookmaking: "I didn't even know it was illegal. How you going to figure it's illegal to bet in one spot when a short distance from that same spot fifty thousand people are shoving their money across a betting counter in open sight?" But before the racing season ended, problems surfaced. He added, "I soon managed to have my troubles at the track . . . being hot tempered and lacking in diplomacy . . . thinking at the time that force and strength were the only ways of throwing my weight."

During this period, Mickey remained in contact with his old supporter and former fight manager Eddie Mead. A beefy middle-aged man with a doughy face and brown hair slicked straight back from a widow's peak,

Mead was doing well. He managed a champion boxer named Henry Armstrong, for Al Jolson. The small black fighter was a phenomenon; at that time he held three world titles simultaneously. Moonlighting as Mickey's fence, Mead took stolen jewelry and disposed of it in the East.

Over dinner at Ruby Foo's on Sunset, Mead spoke to Mickey about moving away from the gun, offering to connect him with an LAPD captain from Hollywood vice. Sanctioned by police, Mickey Cohen's first gambling operation was a card room at Santa Monica Boulevard and Western. Starting out well, the business collapsed when detectives from LAPD robbery-homicide raided the operation without notifying their brethren from the Hollywood station.

Cohen's next foray was a bookmaking establishment in the attic of the Stratford Coffee Shop, 758 South Rampart. Allen Smiley, whom he met at Santa Anita, was his partner. "We had five phones in the office and they all started ringing . . . Smiley and I didn't stop to think that we didn't know how to write a bet down or take off the service," Mickey recalled. "Imagine the panic . . . died-in-the-wool horse bettors trying to make their bets fast, and Smiley and I worrying only about getting past-posted, which was something we understood . . . we had to watch all the time." He admitted it was "a comedy of errors," where countless mistakes were made calculating the odds. But old-timers were there to mentor the neophyte who couldn't count.

Tall and handsome with a thick head of wavy prematurely gray hair, Allen Smiley, was born Aaron Smehoff in Russia. A contemporary of Siegel's, like the boss he was a womanizer and fashion plate with a long criminal history. With Siegel's support, he became a prominent figure in the Hollywood netherworld. While Mickey remained in the background, Siegel and Smiley appeared together in the city's top nightclubs and restaurants, looking like they had just stepped out of a fashion layout. Lauren Bacall recalled her first Christmas in Hollywood, where at the home of producer Mark Hellinger, she and Humphrey Bogart celebrated with Siegel and Smiley.

Another endeavor was Rhum Boogie, a nightclub Mickey operated on Highland Avenue, near Hollywood Boulevard. A novel concept for Jim Crow Los Angeles, the club imported "black-and-tan" entertainers, like the singing, dancing Trenier Brothers, from the Central Avenue ghetto into the white neighborhood. But the sizzling talent and even the nightly patronage of washed-up screen idol John Barrymore, always tipsy and with a party of cleaning ladies from nearby office buildings, wasn't enough to keep the club afloat.

But with ambition burning in his belly, Mickey Cohen was beginning to figure the convoluted angles of the city and county of Los Angeles.

Much activity centered on the world-famous crossroad of Hollywood and Vine. Ben Siegel, on bail for the murder charge against him, continued to hold court daily from a tufted leather booth with a phone at the Vine Street Brown Derby, a movie star haunt. Siegel would kibitz and flash his million-dollar grin to the household names that approached his table. He dined, surrounded by loyal pals: the producer Mark Hellinger, wearing his signature tinted glasses, dark suit, black shirt, and white tie; Warner Brothers gangster star George Raft; theater magnate Sid Grauman, an investor in the Derby and owner of the Chinese, Egyptian, and Million Dollar movie palaces; and the ever-present Allen Smiley.

The Broadway department store, Al Levy's popular eatery, and chic La Conga, the tiny, exorbitantly pricy nightspot, were across the street from the celebrity-packed Derby. Small bars, radio stations, recording studios, and pawnshops filled the treeless Vine Street cityscape. Movie labor racketeer Willie Bioff had an office on the corner in the Taft building, as did Siegel's accountant, Harry Sackman. A short block east was Hollywood Legion Stadium, the boxing mecca.

Mickey's handler, Champ Segal, fronted for Siegel at Le Grand Prix, a luxurious streamline deco barbershop directly north of the Derby. The top action was there, in the twenty-four-hour tonsorial. The nation's major gamblers, from Nick the Greek to Sacramento Butch, were in frequent attendance, as were gunmen, gamblers, grifters, fight promoters, boxers, jockeys, and stars of film, records, and radio.

Budd Schulberg described Vine Street in his Hollywood novel, *What Makes Sammy Run?*: "All along the sidewalk were little knots of poolroom characters who always seemed to be there, holding mysterious conferences. Down the street the playboys were getting out of red Cadillac phaetons or monogrammed town cars at La Conga. There was something savage and tense about that street."

As the Nazis bombed Britain, and Hitler did a jig in the shadow of the Arc de Triomphe, autograph hunters and tourists prowled the crowded sidewalks of Hollywood and Vine, searching for celebrities. An anonymous face entrenched at the fabled crossroad was Mickey Cohen's.

Across from the Derby, Mickey first took on Jimmy Utley, who would become one of his most formidable enemies. A decade older than Cohen, James Francis Utley was tiny and meek-looking, with a round, freckled face, red hair, and horn-rimmed glasses. Dressed conservatively, "he had the appearance of a bank teller," as Mickey tersely described his rival. Mickey dubbed him "Squeaky Voice."

Starting out as a carnival hustler, Utley arrived in Los Angeles in the mid-1920s. He first gained press attention as an informant for reforming cafeteria owner Clifford Clinton, the man whose public crusade proved to be the linchpin in bringing down corrupt Mayor Frank Shaw. A convicted morphine peddler, Utley worked with Jack Dragna. He was involved in prostitution, bookmaking, illegal abortion mills and drugs, and he bossed the lucrative legal bingo parlors at honky-tonk Venice Beach, the Coney Island of L.A. Utley was never shy about his police connections. Mickey despised him for that.

One day at lunchtime, Mickey saw Utley talking to a cop across from the Derby and pointing at him. Told by Siegel to rein in his temper and learn some tact, Mickey still had little impulse control. In the crowded street, he beat Utley badly.

Jack Dragna was furious when he heard about the incident. Siegel severely reprimanded Cohen, repeating it was part of the job to do business with the cops. Mickey was offended. For him a rat was the lowest form of humanity.

Business was Mickey's primary focus, but not the sole dimension of his life. After two years of steady companionship, despite repeated warnings to LaVonne from the LAPD's Jack Donahoe and adamant objections from her parents, on October 15, 1940 — the night before Mickey registered for the Selective Service Act of 1940 — LaVonne Norma Weaver, twenty-three, married the twenty-seven-year-old Mickey Cohen.

Mickey remembered LaVonne was upset when he insisted she come to his attic bookie shop for blood tests and the marriage license. The middle-of-the-night ceremony took place at a for-hire chapel on Western Avenue, and the wedding party consisted of his gangster friends: best man Stumpy Zevon, Joe Sica, and Mike Howard. Mickey later admitted he further angered his bride by demanding the presence of Toughie, his dog, at the ceremony: "The marriage was nearly called off when the minister in the chapel refused to let my toy bull dog . . . be one of the witnesses of the marriage." After threatening to leave, Cohen got his way: "When I finally convince him that I was serious, he consented to leave the dog [sitting] on a chair in the other room."

There was no honeymoon for these newlyweds. The work-obsessed groom left his bookmaking den just long enough to exchange vows.

"I've never regretted marrying Mickey," LaVonne confided to reporter Florabel Muir years later. "No matter what anybody else thinks of him, he's the kindest, most lovable man I've ever known."

Hours after the ceremony, using the name Michael Mickey Cohen, he visited the draft board. A Boyle Heights address, 125 North Breed Street, was given as his residence; his stated occupation was part owner of the Stratford Coffee Shop and fight promoter. Mickey claimed "married" status, which, at that time, could guarantee draft exemption.

According to a later FBI report, the Meyer Harris Cohen file:

> COHEN registered for Selective Service on October 16, 1940 and, in submitting his questionnaire, described himself as a fight promoter. He carefully pointed out his extensive criminal record and was subsequently classified 4-F as being "morally unfit for military service." Later he and his brother apparently chafing under the disparaging comments and subtle insinuations of friends whose sons had already been drafted or had enlisted, made efforts to have COHEN re-classified. An active police investigation of him made at the time failed to substantiate claims that he was of good character and reputation.

Ben Siegel remained under indictment for the Greenberg killing, but a sudden event in New York changed the dynamics at the syndicate's Hollywood branch. In Brooklyn, Murder Inc. assassin Abe "Kid Twist" Reles had turned informant. Slated to testify against Siegel and Frankie Carbo in a Los Angeles courtroom, Reles was being held in round-the-clock protective custody by the New York police at the Half Moon, a Coney Island hotel. On November 12, 1941, Reles "mysteriously" fell to his death.

Frank Costello, who had taken over as head of both the Luciano crime family and the underworld commission after his partner's incarceration, used his incomparable political connections, and a large bribe, to ensure that Reles would never testify against Siegel. With Reles's timely "suicide," the Big Greenie murder case fell apart. Bugsy Siegel was a free man. From three thousand miles away, Mickey Cohen felt the absolute power of the Combination.

Three weeks after Reles's death, on December 7, 1941, the Japanese attacked the U.S. naval base at Honolulu, killing thousands of sailors and sinking much of the fleet. The devastation of Pearl Harbor pulled the isolationist nation into World War II.

6

PICKED FROM THE CHORUS

"Mickey . . . shy as a wild rabbit about
having his picture taken."
FLORABEL MUIR, REPORTER

Unprepared for war and in a panic to quickly ratchet up, the federal government poured vast sums of money into the Los Angeles economy. The aircraft, shipbuilding, and oil industries exploded as soldiers and war workers flooded the region. A major transportation hub and deepwater port, Los Angeles's population skyrocketed during the war years. While the movie studios pumped out patriotism, propaganda, and pinups, the underworld moved in to quickly profit.

A bedroom community just across the hill from Hollywood, Burbank was the headquarters of Warner Brothers, Disney, and Universal studios. An immense Lockheed Aircraft plant and many ancillary businesses were also there. Strategically located in L.A. County, Burbank became the first stage of the incredible rise of Mickey Cohen.

He opened a bookie shop a block from the Warner studio. "I had my sights on organizing the bookmakers," he said. "The Burbank operation gave me a foothold, a starting point." While his partners, Joe and Fred Sica, handled bookmaking operations at the film and aircraft factories, Mickey oversaw Dincara Stock Farm. A horse ranch with a casino, it was a unique take on the mob's rug joints, as their luxury gambling dens were called. "A very beautiful place where they bred horses and . . . kept . . . horses for riding," Mickey proudly described Dincara. Set far into the wooded foothills above the Warner lot, the illegal gambling hall was in a stable at the bottom of a steep incline. A small red light at the end of the driveway meant the casino was in operation.

Mickey recalled, "We opened in a room with one crap table, an old broken down thing. It was so small . . . that when someone wanted to go to the bathroom the dealer had to leave the end of the table to let some lady by. It grew to an air-conditioned $125,000 [nearly $1.5 million today] building." Operating on and off for eight years, Dincara provided free valet parking, and white-jacketed Filipino waiters offered bountiful complimentary food. Mickey said with pride, "We used to pack 1,500 to 2,000 people in every night."

He deemed Dincara "a perfect front." His new connections had solidified a working arrangement for him with Captain George Contreras of the L.A. County Sheriff's Department. Layers of politicians, police, press, and even religious figures were cut in on the horse farm. Distinguished law enforcer Blayney Matthews, chief of the private police force at Warner Brothers studio and onetime head investigator for the DA's office, was on Dincara's payroll. Jack Dineen, a retired police captain, oversaw the operation. With Mickey Cohen using Burbank as a beachhead, the municipality's head police officer, Chief Elmer Adams, suddenly had funds for a yacht.

At the Dincara, reality blurred. Movie people, from legendary stars like Bob Hope and Bing Crosby to grips, came directly from the studio, actors often still dressed in costume. Pirates and cowboys stood next to Egyptian slave girls at roulette wheels, while rajahs and toga-clad Romans played blackjack with Cockney waifs and beautiful ladies from the court of Versailles. Attired in English riding apparel incongruously topped by a wide-brimmed fedora, Mickey flaunted his equestrian skills when riding with his own society woman.

In 1942, FBI agents visited the Cohen home in Burbank. They spoke with LaVonne and interviewed Mickey for the first time. An FBI memo noted, "Siegel began a program of encouraging Cohen."

Mickey recalled that it had become exceedingly profitable to function

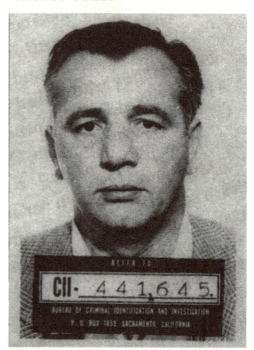

Joe Sica, Mickey Cohen's lifelong partner in crime. Circa late 1950s.

in a businesslike manner. "Siegel would throw me 10 grand, 25 grand — the biggest was 40 grand [more than $500,000 today]. There were no books kept or explanations. All he would say is 'Here, this is for you.'" He added, "At the beginning of my operation Ben Siegel gave me to understand that I was not going to be a fly-by-night hoodlum . . . but that I had the ability, stature and personality to do things in a much more respectable manner and that I should start to pay my taxes so that I could avoid any trouble with the Internal Revenue."

There was reason for concern about the Internal Revenue Service. From Capone on down, many top mobsters had been imprisoned for tax evasion. Cohen was circumspect when he later admitted, "Ben was worried because I wasn't doing any kind of work, but I always had three or four thousand dollars in my pockets and spent money like a drunken sailor. I was such a high spender and liver that he was sure the attention of the Internal Revenue people would be focused on me."

Siegel arranged for his accountant to file taxes for Mickey. The former boxer eventually acceded and filed, but he arrogantly contested, "I was a firm believer that if the government or anybody else wanted any part of my money, they should at least be on hand to help me steal it!"

After the murder indictment was dropped in the Harry Greenberg case, there were new strategies for Siegel. He planned to expand the rackets while personally moving into lucrative gray areas that operated within the confines of the law. More than ever, he maintained a legion of prominent businessmen, politicians, attorneys, accountants, and lobbyists who fronted for him. The special skills of Mickey Cohen's band were reserved for less savory duties.

At the top of Benjamin Siegel's agenda was control of the wire service. The bookies' lifeline, the wire provided essential, instant betting data, making it the key to organized gambling on a national level. Over the years, Siegel had intently observed Moses Annenberg, the owner of the dominant wire, grow into a figure of incomparable wealth and monumental prominence. Annenberg's rise first began with the bloody newspaper circulation wars that plagued Chicago in the early years of the twentieth century. Smart, tough, and volatile, Moe Annenberg served as the head of Hearst's distribution department, where underworld sluggers, fighting newsboys, and gangland techniques were utilized to mandate prime placement of Hearst's tabloids. It was Annenberg's ruthless world that gave birth to Mickey Cohen. Later, he became a Hearst distributor and publisher and owner of the race information sheet, the *Daily Racing Form*. Eventually Moe Annenberg acquired Nationwide News Service. Using whatever rough tactics were necessary to achieve his goal, nineteen competing wire services were soon out of business.

Monopolistic Nationwide was a cash cow and operated legally. Bookmaking was the illegal part of the quotient and was not part of Annenberg's business. By the mid-1930s, Nationwide supplied information from each of the twenty-nine racetracks in the U.S. and into Canada, Mexico, and Cuba. It boasted more than 15,000 subscribers in 223 cities and towns in 39 states, and was one of the biggest customers of AT&T and Western Union. Nearly assassinated twice in 1934 (once by an irate former partner, the second time by the Chicago outfit), Annenberg, who traveled with a bodyguard, soon purchased two major newspapers: the *Philadelphia Inquirer* and the *Miami Tribune*. His arm's-length involvement with syndicated gambling combined with the fiery editorials in his newspapers attracted negative attention from Washington. He raised the ire of several prominent politicos, and in 1938 he was the subject of a six-page memo from FBI Director J. Edgar Hoover to President Franklin Roosevelt. Indicted for income tax evasion, after pleading guilty in 1939, Annenberg bowed out of the wire. He paid an extraordinary $9.5 million (nearly $150 million today) in back taxes and was sentenced to three years in the federal penitentiary in Atlanta. His family legacy became one of great philanthropy.

In Chicago, James Ragen, a fierce old Annenberg loyalist, who was reputed to have killed a man in a fight, took control of Nationwide. Renamed Continental Press, its representatives on the coast were Johnny Rosselli and Jack Dragna, as they had been before the change of ownership. Ragen's son-in-law, Russell Brophy, ran branch offices in Los Angeles.

Seeking ownership and complete control, Ben Siegel set up a competing wire named Trans-America in partnership with the Chicago outfit. Based in Phoenix, it took over the betting parlors in Arizona and Las Vegas with dispatch. With Mickey Cohen handling the organization of the bookmakers, Trans-America successfully moved into L.A. County. But the 1,800 bookie shops doing business in the city of Los Angeles remained with Continental.

Brophy was approached in a friendly manner, but after checking with Ragen, he rejected any alliance with Trans-America. In July 1942, with the agreement of Dragna and Rosselli, Siegel outlined the new order of the L.A. underworld. Cohen was placed in charge of gambling operations. It was prudent for Brophy to join the team.

Again, he refused all overtures. Siegel decided to put Brophy on notice. He instructed Mickey to beat him badly but not kill him. A week later, Cohen and Joe Sica appeared at Continental's downtown headquarters. Using tactics that Ragen had pioneered, it should have come as no surprise when Brophy received a vicious thrashing. Against Johnny Rosselli's orders, the pair also tore out the phones and destroyed the operation.

Still refusing to be intimidated, Brophy swore out a complaint against Cohen and Joe Sica for attempted murder. While Siegel worked to fix the indictment — and placate his associates, Dragna and Rosselli — the two men who had beaten Brophy and wrecked his office disappeared. Sica joined the army, while Mickey left for Phoenix, where he was placed with the influential gambler Gus Greenberg, until the legal case could be resolved.

Months later, Siegel had a fix in place. A trial date was set for Cohen and Joe Sica. Going before the judge, the pair got off with a reduced charge of simple assault and paid a miniscule fine.

★ ★ ★

Upon his return to Los Angeles, Mickey, twenty-nine, ramped up his activity further: "Some of my old time cronies from back East began to join my forces." Given a mandate by Siegel, he and his men began an unrelenting campaign organizing bookmakers. Offering a package of Siegel's Trans-America wire, protection, and debt collection, over a short period of time Mickey Cohen became the partner of more than five hundred bookmakers in the Los Angeles area.

He began to change his mode: "I added some gentlemanly qualities to my actions and started to learn the use of diplomacy. I was a fairly likeable fellow (from what I've been told) and with my new ability . . . to . . . hold . . . my vicious temper, I began to pick up added friends who were to fit in the operations . . . in the future."

Curly Robinson was a man he listened to and respected. According to Mickey, he had helped him in innumerable ways, mentoring him and introducing him to important local figures. The picture of legitimacy, Robinson acted as managing director of Associated Operators of Los Angeles County, Inc. (AOLAC) and West Coast director of the National Organization of Automatic Machine Owners (NOAMO), and he wrote gaming industry handbooks from his office on West Washington Boulevard. At Robinson's behest, Mickey claimed that he and his associates had provided the necessary "persuasion" needed to form a new statewide association of pinball and slot machine operators, a legal gem.

The "Furious Forties of the Brown Broadway," the white-hot strip of nightclubs along Central Avenue, between Fortieth and Fiftieth Streets, was where a galaxy of African-American stars, like Nat "King" Cole and Billie Holiday, performed. A beehive of vice, the area was prime for business. In the manner of Bumpy Johnson, Harlem's legendary Combination-connected gang boss, L.A.'s Elihu "Black Dot" McGee — a tall, trim, impeccably dressed man with an ebony complexion, glistening widely set eyes, sleekly processed hair, and pencil-thin mustache — controlled the rackets in the community. The dapper gambler was friendly with all the top African-American entertainers and athletes and owned the Flame and

Mickey's money machine, the "paint store" on Beverly Boulevard near Crescent Heights Boulevard, where one of the "Shannon" brothers met his death. 1945.

Casablanca nightspots, as well as Turf's Barber Shop and Dot's Bar-B-Que. Mickey Cohen and Black Dot McGee divided the action in the South Central ghetto. For Cohen, McGee also managed the Downbeat Club, where the Stars of Swing, featuring Charlie Mingus, Buddy Collette, Teddy Edwards, and other jazz luminaries played.

In vice-ridden Chinatown, Cohen made a similar arrangement. He recalled his influence had spread to each of the forty-six local municipalities: "The organization eventually spread into every little city in Los Angeles County." He expanded into Orange County and claimed to develop a relationship with Myford Irvine, scion of the wealthiest and most prominent family in the region.

He took pride that his small crew had been able to transcend their lowly beginnings. "Although we started with heists, we eventually set up a bookie empire, a protection empire, and a money-lending empire for the bookmakers and gamblers."

Opening a commission betting office in a paint store at 8109 Beverly Boulevard, he became a bookie's bookie. In the tiny, unassuming one-story building emblazoned with signage for "Kon-Kre-Kota," an asbestos-based

"Wonder Paint," Cohen placed hedges on huge wagers with other syndicate offices across the country and booked off-track for major bettors, usually horse owners and jockeys.

He later divulged the inner workings of the "paint shop": "At the peak of my operation I dealt with from six to eight offices throughout the country, and my transactions with each office amounted to anywhere from $30 to $150,000 a day [approximately $360,000 to $1.6 million today] with each office . . . Some offices paid me from 2½ to 5 percent for the monies . . . Our main source of revenue . . . was the percentage of commission we got for moving the bet." He once confided in Hearst editor Jim Richardson, "You want to know how gambling money is made? . . . We need only one fixed fight or horse race a year in each territory. Ten or twelve of these a year around the country. The word goes out, and you get the big bets down."

The La Brea Social Club, another of his "babies," was nearby in a beautiful Venetian Revival building on La Brea Avenue, near Beverly Boulevard. The private two-floor casino was decorated with photographs of boxing's greatest champions and included a restaurant. Catering exclusively to professional gamblers, and a few affluent Hollywood businessmen "who stuck their noses in," it featured a rich-moneyed, Chicago-style crap game — a first for L.A.

Mickey confirmed, "The money craps were in private quarters so as to give the players a feeling of security, as there were at times a much as $150,000 to $200,000 [$350,000 to $600,000 today] in cash on the table." The operation also doubled as a meeting ground for his men and clearinghouse for his activities.

For eight months in 1944 he ran an exclusive party house at 9100 Hazen Drive, deep in the Coldwater Canyon hills. After midnight, when the wartime curfew shut down the nightclubs on the Strip, the luxury domicile became popular with the rich and famous. Open until dawn, the specialty of the house was high-stakes games of chemin de fer and baccarat. Serving no one without a reservation, Mickey offered gourmet dining, a sommelier, and a swing band with comely girl singers who, "when the occasion called for it," could sing risqué lyrics. Beautiful party girls were employed as shills, steerers, and escorts.

"There was never an evening that we did not turn away thirty to forty couples who were not suitable or did not fit into the surroundings and atmosphere, or with the personalities who were in the club," he recalled. "The operations were so fabulous and high that our investment was quickly recovered."

Neighbors worked to close the enterprise. They leaked the story of the "Mystery House" to the press — although Cohen's association remained hidden. Several nights in a row the media was alerted when residents blocked the revelers from crossing the narrow residential lane. Cohen later sniffed that when the City Attorney's office did not respond to the neighbors' protests "as quickly as they thought the matter warranted, they formed a vigilante committee and took the law in their own hands to form a human blockade of the private road leading to this mystery establishment." He added, "The newspapers made quite a thing out of the affair . . . with the movie names that were intermingled with the situation." Their effort proved successful. The gamblers moved on.

Annexing several suites in the exclusive Ambassador Hotel, he opened a high-stakes "money crap game" for a handpicked clientele. Mickey explained, "At the time I was close to some people at the Ambassador Hotel who had to do with the operation of that establishment. I contacted these people and offered them a deal . . . Most of the boys working at the hotel were friendly to me and, knowing that this operation would add much to their own pockets, were very cooperative. We had quite a run in the Ambassador."

Wartime shortages proved profitable. He made fortunes in silk and nylon stockings, quality liquors, perfumes, gas, and food-ration stamps. Prime-cut steaks were a black market rarity he provided for the right price, or favor. Even spaghetti sauces were big business for Mickey Cohen.

Operating in labor enforcement and strikebreaking, his loan shark operation grew to "the size of a legitimate bank." Top restaurants, nightclubs, and bars were all in his web of influence and proved to be another area of profit. And he recalled, "As sort of a hobby I retained . . . interest in one of my first loves . . . boxing." With a wealthy businessman fronting, he controlled the career of a leading lightweight contender. During the war years, the fighter, Willie Joyce, was matched with champions Henry Armstrong, Ike Williams, and Willie Pep. Mickey also sponsored a heavyweight who fought Joe Louis, the most important champion of the era. Looking extremely content, Mickey posed with the legendary Louis for a photograph. Cohen recalled, "Many other leading fighters tried to interest me in managing them, but it was impossible for me to really make it a full-time operation."

Mickey would deny it, but prostitution, extortion, and drugs were also major parts of his operations. "He knew every whore in town, mainly for protection," a Cohen lawyer acknowledged.

LaVonne and Mickey relocated in 1944, to a grand apartment in Beverly Hills. Another step into the big time, each new residence was more spacious and luxurious than the one before, with ample closet space to contain Mickey's constantly expanding wardrobe.

Bugsy Siegel had made a mensch out of him, and during the process Cohen grew from ambitious thug to cunning racketeer. Through his alliance with Siegel, the ex-boxer became closely associated with all the royalty of gangland. Mickey admitted to admiring Siegel, but as time went on it became harder for him to accede to Siegel's demands.

By 1945, Siegel had it with L.A. The previous year, after an unprecedented roust in Allen Smiley's Sunset Tower apartment, Benjamin Siegel was put on trial, again. This time it was for a demeaning, nickel-and-dime bookmaking complaint. Los Angeles County District Attorney Fred N. Howser added a conspiracy charge to the indictment, which changed the misdemeanor offense to a felony. Curiously, Mickey and film star George Raft were present in the apartment at the time of the arrest, but they were not charged. Clearly, it was Siegel who was the target.

With movie idol George Raft as the star defense witness, the Bugsy Siegel bookmaking trial was a media circus. A few well-connected figures from the East that had known Siegel since his youth also showed up at the proceedings. Reporter Florabel Muir mused, "Losing face is as distasteful to denizens of the underworld as it is to Orientals. If it happens too often to those in the high spots it . . . becomes dangerous. When a whispering campaign starts about a guy being through, it often happens that he is."

The episode was a rude awakening for Siegel. He sold the Holmby Hills mansion, his eye cast toward more salubrious pastures. In 1945, he handed the operational reins of the byzantine Southern California empire to Mickey Cohen.

Benjamin "Bugsy" Siegel accompanied by the most powerful criminal lawyer in Los Angeles, Jerry "The Magnificent Mouthpiece" Giesler. 1944.

The Mick could see the finish line.

Running fast, hard, and long, Cohen had made many enemies coming up. With his thick bankroll and newfound authority, he *really* began to make waves. "The only thing they respected was fear," he said of his rivals. "It was really a matter of dog eat dog."

Mickey had grown up in Boyle Heights with a family named Shaman. As adults they were also known as the "Shannon brothers." Mickey acknowledged they were strictly local, adding, "they thought they were tough . . . knowing me they thought they could get away with a lot of things." After a dispute at the La Brea casino, Joe, the youngest "Shannon," was badly beaten by one of Cohen's men. Angry and armed, Max Shaman came looking for Mickey at the paint shop. The California Crime Commission reported: "The record shows that on May 16, 1945, he [Mickey Cohen] shot and killed Max Shaman in the office he maintained as 'front' for his fast-growing bookmaking business. There were no witnesses."

Impressed by Mickey Cohen's rising power and ability to handle the lucrative territory, New York underworld czar and Siegel partner Frank Costello hired attorney Jerry Giesler to represent Mickey in the Shaman matter. Nicknamed the Magnificent Mouthpiece, Giesler now had an unparalleled reputation, having successfully defended such Hollywood luminaries as Charlie Chaplin, Errol Flynn, Busby Berkeley, and theater tycoon Alexander Pantages in criminal complaints, as well as Bugsy Siegel. In Los Angeles, if you had wealth, power, or were merely famous — and you were in trouble — the first call: "Get Giesler."

He earned his fat retainer by satisfying DA Fred N. Howser that the killing of Max Shaman was self-defense. Mickey recalled, "Although the coroner's jury brought in a verdict of homicide, when the situation was finally evaluated . . . I was given my freedom."

But the paint shop was on a busy boulevard, at the center of a well-populated residential neighborhood. The Max Shaman killing was too public to keep hidden. For the first time since his boxing days, Mickey Cohen appeared in the papers. "As shy as a wild rabbit about having his picture taken, [Mickey] dummied up and wouldn't tell anybody anything," Florabel Muir observed.

7

HOLLYWOOD BYZANTINE

"I'll make sure that c . . . s . . . . . tells
me how he got his information."
BUGSY SIEGEL, SPEAKING OF
FBI DIRECTOR J. EDGAR HOOVER

In 1946, for a second year, the narrow world of Hollywood was rocked by violent strikes. Two unions were going head to head: the well-entrenched and mobbed-up IATSE and leftist Herb Sorrell's Conference of Studio Unions (CSU). Eight studios were at stake, each grinding out a picture a week. Sorrell called his ten thousand tradesmen to strike. IATSE's leaders promised studio negotiators that their members would break Sorrell's picket lines and keep the film factories rolling.

A major clash broke out at the Warner Brothers gate. CSU strikers slammed IATSE workers with bricks and rocks when they tried to break the picket lines. More violence erupted in Culver City, outside MGM. Each union accused the other of calling out underworld goon squads. Eventually IATSE demonstrated it had the strength to keep the studios open. The moguls bowed in gratitude to Mickey Cohen's muscle.

Work went on, but the town remained tense as strikes continued. Reacting to the prevailing mood, Ronald Reagan, the liberal Democrat who had recently been elected president of the Screen Actors Guild, began packing a Smith & Wesson in a shoulder holster.

During this highly volatile period, MGM glamour girl Lana Turner was unperturbed. Fresh from a second divorce and enjoying the success of *The Postman Always Rings Twice*, she hit nightclubs on the Sunset Strip. She told *Photoplay*, "The war had just ended, and the men were home. They seemed to catch your eye everywhere you went, like a greening after a thaw. How I loved to dress up and go dancing with a handsome dark man."

The studios were having problems, but Siegel and his partners were looking toward a cloudless future. The Combination was richer and more powerful than ever, having profited handsomely during the war. Their postwar strategy was to continue in the rackets while expanding into safer, legal propositions. According to a government report, the aristocrats of the mob were already invested in a startling number of legitimate businesses. They wanted more.

According to FBI reports, on the immediate agenda was mob control of leases and concessions of three New York airports — Newark, LaGuardia, and the rapidly expanding Idlewild, later called JFK. They were buying into luxury hotels — like the Beverly-Wilshire, the Sunset Tower, and the Town House in Los Angeles, New York's Waldorf-Astoria and Sherry-Netherland, as well as prime locations in other major cities — through the Kirkeby Hotel chain. They were underwriting extravagant hotels along the oceanfront strip in Miami Beach and widely expanding their Cuban enterprises. The Flamingo Club, the Las Vegas gaming resort that Ben Siegel was building, was another project they believed would be lucrative. It was special — and one hundred percent legitimate.

With his own agenda as acting operations manager of Southern California, Mickey Cohen was not involved in these ventures. He was now a mobster with considerable power and supreme connections, and 1946 would prove to be a deadly year for his foes.

A team of prominent gamblers tried to assassinate him. Soon the coroner's wagon carted the tommy gun–riddled bodies of the plotters, Benny "The Meatball" Gamson and George Levinson, to the morgue. Their partner, Pauley Gibbons, who once had the temerity to enter Cohen's apartment and slash his wardrobe to shreds, was shot and killed as he entered his Beverly Hills flat.

Beverly Hills Police Chief Clifton Anderson was "looking for leads" when he attended Gibbons's funeral. He watched as a drunken bum delivered a large box with an elaborate card that read: "To My Pal."

"The mortician unwrapped it carefully, fearing a bomb or other instrument of death," Anderson noted. "With utmost caution he lifted the lid and revealed the contents of the box. It was filled with horse manure."

The Beverly Hills cops questioned Mickey about the gift honoring Gibbons's demise and then released him: he had an alibi. His top lieutenants, Harry "Hooky" Rothman and Edward "Neddie" Herbert, were held as suspects then released as well.

According to the California Crime Commission, "Gibbons had long been battling with Cohen over their competing gambling operations . . . Gamson and Levinson had been bookie colleagues of Pauley Gibbons. Their deaths automatically removed three potential obstacles in the path of Cohen's plans for building his gambling empire."

Mickey had won several big rounds, but one enemy still rankled him. Now racketeer Jimmy Utley, whom Mickey had always disliked for his police connections, was not only snitching to local authorities, he had become an informant for the California attorney general's office and the FBI. A predator alleged to having sexually assaulted young women in his abortion parlors, Utley had grown powerful and prosperous. He owned the Tropics, off Hollywood Boulevard, and ran the hidden casino in Mark Hansen's Florentine Gardens, and there was much action at his exclusive, star-packed restaurant. At Venice Beach he strolled along the crowded boardwalk, surveying his businesses. A quarter would buy a card at one of his bingo parlors, like the Fortune Club, the Surf, or the Rose. Now Mickey flexed his political muscle to shutter the games at Venice Beach, which were among Utley's prime rackets. Lucrative and legal, the bingo games were suddenly outlawed in the beachfront stronghold.

Cohen recalled, "Utley . . . had a connection to do things, to operate. Naturally, when my operations took over he was pushed aside completely, as I consider a stool pigeon the lowest type of vermin." Utley was then arrested and charged with violation of state gaming laws in relation to the bingo concession on the *Lux*, Tony Cornero's newest gambling ship.

The *Lux* opened for business on August 7, 1946, with immense fanfare. A vivid billboard graced the Sunset Strip. Skywriting planes etched the ship's name into Southland skies, and full-page newspaper ads announced its debut. Days later, it was hit. Governor Earl Warren, Cornero's longtime nemesis, commanded the Long Beach Port Authority to shut down water taxi service to Cornero's ship. Without means to transport gamblers to the *Lux*, the era of California's offshore party boats abruptly ended.

To counter Cohen, Jimmy Utley, and his numerous allies, began an assault on all of his enterprises. Mickey recalled his foe as "quite upset about not being able to operate. Utley started to put on a heat campaign against all of the operations."

A "political roundtable" was called to counter the attack. Mickey wanted to kill Utley, stressing it was the only solution. He recalled, "My vote, and which would have been the easiest way to handle it, was to put his lights out. Most of the others at the meeting became panicky at this severe decision, and voted that he should be taught a lesson . . . that would cause him much embarrassment."

The final decision: Mickey would personally deliver the warning.

Utley owned Lucey's, a popular restaurant located directly across from the Paramount lot on Windsor Boulevard at Melrose. A movie-crowd hangout, it also harbored a drug bazaar and was frequented by Utley's associates.

At lunchtime on August 16, 1946, Mickey Cohen and one of his men brazenly walked into Lucey's. In front of scores of customers, including producers, directors, film executives, and stars like Joel McCrea and Eddie Cantor, Cohen pistol-whipped Utley while an associate held a gun on the diners. Watching in silence, many tourists thought the scene was staged for a film. Cohen and his accomplice, dressed for the scorching weather in Hawaiian shirts, stepped over the unconscious victim, tipped their hats to the diners, and leisurely strolled out. Tracking blood through the fashionable restaurant, the pair pushed past the crowd of autograph hounds lurking at the entry and sped off in a waiting car.

Utley was hospitalized for two weeks. He refused to identify his attackers, and none of the restaurant's patrons came forward to report what they had witnessed. But that was not the end of the matter. After the beating, Mickey phoned his rival and demanded a heavy "loan."

Jack Dragna was livid. Jimmy Utley vowed vengeance. With Mickey in control of Los Angeles, it was now clearly apparent that Dragna and his associates were being squeezed out.

Gambling became legal in Nevada in 1931. Los Angeles mobster Tony Cornero was the first to see a future in the barren desert of southern Nevada: that year, he opened a casino near Boulder City. In short order, the joint burned down, and Cornero's interests remained in Los Angeles. But the old L.A. gambling fraternity, headed by Guy McAfee, had been successfully established in tiny Las Vegas since L.A.'s city hall scandals of 1938.

After his bookmaking bust, Ben Siegel saw Las Vegas as the second key to his legitimacy. Already entrenched there with Trans-America wire, he decided to colonize the desert. As he once fantasized about movie stardom, Siegel now envisioned an air-conditioned El Dorado. Casting himself as the mogul of Las Vegas, he would bring luxury, style, and top entertainment to the dusty, inhospitable whistle-stop.

With Mickey Cohen running Los Angeles, Siegel was able to focus on the Vegas project. Following his destiny as his fortieth birthday approached, the Flamingo Club became his obsession. With backing from Meyer Lansky, Frank Costello, Joe Adonis, Longie Zwillman, Al Capone's cousins — the Fischettis of Chicago — and members of the Minneapolis mob, for the second time Siegel began his push into Guy McAfee's domain. Given a free hand, anything he wanted appeared. Construction began in early 1946.

Originally the exclusive gambling resort was the idea of Billy Wilkerson. Famous as the man who discovered Lana Turner, Wilkerson was a compulsive high-stakes gambler. He owned the influential movie trade paper *The Hollywood Reporter* and was also the creator of the most spectacular supper clubs on the Sunset Strip. A smooth and sophisticated entrepreneur, Wilkerson was an experienced operator. A supporter of Siegel's since the mobster arrived on the coast, it was rumored that Wilkerson fronted for syndicate interests.

During the early days of the Flamingo project, the relationship between Siegel and Wilkerson became turbulent. Soon after ground was broken, Siegel threatened to kill Wilkerson if he did not relinquish control of the project and sell back his shares. Wilkerson acquiesced. He began driving a robin's egg blue bulletproof Cadillac, on loan from Tony Cornero, and eventually hid out in Paris.

Except for the stress and heavy publicity the divorce from his long-suffering wife of eighteen years created, things appeared to be on course for Siegel. Then a seeming insignificant gossip item nearly brought him down. On July 14, 1946, Walter Winchell, the enormously popular newspaper columnist and radio star, blared in his trademark staccato to his audience of fifty million listeners: "According to the FBI, a prominent West Coast racketeer is endeavoring to muscle a prominent West Coast publisher out of his interest in a West Coast hotel." Clearly referring to Siegel and Wilkerson, the explosive blind item had been given to Winchell by his close friend FBI Director J. Edgar Hoover.

Revealed here for the first time, this information struck deep into Siegel's self-destructive nature, igniting a firestorm. According to the Benjamin "Bugs" Siegel FBI file #62-81518, July 21, 1946:

> SIEGEL stated that he was going to New York to have Winchell get hold of the Director [J. Edgar Hoover] and bring the Director to him [Siegel]. Referring to the Director, SIEGEL shouted, "I'll make sure that c . . . s . . . . . tells me how he got his information." SIEGEL implied that he would take care of the people who furnished the information to the Director when he learned their identity. SIEGEL ranted that all of his money and his friends' money, everything he had, was tied up in the Flamingo Hotel, and the publicity given this venture by Winchell might prevent him from getting the licenses, hotel, liquor, gambling, et cetera.

FBI Director J. Edgar Hoover was a closeted homosexual and reputed cross-dresser with a gambling habit. The mob was privy to this information. Hoover had always insisted: "There is no organized crime."

But calling Hoover an obscene name that indicated a sexual act, on a tapped phone, was not in Siegel's interest. When Hoover became aware of the information, using the auspices of an FBI investigation — CAPGA, which stood for the "reactivation of the Capone gang" — Hoover immediately assigned ten agents to follow Siegel, observe his activities, and listen in to all his conversations. Orders went out for all his domiciles and offices to be wiretapped and his correspondence monitored. Within days the Civilian Production Administration, a federal agency, shut down construction at the Flamingo and started an investigation into fraud against the government, in connection with the hotel's construction.

Handsome, dapper Allen Smiley was constantly seen with Bugsy Siegel at the best places in Hollywood. Smiley was sitting very carefully on a sofa with Siegel at the time of Siegel's execution. 1947.

Battling to clear his name from allegations intended to constitute a federal indictment and restart building, Siegel, accompanied by Allen Smiley and a costly team of architects and attorneys, spent most of August 1946 in San Francisco, at hearings. More than a month after construction was halted, building restarted. But the FBI continued utilizing every asset in its arsenal to ascertain violations of federal statues against him. Investigations into narcotics distribution, tax evasion, draft dodging, and more were instituted.

A reckless frenzy to complete the delayed undertaking ballooned the Flamingo's cost to nearly $6 million (more than $66 million today), an extraordinary figure for a 120-room hotel. Siegel spent the next months traveling the country, raising funds for the over-budget project. Selling over a hundred percent of the shares, Siegel put the mob hierarchy into awkward partnerships with Beverly Hills businessmen.

Lansky's Swiss banking sources made allegations. They told him that Virginia Hill, the female mobster whom Siegel had secretly married, visited Zurich and deposited an enormous sum of money in a clandestine numbered bank account. She also signed a long-term lease on an apartment in the Swiss city. Siegel's partners believed the money banked in Switzerland was siphoned from construction overruns at the Flamingo. It appeared that

Siegel was complicit with Hill in the larceny, and if confronted, Siegel had plans to flee.

Mickey later said, "I knew that Benny's Vegas propositions and the Flamingo he was building took off badly. Any time any proposition in the racket world goes bad . . . you wonder if the person knows what he's doing or if what's going on is the right thing. That's especially if you've been bankrolled, like Benny was, by the organization."

Though construction was only partially finished, Siegel was forced by his partners to open the Flamingo on December 26, 1946. The casino was serviceable, but there were no completed guest rooms. A star-studded show and the best of everything was provided for the nightclub patrons, and on the gambling floor, Siegel employed a carefully selected crew of croupiers. These handsome Greeks, imported from Havana, stole huge sums of money from the house, while Guy McAfee's wife, starlet June Brewster, and other black-chip gamblers won heavily.

Siegel became frantic. As the losses mounted and the pressure grew, his legendary temper raged. Poor attendance, shortfalls and rubber checks, violent outbursts, and outrageous public embarrassments were common occurrences. Bleeding capital, the Flamingo shut down a few weeks after opening. Given an influx of new funding from mob partners, the Flamingo reopened on March 1, 1947, after a dress rehearsal by the entertainers, staged before Siegel and Lansky. The three singing Andrews Sisters, one of the nation's most popular acts, headlined the bill. The hotel rooms were finished; the casino re-staffed. This time, the dealers were arrow-straight and folksy. The Monte Carlo pretensions, dress code, and haughty waiters in formal uniforms and white gloves that Siegel had demanded were out. In were waitresses, friendly and pretty, bingo games, and raffles.

Business began to improve, but the Flamingo was not Siegel's only monumental problem. From late summer 1946, a wire war raged. The bookies were furious, screaming they were now forced to pay twice for service, once to Continental and, again, to Trans-America. Years in the making, Trans-America had become wildly profitable for Siegel. Thanks to Mickey Cohen's skills, according to a Continental insider, "[Trans-America] damned near licked us . . . to tell you the God's honest truth, we were expecting to go out of business."

In May 1947 the picture abruptly changed, making Trans-America unneeded. James Ragen, the head of Continental wire service and Siegel's bitter rival, had been shot in an assassination attempt. He survived, only to "mysteriously" expire in the hospital. Arthur "Mickey" McBride, a well-connected Cleveland sportsman who was starting a professional football team, the Browns, officially bought out Ragen's heirs. A wire service veteran from the Annenberg days, McBride claimed he was buying Continental for his son. Everyone seemed content with the new arrangement, and the Cleveland man. Everyone except Ben Siegel. Adding to Mickey's importance, his longtime mentors from Cleveland were reputedly the hidden faces behind the newly reorganized wire.

Cash-strapped and desperate, Siegel over-stepped all boundaries by demanding $2 million (more than $22 million today) from his Chicago partners to fold the now-redundant Trans-America. Already furious about the Flamingo, the wire war, and the FBI situation, the outrageous ultimatum sealed Benny Siegel's fate.

Standing in the wings, Cohen bided time as the Siegel murder plot unfolded. With his close connections to both Cleveland and Chicago, and the invaluable associations he had forged with the New York bosses, Mickey Cohen was primed to permanently become the man on the coast.

In the early morning hours of June 21, 1947, Siegel landed in Los Angeles on a flight from Las Vegas. Business meetings were on his agenda. Also Barbara and Millicent, his teenage daughters, were en route from New York; he had planned a vacation with them at Lake Louise, the beautiful resort in the Canadian Rockies.

In an action sanctioned by Lucky Luciano, Frank Costello, and Meyer Lansky, before midnight, Benjamin Siegel, forty-one, was assassinated in the living room of Virginia Hill's Beverly Hills mansion. In a final act of retribution, the assassin expertly shot out both Siegel's prided baby-blue eyes.

Ushered to the seat of his impending death by his favored companion, Allen Smiley, the executioner was rumored to be another of Bugsy Siegel's longtime friends: his codefendant in the Big Greenie murder case, boxing kingpin Frankie Carbo.

Beyond a doubt, Mickey Cohen was complicit in the plot.

ACT II

KING OF THE
SUNSET STRIP

8

PUTTIN' ON THE DOG

"To be honest, his [Bugsy Siegel] getting
knocked-in was not a bad break for me."
MICKEY COHEN

By July 1947 the sensation surrounding the Siegel execution began to
fade, but another grisly murder still gripped the metropolis. The victim,
aged twenty-two, was a striking brunette named Elizabeth Short. One of
countless fetching young women who existed in the cheap bars and seedy
nightclubs of Hollywood's underbelly, she had dreamed of stardom. Her
elusive reverie ended the past January when she was tortured, murdered,
and then dumped in a vacant lot in the Crenshaw district. Cleanly bisected
at the waist, her mutilated and defiled body parts were naked and bloodless.

The unfathomable crime was the most heinous in Los Angeles history.
The tabloids exploited it wildly, and the brutal slaying of the beautiful young
woman instantly became notorious. The shocking murder galvanized the
citizens of Angel City, both terrorizing and fascinating them. In death Beth
Short became legendary as the Black Dahlia: the first celebrity victim.
Putting stress on law enforcement, like the gangland murders of 1946 and
Bugsy Siegel's assassination, the Dahlia case remained unsolved.

At the studios, the pressure was on to respond to the changing tastes
of postwar America. From the smaller studios came the next wave of

gangster films. Stylized and mysterious, often set in the shadowy L.A. netherworld, their themes were dark, the characters nihilistic — tough guys, dirty cops, racketeers, and cold-blooded femme fatales. Shot in haunting black and white, the plots were thinly veiled variations of headline stories. And the bad guys no longer died in the last reel: they were heroes now.

Thirty-three and no longer a supporting player, the *real* story was about Mickey Cohen: Hollywood's new king of gambling, dope, and prostitution.

After Benjamin Siegel proved dispensable, Mickey recalled, "I took over from Benny right away, on instructions from *the people* back east." Approved from the top — Meyer Lansky and Frank Costello — the *pisher* had influential sponsors all over the country. Deported underworld kingpin Lucky Luciano sent his approval from Italy.

After a decade under Siegel's thumb, the ex-boxer claimed to miss his murdered boss. Mickey respectfully remembered the god-like station Siegel held and what the master had taught him. But he was the first to admit, "To be honest, his getting knocked-in was not a bad break for me." Years later, he would reflect that eliminating someone of Siegel's "ilk and high echelon" undermined the entire foundation of the organization.

Although relishing his important new role, Cohen remained a vassal to the eastern bosses he idolized. He was the "fair-haired boy" of New York syndicate leader Frank Costello, and his Cleveland mentors, represented by the Mayfield Road Gang's Lou Rothkopf, and the Steel City's godfather, Anthony Milano, continued to be deeply involved with him. Rothkopf made frequent trips to Los Angeles as the Cleveland syndicate acquired a Las Vegas gambling resort, Wilber Clark's Desert Inn. The DI was the first asset in what would become the largest hotel-casino portfolio in Las Vegas. Tony and Frank, the "retired" Milano brothers, had taken up permanent residence in Beverly Hills. Ensconced in a sprawling hacienda-style mansion at 9451 Sunset Boulevard, just a few blocks west of the Sunset Strip, the presence of the powerful Milanos made the Dragnas very uncomfortable. It was apparent that Mickey Cohen had moved his own Mafia family into Los Angeles.

Devoted pet owner Mickey Cohen poses with his bulldog.

★ ★ ★

In 1947 Mickey Cohen was connected on the city, county, and state level. He owned law enforcement, judges, DAs, and politicians. A firm believer in *whatever it takes*, he showered the meagerly compensated civil servants with a tidal wave of cash. "I shake one and give notes to others, and it keeps me outside," Mickey boasted.

His finger in every pie, his hand in every wallet, Cohen's influence reached from downtown, Chinatown, and South Central to the Sunset Strip, Hollywood, Culver City, Beverly Hills, Santa Monica, Burbank, Long Beach, San Pedro, and Glendale. He controlled activities in Gardena and Pasadena and out to Orange County, Lake Arrowhead, Palm Springs, and into Mexico. There was talk that San Francisco, Honolulu, and Manila were in his grip.

His latest front was called Michael's Exclusive Haberdashery, which operated from a two-story building at 8804 Sunset Boulevard, in the county territory of the Sunset Strip. On the ground floor was an elegant men's clothing shop paneled in rich dark wood. Extravagantly expensive items for the discerning sporting gentlemen were the store's hallmarks. The

commission bookmaking operations and the racketeer's private office were
below street level. In adjacent storefronts were his other setups, Courtley's
Exclusive Jewelry and a tailor shop that fabricated custom items for his
personal wardrobe and the men's clothing shop. His friend Barney Ruditsky,
a retired NYPD detective licensed in California as a private detective,
worked out of a fourth storefront. Nearby Mickey secretly owned a used-car
lot, where the garage was used for special purposes, such as quickly converting a black Ford sedan into an exact replica of a police car.

In a fine example of the Combination, the Mickey Cohen outfit was
an ethnic mix that worked together successfully. Some of New York's toughest Jews, a strong crew of Italians — mainly from Cleveland's Milano gang
— associates from Chicago, St. Louis, and a few pugs of WASP origins
attended him.

In the top tier of associates was New Yorker Mike Howard (born Meyer
Horowitz), a nattily dressed, tough-looking man in his fifties who was his
"business manager" and buyer for the men's clothing shop. Curly Robinson,
the influential and legitimate gaming machine czar, was the local who held
great importance. Tough Joe Sica, FBI #343378, was another partner, but,
like Robinson, was not part of his entourage. A stocky, inconspicuously
dressed man of medium height with thick black crescent-shaped eyebrows,
large nose, and passive expression, Joe Sica, and his brother Fred, now
occupied the Savoy Shirt Shoppe at 8470 Melrose Avenue. Situated in the
heart of the city's tony art and antiques district, not far from Cohen's Sunset
Strip businesses, authorities claimed the custom-made shirt establishment
was the front for a giant wholesale narcotics business.

Mickey's ever-present crew included two New Yorkers who had known
him from his days as a boxer. His "right-hand" was Harry "Hooky"
Rothman, a dese-dems-and-dose character who was "built like a bull," and
"left-arm" Edward "Neddie" Herbert was a man with top syndicate connections and expertise with firearms, including machine guns. With
Mickey since Cleveland, Frank Niccoli had his trust and was another
respected member of this second tier.

The core of the Mickey Cohen gang was a sinister assortment of seasoned criminals consisting of ex-convicts, muscle guys, bust-out gamblers,
and killers. Among the group were Toledo, Ohio, gambler Al "Slick" Snyder;
massive Sam Farkas; Roger K. Leonard, who had aspirations of becoming

Attorneys Vernon Ferguson, left, and Sam Rummel, far right, confer with their client Mickey Cohen. 1949.

a producer like his brother; cardshark Joseph "The Egyptian" Kaleel; old cigar-chomping thief Abe "The Goniff" Brieloff, who drove Cohen; Jimmy Rist, a former heavyweight boxer who was "very reliable"; tiny, middle-aged Willie "Stumpy" Zevon, FBI #529512, who handled volume bets and dice games and had an infant son later famous as '70s rock star Warren Zevon; gambler Roughy Goldenberg; Joseph "Scotty" Ellenberg, who "took orders explicitly"; and quiet, meek-looking, but tough, Jimmy Regace, whom Mickey deemed "meticulous" in whatever assignment he undertook.

Other associates included shrewd old racketeer Max Cossman; middle-aged Sol Davis, a careless man sponsored by Neddie Herbert, who was alleged to have been with Murder Inc.; and young "showoff" Dave Ogul who was another "irresponsible guy" only used as fill-in. From Cleveland came a favorite: Dominick "High Pockets" Farinacci, a tall, lanky worrier who was going blind. He loved Mickey and was "ruthless" when it came to him. "Muscle" Tony Civetta was another Cleveland associate who garnered Mickey's regard.

Two new members of Mickey's shadowy cast appeared in 1948 and rose quickly. "Happy" Harold Meltzer came west from New York under the cloud of the ice-pick murder of Charlie "The Jew" Yanowski, a New Jersey underworld power. The second man, a twenty-two-year-old Casanova, was named Johnny Stompanato. Mustered out of the marines, he turned up in L.A., where Mickey quickly conscripted him. Slickly handsome and superbly endowed, he held an envious position: his duties were said to involve moving cash for the boss and overseeing beautiful women used in big-money sex and blackmail schemes.

To make a proper impression and keep the tailor shop busy, Cohen's top men dressed like fashion plates. Maintaining pretense, the Cohen boys occasionally doubled as clothing salesmen, but they were mainly occupied with countless, highly specialized duties.

Mickey said that his small, tight organization served its function. "I didn't need crowds. They added heat to me." To keep his boys in line, Mickey would personally beat them for various infractions: bullying bookies unnecessarily, lackadaisical performance, or getting high on their own supply.

A key to Cohen's astounding ascent was a stellar legal team. Going for the best money could buy, he hired Samuel Rummel, who had a long and successful history in Los Angeles representing top underworld figures, as his counsel. The underworld lawyer, fiery and outrageous, would theatrically gesticulate, coo, and bellow to persuade a jury. Mickey teamed Rummel with Vernon Ferguson, a tall courtly older gentleman with receding white hair. A long-time advisor to the L.A. County grand jury, Ferguson had been the sympathetic deputy DA who first moved to dismiss Bugsy Siegel's murder indictment.

Siegel's accountant, Harry Sackman, was now on Mickey's payroll, while many legitimate businessmen who had once served Siegel switched their allegiance to Cohen. Mickey was a master of power networking, and a crime expert observed, "[In] his enterprises, he had as partners men and women of considerable wealth and social standing in Los Angeles . . . He was a miniature colossus."

"Nothing moves unless I give the word," Mickey trumpeted, cruising his immense fief in shiny new Cadillacs. Huge sedans with aerodynamic fenders and torpedo fins, Cohen's cars were always navy blue, spotless, and flashing with chrome. They were customized for speed and also featured hidden compartments that stashed guns and cash. The heady image of stray money fluttering around his car's interior remained an indelible memory for Cohen: "I remember one night when I collected so much dough that I couldn't stuff it all into the secret pockets, and there was fifty-dollar bills flying all over the inside of my car."

The Mick proved insatiable. He began utilizing a swindle that had been a highly lucrative racket of Bugsy Siegel's. Using oblique threats of blackmail or violence, he began asking people for "loans." Although he had an incredible cash flow, he quickly became the town's biggest debtor. Repayment was not part of the scenario. In a variation of the scheme, he began laundering illicit money by recording phantom loans, where in actuality no money was received from the lender.

A prominent bookmaker mused, "Meyer Harris Cohen was, in his own way, a philosopher. His message was functional rather than inspirational and could be summed up in one sentence: get the buck no matter how.

"He practiced this with a concentration as great as that of a hungry hyena. If he had a coat of arms, it probably would have shown $100 bills rampant on a field of double crosses."

★ ★ ★

Just a few years "off the heavy" (armed robberies), the former boxer was interested in making money and spending it. Referring to himself as a "plain, vulgar heist man," unlike Siegel, Mickey Cohen had no social aspirations. But there were other objectives. "I wanted to be a gentleman and go first class," he said. "The rackets . . . was one of the ways to get to the top and go first class."

But he clearly understood the rules of the game and his place in it. Located immediately west of Beverly Hills was Holmby Hills. With vast manicured estates hermetically sealed behind walls and gates, the tiny enclave represented the city's most rarefied world. It was an environment inhabited by those too grand for Beverly Hills: Hollywood's moguls, industrialists, and the late Mr. Benjamin Siegel. This was not a place for Mickey Cohen.

On the far west side of town was the community of Brentwood, decades later made famous by the trials and tribulations of O.J. Simpson. In the 1940s, the neighborhood was strictly white bread, until the flashy

Built in late 1946 through early 1947, Mickey Cohen's modest appearing, but meticulously designed, ranch house at 513 Moreno Drive in affluent Brentwood. The Gangster Squad illegally planted a bug during construction. 1951.

hoodlum from East L.A. moved in. Although distinctly upper-middle class, it was rustic, homey, and sparsely developed. A place where kids rode bikes and people spoke to the folks next door. Quiet and close to the beach, the bedroom community attracted professionals, businessmen, and divas Joan Crawford and Greta Garbo, but it was mainly inhabited by less pretentious movie types. Living in the area was an auspicious array of exiled European intellectuals, including Thomas Mann, Bertolt Brecht, Arnold Schoenberg, and many others.

Located a short distance from the newly built Brentwood Country Mart and the verdant fairways of the Brentwood Country Club, the rumored site of a large bookmaking operation, Cohen's house, at 513 Moreno Drive, was hardly a mansion. Built before Siegel's death, the postwar ranch consisted of seven moderately scaled rooms plus a maid's quarters. It looked like the dream home a returning GI might buy with a Federal Housing Administration loan. But the scale and modesty of the exterior was misleading. It had been built, with no expense spared, to suit all the needs, whims, and rapidly growing obsessions of Mickey Cohen.

Den of iniquity: the perfectly appointed room in Cohen's Brentwood home where meetings were held. Note the vintage British boxing print. 1951.

Working closely with a topflight decorator, Mickey created the house to his only standard: perfection. The interior design was tasteful and traditional. A monochromatic color scheme was used in each room. The living room featured soothing tones from celadon to spruce. The dining room palette was muted blues. In the den, the decorator acquired a library of classics for the barely literate mobster. At the soda fountain, the immaculate racketeer — who didn't smoke, drink, or take drugs himself — loved confecting hot fudge sundaes for his guests.

LaVonne and Mickey occupied separate bedroom suites. Hers was mauve: a luxurious boudoir made for a movie star, with European flair and the requisite tufted bed. The dressing room walls were beveled mirror, 3/4 inch thick, and there was a chaise longue, a makeup counter surrounded by lights, and a walk-in vault for furs and jewels. His was modern in design, done in masculine neutrals and complemented by natural leather and honey-colored wood. The bedspread was monogrammed with a giant MC.

Toughie, Mickey's bulldog, slept in his quarters. Resting on the end table was a silver framed photograph of the dog, posed with his look-alike master. The pampered pet had a bed that was a miniature of Mickey's, complete in every detail, down to the bed covering monogrammed TC. Just like the boss, Toughie's sheets were changed daily.

In the dressing room, the fantasies and fetishes of Mickey Cohen were completely indulged. The cedar-paneled walk-in closet housed dozens of tailor-made suits, some with hidden holsters built into the left shoulder linings, hundreds of Czech cotton shirts with MICKEY emblazed on the breast; scads of suspenders, display hankies, and fashionably patterned ties; scores of custom-made shoes in wooden trees; and dozens of neatly boxed fedoras including many Borsalinos. Sports clothes, outerwear, and sixteen hundred pairs of cotton lisle socks, along with sundry notions, lotions, powders, and potions — all were arranged in perfect order.

It was enough to make Jay Gatsby weep.

Secretly overwhelmed by profound and deeply rooted phobias, Mickey Cohen was terrified of germs. An acute cleanliness obsession had taken hold, and his long growing compulsions now reached colossal proportions. Showering and changing outfits several times a day, Mickey wore clothes a few times and then gave them away. He scrubbed his hands every few minutes and touched no surface unless protected by tissues. Conversations or meals would be interrupted to quench his compulsions. Refusing to wear a soiled garment, he once delayed a dinner party for hours after noticing a small water spot on his suit. Even with money, Mickey was phobic. Every day the bookkeeper replenished his bankroll with clean, crisp bills.

In the Brentwood house, his needs were addressed. A water-heating system large enough for a hotel was installed. A housekeeper cleaned every surface of his bathroom and sanitized it with alcohol each time it was used. After spending an hour showering, clean towels were spread to insulate the floor before his bare feet touched it. "Air-drying" his body, a process that took at least fifteen minutes, the first article of clothing he donned was a fedora. Next, he covered himself with such copious amounts of talcum powder that he resembled a snowman wearing a hat. Running from wall to wall to remove excess talcum powder, he then stepped into his clothing. His shoes were the last items he touched. After handling them, he found it necessary to wash again. The ritualistic dressing custom often took three hours to complete. In the course of a week, the mobster went through thirty bath towels, twenty-one large boxes of tissues, two large containers of Johnson's baby powder, seven bars of Cashmere Bouquet soap,

Mickey Cohen cleans up for the press photographers. His obsessive behavior remained a secret until 1958 when it was revealed in the heavily circulated weekly magazine The Saturday Evening Post.

and a bottle each of Lilac vegetal and Floris's English Lavender aftershave.

For the kid from Boyle Heights, everything had unfolded just as he had envisioned it. The Moreno Drive house was a major dream realized. When he and LaVonne moved into the house on a perfect April day in 1947, the furniture was in place, the kitchen and bathrooms had been stocked, clothes were hanging in the closets, and cars were parked in the garage. Willa Heywood, their African-American housekeeper, greeted them with Mickey's favorite chocolate cake.

As if to puncture the reverie, some cheeky members from the LAPD provided Mickey with a special housewarming gift. Planted in the living room while the house was under construction: a bug.

★ ★ ★

After Siegel's death, Cohen renounced all ties to Jack Dragna and his Mafia family. Never highly profitable or enterprising, Dragna had been forced to accept Siegel's demands. But the Dragnas were not going to roll over for the conniving little Jew from Boyle Heights. With Siegel's death, the time had come for a new arrangement.

While Cohen was making enormous amounts of money, the Dragna family, now without wire service, was forced to exist on ever-diminishing returns. In contrast to Cohen and his associates, who inhabited the city's most fashionable clubs and restaurants, when Dragna hoodlums dared to venture onto the exclusive Sunset Strip they hung out at a pizza parlor.

Cohen also had to contend with Jimmy Utley, who was primed for revenge. Utley worked with factions of the LAPD, Jack Dragna, and Tony Cornero. Mickey later stated that in 1946 after he publicly beat Utley in his restaurant and shut down his operations, his foe put a substantial bounty on his head: "He . . . offered two policemen . . . an apartment building worth $200,000 [approximately $2.5 million today] if they would use their badges to shoot me in the head, or do anything to get even with me."

In August 1947, a powerful and respected figure from the Dragna family, absent during the rise of Mickey Cohen, returned: Johnny Rosselli was again on the Sunset Strip. Since 1943, he had been serving time in a federal penitentiary for his role in the labor conspiracy that extorted millions of dollars from Hollywood moguls to secure union peace. Rosselli, and the Chicago bosses behind the extortion, had curiously been paroled early, after serving only four years of a ten-year federal sentence. In the early 1940s, during his brief marriage to the beautiful Fox ingenue June Lang, Rosselli had been mentioned in the columns as a "mysterious" man-about-town. Now labeled an ex-con, directly tied to the hierarchy of the Capone outfit, he kept a low profile as parole authorities scrutinized his movements.

For years, Rosselli's great friend was Harry Cohn, the boss of Columbia Pictures. Meeting in the mid-1930s, the pair became so close both lived in the luxurious Sunset Plaza apartments and frequently traveled together. Early in their friendship, Cohn magnanimously offered the gangster a much-coveted position as a Columbia producer. The starting salary: a princely five hundred dollars a week. Rosselli demurred, informing his pal he got that much from waitresses taking bets for him. When IATSE moved

Based in L.A. since the 1920s, "Handsome" Johnny Rosselli, a top member of the Dragna Mafia family, strategized to assassinate Mickey Cohen during the L.A. gang war. 1948.

to strike against Columbia in November 1937, Rosselli interceded for his friend. Harry Cohn was the only studio head that received special treatment in the shakedown plot and paid no extortion money.

Under the iron fist of Harry Cohn, Columbia had rapidly moved beyond its poverty-row beginnings into the ranks of the major film studios. By 1947, Columbia boasted multiple Oscars, and Rita Hayworth, Cohn's incomparable creation, had just ignited the screen in *Gilda*. A respected movie mogul and the father of two young sons, Harry Cohn still wore the ruby ring Rosselli had given him, but he distanced himself from his once intimate friend. As a parolee, Rosselli needed to show gainful employment. Now the mogul refused to place him at Columbia. Another friend put him on the payroll as an "artist consultant" at Eagle Lion, a miniscule operation that cranked out B pictures. Sleek, attractive, and a notorious womanizer, Rosselli held many "casting sessions" but never appeared on an Eagle Lion set.

His real job, as a leader in Jack Dragna's Mafia family, consisted of planning the strategy to wrest control of the L.A. rackets from Mickey Cohen. Rosselli complained to a girlfriend, "That Mickey Cohen is a disgrace to the underworld."

★ ★ ★

In the fall of 1947, rumblings were felt from Mulholland Drive to Malibu. The House Committee on Un-American Activities (HUAC) had begun an investigation into Communism — Hollywood-style — that created an atmosphere of suspicion and paranoia, resulting in the blacklisting of actors, writers, and directors.

During this time, tremors were felt from another group, also secretive and subversive, but of a different hue. In response to Mickey Cohen's growing empire and powerful outfit, the L.A. Mafia moved to strengthen its ranks for the first time in years. At a small downtown winery, Jack Dragna, with Johnny Rosselli at his side, "touched" five new men. The initiates included Louis Tom Dragna, the Mafioso's twenty-eight-year-old nephew, and a newcomer to the coast, Jimmy "The Weasel" Frattiano, from Cleveland.

Violent and ruthless, the tubercular Frattiano was a small-time hood recently released from an Ohio prison after serving eight years on a robbery conviction. Now in L.A., the ambitious Weasel was prepared to accept any assignment from his Mafia boss. Dragna ordered him to infiltrate Cohen's organization.

"At first Jimmy had not understood the reason for Dragna's move against Cohen, other than he personally disliked him," Ovid Demaris noted in Jimmy Frattiano's biography, *The Last Mafioso*.

When the Iron Man, George Contreras, died in 1945, Cohen's faction approved the man who would take over Contreras's activities as conduit from the sheriff's department to the organization. But the new man was not loyal to Cohen. Demaris explained, "Jimmy [Frattiano] later discovered that Al Guasti, undersheriff [sic] of Los Angeles County, told Dragna if Cohen were out of the way, they could control most of the juice in the county, which he estimated at $80,000 a week [$850,000 today]. That was the kind of motivation Jimmy understood."

Dropping some names from Cleveland, during the warm California winter the Weasel moved in. Welcomed to Sunday bagel noshes at Cohen's Brentwood house, Frattiano began working at a Cohen-controlled bookmaking operation. Mickey even took care of a hospital stay for the consumptive thug. All the while, Frattiano continued spying for the Dragnas.

"Twice a week we met," Frattiano told Demaris, "usually at Napoli's,

Mickey Cohen and members of his outfit photographed at the sheriff's station after an attempt to assassinate Cohen went awry and his top lieutenant, Harry Rothman, was shot and killed. (L to R) Mike Howard, "business manager" and buyer for Cohen's men's shop; a glaring Mickey Cohen; Sol Davis; and Jimmy Rist, whose injury was collateral damage. August 18, 1948.

a place across the street from Columbia Studios. Johnny [Rosselli] couldn't be seen with me, so we didn't sit together at the same table. But I'd see him get up and go to the toilet and I'd follow him in, and we'd bullshit about what was going on. If I had any problems, he'd take it to Jack [Dragna] and straighten it out."

In late 1946, the LAPD formed a secret Intelligence Unit, known by the brass as the Gangster Squad, led by Willie Burns. The names of the seven handpicked recruits suddenly disappeared from police rolls. Working deep undercover, they had no office, just two unmarked sedans. Given a "no holds barred policy," they did whatever was considered necessary to implement their mandate: stop Mickey Cohen. Gangster Squad member Jack O'Mara recalled decades later, "We did a lot of things we'd be indicted for today."

It didn't take long for Mickey to hear about the clandestine and elite intelligence division. Mockingly, he called them the "Stupidity Squad." But they had already done damage. O'Mara had infiltrated the Brentwood house. Posing as a technician who appeared weekly to service the TV, he had secretly checked the wiretap and spied. The mobster was apparently pleased with his service; he always greeted O'Mara cordially and tipped him lavishly.

By the time of Siegel's death, Cohen had eliminated much of his competition. Although Guy McAfee allegedly still maintained rackets in Los Angeles and kept a mansion in Beverly Hills that he visited on weekends, the only major independent operator still residing in the city was Tony Cornero.

On February 9, 1948, at 6:45 p.m. at 312 South Elm Drive in Beverly Hills, Tony Cornero answered the door at his bungalow. He faced two men, one holding a box. The man with the carton said to him, "Here, Tony, it's a package for you!" Then five slugs were discharged through the package into Cornero's belly.

Thick black headlines:

BIG-TIME GAMBLER

FIGHTS FOR LIFE AFTER OPERATION

UNIDENTIFIED PAIR ESCAPE

Although it seemed clear to authorities that Mickey Cohen had ordered the attack, when questioned by police he expressed "great surprise." Claiming that he wasn't well acquainted with Cornero, Mickey commented, "I always knew him as an amiable and civil fellow. I'd say it was a personal grudge deal and can't comment to anything. I understand Tony's new interest was a Mexican meat deal."

Cornero survived but moved to Las Vegas. Cohen's domination meant there was no room for him in L.A.

Just as Johnny Rosselli was reestablishing himself in Los Angeles, a scandal involving him cast aspersions on the Justice Department and reverberated to the White House. Improprieties regarding the early prison release of Rosselli in the studios extortion case came under congressional investigation. On July 28, 1948, Rosselli turned himself in when a Washington, D.C., parole office issued a warrant, charging him with associating with "unsavory characters."

But Rosselli had a foolproof scheme in place to deal with the Cohen problem. Jimmy Frattiano, his unwitting wife, and their eleven-year-old daughter became the centerpiece of the plan to assassinate Mickey Cohen.

On Wednesday evening, August 18, 1948, the Frattiano family had a cordial meeting with Cohen at his Sunset Strip shop. Stepping out onto Palm Avenue, the Weasel signaled a lookout for Dragna's gunmen. As Frattiano and his family walked to their car, gunfire boomed in the background.

The next day, when Frattiano read the morning papers he learned that the plot had gone awry. Mickey Cohen was very much alive. Hooky Rothman, Cohen's top lieutenant, was on a slab at the morgue. Frattiano realized that by shaking Cohen's hand in parting he had inadvertently foiled the plot: he'd triggered Mickey's hand-washing compulsion, which placed the mobster in the bathroom and out of harm's way.

Nevertheless, a strong, clear message had been sent. The newly reigning King of the Sunset Strip may have appeared cockier than ever, but treachery was now a constant danger. The house and haberdashery were fortified, and an order was placed for a bulletproof Cadillac.

But a new piece of obsessive behavior would once again decide Mickey Cohen's fate.

9

A THOUSAND HINKY PLAYS

"In such close proximity to a real underworld
insider, my imagination raced."
SHIRLEY TEMPLE BLACK,
REMEMBERING MICKEY COHEN

Television was in its infancy. Comedian Milton Berle made his debut on the new medium in June 1948, creating a sensation. With him, a revolution began. Because of the popular new diversion, both movie attendance and newspaper sales plunged. Los Angeles had five major dailies, each publishing several editions, and the papers were constantly looking for ways to boost circulation. When the bungled Mickey Cohen assassination hit the headlines, editors realized that Cohen's exploits made sensational copy. Overnight, the former newsboy became a source for headlines that sold newspapers. The press came courting.

Once forced to remain subservient by Bugsy Siegel, times had changed: Cohen was now the boss. Lured from relative anonymity to bask in the limelight, he welcomed his newfound status and celebrity. Autograph seekers, who haunted the Sunset Strip looking for marquee names, started asking for his signature. Inebriated with the massive amount of attention, like so many before him, Mickey Cohen began marching to the siren song of the Hollywood dream machine.

★ ★ ★

For the next ten days the papers milked the story of the men's shop execution. It took another red-hot extra featuring one of Hollywood's hottest young actors to knock the mobsters off the front page. The scorching new story told how officers interrupted a marijuana party at the hillside cottage of Lila Leeds, a stunning blonde starlet. The police arrested the scantily dressed hostess, a Lana Turner look-alike, along with a girlfriend, Vicki Evans, and two male companions, one of whom was Robert Mitchum, the brightest star at RKO Pictures. All four were booked on narcotics possession, a felony that carried a penalty of six years in prison.

In the strict social climate of the time, drugs were considered a forbidden pleasure. Fearing repercussions from his arrest, when the booking officer at the county jail asked Mitchum his occupation, he answered, "Former actor."

Syndicated-columnist Hedda Hopper, sensitive to the perishability of stardom, served up a scoop: "A wild rumor behind the scenes here that the police decided to pull this caper with Mitchum in order to draw the heat off the department because of their inability to deliver any kind of a case on last week's gangster killing of one of Mickey Cohen's hoodlums."

The reefer scandal rolled on for months, and even the adored Shirley Temple was pulled close to the vortex. As a child, a decade before, she had been the greatest star of all, celebrated by presidents, kings, and J. Edgar Hoover. Now imprisoned in a troubled marriage and with her career sinking, America's sweetheart drifted into a habit of frequenting after-hours clubs on the Sunset Strip. It was there, in the half shadows of Dave's Blue Room, that the petite film legend encountered the notorious Mickey Cohen.

"We met at mid-stairway," Shirley Temple Black revealed in her autobiography, *Child Star*, "his chunky body pressed sideways facing me. As we stood fitted together like sardines, he said he had noticed me with his friend Ruditsky, and how much he liked my films. In such close proximity to a genuine underworld insider, my imagination raced ahead but he was gone."

Barney Ruditsky was a ubiquitous presence on the Sunset Strip. Although Shirley Temple thought he looked as innocuous as a "refrigerator salesman," the former New York police detective was a tough and cagey character who once reputedly collected debts for Bugsy Siegel — and was suspiciously present at his murder scene when the police first arrived. While operating Hollywood's most popular private detective agency, Ruditsky befriended local lawmen, and managed Sherry's, a Cohen hangout on the Strip.

"When Ruditsky recognized how impressed I felt near seedy characters like Cohen, he whispered that he had a treat in store," Shirley Temple Black wrote. "A combined posse of Los Angeles police and county sheriffs was planning a marijuana bust at a . . . hideaway of actor Robert Mitchum and actress Lila Leeds. Would I like to come along in his unmarked car?"

Although tempted by the provocative invitation, the former child star had second thoughts. She wisely passed.

The arrest threatened to end Bob Mitchum's career. He had recently learned that his former business manager, Paul L. Behrmann, had left him insolvent and the subject of ominous threats. Although he decided not to pursue legal remedies against Behrmann, Mitchum later commented, "My best friend and trusted manager admitted the complete disappearance of my funds and refused an accounting."

Howard Hughes, the owner of RKO Pictures, had a vested interest in Mitchum's career. Hughes hired Jerry Giesler, the celebrated attorney who saved Mickey Cohen from prosecution in the Shaman case, to represent his star. Giesler managed to arrange a plea deal for the actor.

After sixty days at the sheriff's Wayside Honor Rancho, Mitchum was back on an RKO stage, finishing *The Big Steal*. But conspiracy theories continued to circulate. Beside the Ruditsky connection, a year later revelations would surface that spoke of Mickey Cohen's involvement in Mitchum's drug arrest.

Accompanied by Cohen's new associate, Johnny Stompanato, Sir Charles Hubbard, a wealthy Englishman, appeared in Los Angeles in 1948. Soon after his arrival in the city, like Mitchum, Hubbard was also in need of counsel, after finding himself in a compromising position and serious trouble with the law. Arrested at a Hollywood marijuana party, Sir Charles Hubbard was convicted of a drug charge. And like Mitchum, he served his six-week sentence at the sheriff's accommodating Wayside Honor Rancho in Castaic.

But Sir Charles and Stompanato remained in communication. The socialite thoughtfully "donated" $85,000 (more than $760,000 today) as "loans" to Stompanato. Unlike Mitchum's, Hubbard's arrest went unpublicized.

★ ★ ★

Feeling secure in his impregnable office, Mickey Cohen held court in his carefully designed "throne room." Between fittings with his personal tailor, he met visitors. Courtiers, including many legitimate businessmen, sought funding, protection, and favors for a variety of legal and illegal enterprises. Involved in a full complement of investments that included real estate and oil ventures, he reputedly funded a small airline with surplus planes that eventually grew into a business empire. Cohen's taste on situations outside of syndicate business amounted to sixty percent of the proceeds, with twenty percent forwarded to the eastern bosses.

Mickey invested in a start-up publishing venture offered by Jimmy Tarantino. A former stringer for the boxing trade *Knockout*, Tarantino was a member of the Varsity, Frank Sinatra's original entourage of hangers-on. Privy to confidential information, the gofers and goons of the Varsity did the crooner's bidding for a pittance and the opportunity to bask in the star's reflected glory. Tarantino planned to put his insider assets to work as editor of a scandal sheet that printed salacious articles about stars. To burnish the enterprise, Sinatra manager Hank Sanicola's name appeared on the masthead as publisher, while Mickey Cohen was the extortion vehicle's hidden angel.

As *Hollywood Nite Life* began airing stars' most intimate secrets, shock waves were felt throughout the film community. Available by subscription only, the magazine was planted on the desks of studio chiefs and top producers. "Salesmen" for *Hollywood Nite Life* began extorting celebrities with indiscretions to hide, giving them the option of either advertising or becoming the subject of an exposé. Even Sinatra was preyed upon. He reportedly advertised to keep his torrid extramarital affair with gorgeous new star Ava Gardner hidden from the public, and allegations of a sexual assault in Las Vegas also remained secret.

Whenever Judy Garland had problems with her husbands, she went to Mickey Cohen. He liked Judy and knew how to persuasively speak to the men on her behalf. Again, Garland came to Mickey for help. This time it was after four installments of an ongoing series in the mobster's scandal sheet, which exposed her sexual peccadilloes and drug addiction. Although not involved in the content of the articles, Mickey later admitted feeling a tinge of shame that Garland had been disgraced. He never revealed to the star that he was behind *Hollywood Nite Life*.

Tarantino finally met his match in Louella Parsons, Hearst's Hollywood columnist. With an audience of forty million readers, for more than twenty years Parsons' own poison pen had struck fear in the greatest stars and moguls alike. Cohen stopped Tarantino from writing about the news-woman. He would not alienate the mainstream press, and her surgeon husband, Henry W. "Docky" Martin, MD, held a prominent post as state racing commissioner.

Hollywood Nite Life ceased publication. Cohen sent Tarantino to San Francisco, where he was expanding his fief.

From the beginning Hollywood was unique: a place where the beautiful, but common and uneducated, could ascend, overnight, to lofty heights. The studios maintained in-house finishing schools to teach contract actors grammar, elocution, the social graces, and novel skills, like fencing. The publicity departments fabricated new names and birth dates, as well as "proper," even "aristocratic," backgrounds for the human assets. From waitress to Wellesley girl, from grease monkey to gent, the film city was a phony world replete with glittering surfaces.

As the gag went, the men who owned the film factories had gone directly from Poland to polo and, early on, were caught up in self-improvement frenzies. With private tutors, they smoothed out their accents and learned to handle the cutlery and speak a smattering of French. Starting to come into contact with people of education and rank, Mickey Cohen felt he was out of his element. Painfully self-conscious about his lack of education, he remained silent among the social elite. "I was able to keep my mouth shut so nobody would know I was stupid," he later divulged. Acknowledging that he had been "living like an animal," he wanted to improve his language skills and manners. "There was plenty someone could still add to my finesse," he said.

Possessing the manners and diction of a lady, LaVonne was thrilled that her husband had plans to elevate himself. Further cementing the goodwill of Florabel Muir, the newspaperwoman who had become his most outspoken ally, Cohen hired her husband, Denny Morrison, as his private tutor. An accomplished journalist, Morrison accompanied the mobster on his rounds. Coaching him during open time slots, he gave his student several "hundred-dollar words" — like balneotherapy — to learn each day.

"Mickey picks them up and repeats them like a parrot, but because he has a quick mind he puts most of them to use in the right places," Muir noted. "He has been astounding his attorney, Sam Rummel.

"'Where have you been getting this kind of talk?' Rummel finally asked.

"'I got me a tutor,' Mickey answered proudly."

He even claimed to be reading *War and Peace*.

Muir recalled her husband asked to borrow Mickey's richly bound edition of the classic, only to be told that it must be quickly returned. She asked Cohen if he really had plans to read it.

"No," he answered, "not in a thousand years. I got a war and peace of my own to worry about. Why should I worry about Tolstoy's troubles? I want it back 'cause it leaves a hole on the shelf when it's gone. It matches the color of them other books."

A former newsman who had long been the highest-salaried screenwriter in Hollywood, Ben Hecht was acclaimed for gangster movies *Underworld*, for which he won an Academy Award, and *Scarface* as well as classic titles like *The Front Page*, *Gunga Din*, *Spellbound*, and *Notorious*. He received no screen credit for his most prominent work: the final rewrite of *Gone With The Wind*.

During World War II, Hecht became politically radicalized after learning of the Nazi atrocities against the Jews. He subscribed to the existence of an explosive and far-reaching conspiracy that claimed calculated policies were behind the plight of European Jews during World War II. The highly controversial theory advanced that the British government preferred the European Jews dead, fearing they would immigrate to Palestine and upset British and Arab oil interests. The theory went further, claiming that

Britain's ally, the United States government, passively heeled to British needs while the Palestinian Jews were placated by promises of small pieces of British Palestine. Hecht allied himself with Peter Bergson, the head of the extremist group Irgun Zvai Leumi. Labeled assassins and terrorists, the Irgun committed acts of extreme violence in their goal to drive the British and Arabs out of Palestine and form the new state of Israel.

According to journalist Sidney Zion, members of the group were "informed against, kidnapped, and tortured" by the less radical Jewish groups and the British army. "The Irgun — and its tiny but extraordinary sidekick, the Stern Group — eschewed civil war and fought on, blowing up British installations, copping British arms, liberating British prisons, and flogging and hanging — in retaliation — British soldiers. The Haganah, the official Jewish underground, laid down its arms in the midst of the Revolt, while the Irgun, never more than 7,000 strong, had . . . 80,000 English soldiers living in military ghettoes afraid to patrol the streets."

In 1946, the Irgun was alleged to be behind the bombing of the British Embassy in Rome, where half the building was destroyed, dozens of people were injured, and three died, as well as the internationally notorious bombing of Jerusalem's King David, the five-star hotel that headquartered the top command of the British forces in Palestine. The bombing of the King David Hotel killed ninety-one people and injured forty-six.

Although the majority of Israelis and established Jewry worldwide condemned the Irgun as outlaws, Irgun leader Peter Bergson, the nephew of the chief rabbi of Palestine, managed to enlist Hecht as advance man, fundraiser, and voice of the group in America. Heading up the Irgun's U.S. branch, the American League for a Free Palestine, Hecht would turn to Mickey Cohen for help.

When first approached Mickey was skeptical, thinking the cause was just a racket: "When *you're* kinky, your mind runs kinky." Then Hecht invited the mobster and his "business manager," Mike Howard, to his beachfront villa in Oceanside. Speaking for the boss, Howard said that Cohen was interested in the Jewish cause but wanted to make it clear: he was no mark. For a handsome sum, he had recently acquired a bronze plaque from a "Jewish patriot" who turned out to be a grifter from Chicago. Hecht noted the exchange in his memoir, *Child of the Century*: "'As soon as Mr. Cohen's friends catch this thief,' said Mr. Howard, 'they will break his head. In the meantime, we would like to be of some help to the Jewish situation — if we can be assured we are not goin' to be trimmed.'"

Howard asked Hecht to explain the Irgun and what he wanted from them. As Mickey Cohen silently contemplated the ocean, the esteemed writer described the situation in Palestine, his fundraising difficulties, and ways in which the Hollywood mobster could be of assistance to the Irgun. When the situation was clarified, Howard expressed great surprise that funding for the cause was not readily available.

Hecht wrote:

"I can't understand why you are having any trouble raising finances in Hollywood for your outfit," Mr. Howard said, very businesslike. "The movie studios are run by the richest Jews in the whole world. They could underwrite this whole Irgun matter overnight."

I explained that all the rich Jews of Hollywood were indignantly opposed to Jews fighting and were working very hard to keep us from helping them. Mickey Cohen spoke for the first time.

"Knockin' their own proposition, huh?" he said.

Mickey decided to lend his support, and Hecht later attested to Mickey Cohen's deep involvement in the Zionist cause. Inspired by Jews fighting "like racket guys" to establish their homeland, he called on the national syndicate to subsidize, supply, and train the Irgun. Cohen recalled that fundraising dinners were held in Boston, Philadelphia, and Miami, and he held a major event at his elite nightclub, Slapsy Maxie's. He said, "There were judges there, people from all walks of life — every top gambler that was in the city or nearby." Texas Mafia boss Sam Maceo came from Galveston and provided one of the largest donations.

Working closely with mobsters who controlled the docks in New York and New Jersey — Albert Anastasia and Charlie "The Jew" Yanowski, respectively — rumors swirled that Cohen's involvement was not purely an act of charity. There were allegations, never proven, that he kept large sums of money raised for the cause and that the mobsters were using the Irgun as a front for their own operations.

Already deeply mortified by the mobster's unsavory, headline-making activities, the local Jewish community feared Cohen would spawn more anti-Semitism. Cohen complained of complacency among the wealthy, respectable Jews who rejected the Irgun — and him. He snorted, "I was an out-and-out hoodlum . . . I guess these powerful Jews felt I was a . . . detriment . . . So these Jews held a meeting about me. I. Magnin [prominent 'rabbi to the moguls' Edgar F. Magnin, of the I. Magnin department store family], Saks Fifth Avenue, Louis B. Mayer, people like that got together."

Attorneys Rummel and Ferguson were warned that if their showboating client didn't curtail his activities — years later Mickey would shamelessly claim *only* his actions involving the Irgun were criticized — the influential establishment Jews would see that he was sent to prison.

10

HIGH JINGO

"You know what it means when a case has high jingo? Yeah, it means it's got command staff's fingers in the pie."
MICHAEL CONNELLY'S *THE CLOSERS*

Mickey claimed two LAPD police officers, Lieutenant Rudy Wellpott, the powerful head of administrative vice, and Sergeant E.V. Jackson, his trusted right-hand man, had been targeting him. Having instituted the "bug in the rug" at Cohen's house, Wellpott led the raid that closed the La Brea Social Club and removed one hundred decks of costly marked cards from the premises. Mickey's sources told him these cops were also behind a break-in at his home where his personal phone book was stolen.

"Mickey knew I intended to kill him," Lieutenant Wellpott admitted years later to journalist Dean Jennings in the *Saturday Evening Post*. "I was hair-triggered to get him." Softening the threat he added, "But not without justification."

Cohen began looking for a way to neutralize the cops, presumed to be allied with Jimmy Utley, and to rid himself of the wiretap.

Brenda Allen was now Los Angeles's leading madam. She had 114 beautiful prostitutes and a list of the city's most prominent clients. From the switchboard of her telephone answering exchange, "Hollywood 5-255," she dispatched the most prized call girls in the City of Angels. A sergeant in LAPD's Hollywood vice authorized a freelance electronic expert, James A. Vaus Jr., to institute surveillance on the madam.

A typical example of the conversations overheard on Brenda Allen's phone: A male voice is heard first. "This is Harry. Got anything good tonight?"

The madam replied coyly, in a lilting Southern accent,

> "We've got some mighty nice books. The heroine in one you'd like to read is a beaut! She has long black hair, is about 5'3", and would make your reading most enjoyable."
>
> "Where can I get that book?"
>
> "On the corner of Sunset and La Brea. There is a picture on the front cover of a gal in a long mink coat. How about being there about nine o'clock?"
>
> "Okay."

The saga of Brenda Allen, née Marie Mitchell, alias Brenda Allen Burns, aka Marie Balanque, began during the Great Depression, when she was turned out in San Bernardino then turned up in L.A., where she joined Guy McAfee's prostitution ring. For a time she plied her profession on a downtown beat. She was arrested in 1940, along with two pimps and McAfee's notorious madam, Annabelle Forrester. Tried and convicted, Madam Forrester served her time in the women's correctional facility at Tehachapi while Brenda Allen, a chief prosecution witness, went on with her business.

After the war, Allen moved into the big time. At thirty-five she held the top spot with a winning combination of quality product, unchallenged protection, and bold business techniques. Cabbies on the Westside were paid to pass out her card, while bell captains and bartenders at the best hotels all knew her number. Allen often dispatched prostitutes to more than a hundred wealthy and meticulously screened clients in a twenty-four-hour period.

Soon, the wiretap picked up a conversation that merited special attention. After dialing the confidential number of the LAPD administrative vice squad, tall, red-haired Allen asked to speak to one of the very officers

Whore of Babylon: criminal lawyer Max Solomon (left), part of Mickey Cohen's coterie of attorneys, represents Hollywood's premier madam Brenda Allen, alleged to be in bed with law enforcement, literally and figuratively. Summer 1949.

who was in pursuit of Mickey Cohen. Told that Sergeant E.V. Jackson was out, she left a message for him to call "Mrs. Johnson." Further tapped conversations reportedly established a direct line of corruption between the madam and the vice cop, proving that Brenda Allen and Sergeant Jackson were sexual intimates and partners in the call girl ring.

This was exactly the type of information that Mickey Cohen was seeking.

★ ★ ★

Sent by Barney Ruditsky, wiretapper Jim Vaus was highly impressed as he passed through a steel-plated door at Mickey Cohen's clothing shop.

Entering the private office, the electronics expert noticed the mood of quiet luxury the gleaming walnut walls and indirect lighting created. A television set hung suspended from the ceiling, and at the end of the large room was a circular desk. Behind the desk, under an oil painting of President Franklin Roosevelt, sat a small, stocky man in his thirties with receding black hair.

Mickey Cohen eyed Jim Vaus and coldly demanded if he had planted the wiretap in his home. With relief, the electronics expert told the mob boss he didn't even know where he lived.

Vaus was then sent by Cohen to look for the bug in his house. As Neddie Herbert and LaVonne watched, Vaus spent that afternoon sweeping Cohen's home for wiretaps. Like at the Sunset Strip shop, he was impressed by the luxurious "creature comforts" he saw in the Brentwood house and the mobster's "reel-sized roll" of cash. At his workshop Vaus tinkered with a supersensitive pickup coil and a high-gain amplifier he hoped would detect the current from the bug. Locating the electromagnetic flow, Vaus cut a hole in the living room floor. Lowering himself into the crawl space beneath the house, the electronics expert pulled the hair-thin wires that connected microphones to a main transmitter from a termite-size hole in a wood box near the fireplace.

After thirteen months the wiretap maintained by the LAPD Gangster Squad was gone. And on that day in May 1948, Jim Vaus accepted a job offer from Cohen. Setting up shop in the basement of the Sunset Strip clothing store, Vaus's electronics wizardry continued to be in demand with the police, both city and county, and PI Barney Ruditsky. Vaus continued to monitor Brenda Allen for both the police and the mobster. For Ruditsky, Vaus listened in on lines for suspicious Hollywood husbands, including Errol Flynn, Mickey Rooney, and Latin bandleader Xavier Cugat, who were eager to catch cheating spouses. Vaus also planned a spy system that studio head Harry Cohn wanted for the Columbia lot.

With Vaus providing Cohen knowledge that Sergeant Jackson was Brenda Allen's partner, the mobster could now defend himself against his foes in the LAPD. That summer of 1948, Brenda Allen was indicted for the misdemeanor of running a house and the felony of pandering. Convicted, she began serving a year in county jail.

★ ★ ★

The Battle of the Sunset Strip continued: the elimination of Mickey Cohen remained the prime focus of the Dragnas. Trying to reclaim the territory, Jack Dragna received affirmation from his relative, New York boss Tommy Lucchese, and certain Chicago factions began to ally themselves with him. Bugsy Siegel's lieutenant Allen Smiley affiliated himself with the Dragnas. Russian-born Smiley was now in Houston, living at legendary oilman Glen McCarthy's luxurious new Shamrock Hotel and fighting deportation. As the Dragna coalition strengthened, Mickey's archenemy, Jimmy Utley, readied himself to take over Cohen's empire.

★ ★ ★

On a rainy evening a few weeks after the men's shop ambush, shotgun fire erupted from both sides of the street near the Brentwood house. Shells blew out Cohen's windshield and ventilated his Cadillac, but Mickey was not injured. Late for a dinner party he was hosting for film star George Raft, Mickey arrived home covered in broken glass and hungry. He profusely apologized to his dinner guest for his tardiness and disheveled appearance.

On another night, LaVonne drove to a gambling club to pick up her husband. She found him staggering down a Santa Monica street, holding his head in his hands. Minutes before in the crowded club Mickey had been hit from behind with an iron pipe. He fled from his assailant by jumping out a nearby window. Dazed and bleeding profusely, Cohen was treated at a hospital.

Cohen's bodyguard noticed a wire that protruded from the crawl space under the Brentwood house. It was attached to a bomb planted by the Dragnas. They were again unsuccessful; the bomb's fuse had fizzled.

Mickey confirmed years later that whenever possible he defended himself: "We got some of their people in retaliation." Downtown, on North Broadway, an automobile approached Cohen's Cadillac. Traveling at high speed, the vehicles careened side by side. Maneuvering into a position where it was possible to attack, Mickey recalled, "There were many shots fired, but nobody got really hurt. Just a lot of noise. They fired back, also. If the police got the report, nothing came out of it."

Cohen admitted to a skirmish that took place in the exclusive Bel-Air neighborhood: "Neddie and I were driving home from the Strip about 3 a.m. A big black car pulls out . . . Neddie says, 'It don't look good to me.'

"I opened the trap door in the car and we got equipment out . . . numerous slugs were fired at each other. We think they used a Tommy. They didn't try to go through with the play when they saw we had them pretty well covered." After the incident Cohen noticed a small newspaper article stating that possible gunfire had been heard in the neighborhood.

Mickey sent Jimmy Frattiano, the Cleveland hood who had infiltrated his gang for the Dragnas, to the City of Hope hospital to be treated for tuberculosis. Recovering there for months, double-crosser Frattiano plotted Cohen's assassination. The plan called for Cohen to be executed in the hospital parking lot when he arrived for a scheduled charity appearance. Frattiano was furious when it became apparent the Dragnas scuttled the scheme.

Unlike the highly publicized ambush at the men's store, Mickey Cohen's ongoing brushes with death remained underworld secrets.

Then 1949 began with more headline-making news stories involving Mickey Cohen. On January 15 LAPD vice officers Wellpott and Jackson arrested "Happy" Harold Meltzer, the prominent newcomer in Cohen's gang, on gun charges. Cohen was outraged, claiming the cops planted the pistol. Released on bail, Meltzer awaited his trial date.

Two months later another event would prove to have profound repercussions not only on Mickey Cohen and his men, but also the brass of the LAPD and powers at city hall. It unfolded in the West Adams neighborhood; at the center was Alfred Marsden Pearson, fifty-three, who ran Sky Pilot Radio, a tiny electronics shop. Over a fifteen-year period, hundreds of dissatisfied customers had complained to the LAPD about being cheated by Pearson. Known for overcharging, he earned a disreputable reputation in the neighborhood, as well as unfavorable ratings with the Better Business Bureau and the Federal Office of Price Administration. Pearson had also been charged with assaulting two female customers during arguments over bills.

LAPD Captain Harry Lorenson, the influential chief investigator for the police commission, accused Pearson of being "the most dishonest businessman in the city" after arresting him five times in a brief period.

Public indignation was aroused when a story appeared on the front pages of the *Examiner*, stating that Pearson had legally managed to turn an unpaid repair bill into a huge windfall. After haggling with the repairman, Mrs. Elsie Phillips, a sixty-three-year-old widow, refused to pay him $8.91 for fixing her radio. Pearson sued, winning an $81 judgment against the widow, which she was unable to pay. He rapaciously forced the sale of Mrs. Phillips's one-story frame house to satisfy the judgment. He then bought the house at auction for $26.50. Pearson allowed the poor widow, who was caring for her grandchild, to rent the house back from him.

A group of LAPD officers from the Wilshire station took pity on the elderly woman. They pledged to pay her rent, while Captain Lorenson found an attorney to represent her in a suit to recover the house. In a crosscheck, Pearson sued Lorenson for $45,000, claiming the police officer had conspired to destroy his business.

As chief investigator for the police commission, Captain Lorenson was extremely important to Cohen. The mobster asserted years later, "I had the police commission in Los Angeles going for me. A lot of the commissioners didn't have any choice. Either they would go along with the program, or they would be pushed out of sight." Cohen added, "I had . . . what you would call the main events. It was all the way to the top of the box at different police stations."

Captain Lorenson met Mickey Cohen and a businessman at Goodfellow's Grotto, a downtown restaurant frequented by politicians. When the heavy draperies were drawn around booth #12, Alfred M. Pearson was discussed. The situation with the electronics expert was mysterious and deeply rooted, but the mobster's solution was simple and final: he wanted to kill the man. But he agreed on a "civic-minded" way to deal with Pearson. And Cohen later claimed the scheme had the seal of approval from Mayor Fletcher Bowron. Mrs. Phillips's plight would be used to organize disgruntled West Adams businessmen and residents to protest in front of Pearson's shop. Like Jimmy Utley, Pearson would be issued a strong and public warning: Cohen's associates would brutally assault Pearson at the neighborhood protest.

The demonstration occurred on a crisp, clear Saturday afternoon, March 19, 1949. Seven of Cohen's most seasoned boys made personal appearances. As a large contingent watched, Cohen's hoodlums, armed with picket signs, paraded in front of Pearson's shop at 5120 West Adams Boulevard. Cohen passively observed from the sidelines. Responding to the noisy crowd, Pearson peeped out of his well-barricaded storefront, shouting for everyone to get away from his business. The throng wildly cheered as Cohen's seven picketers moved into the shop and savagely beat Pearson. Mickey then drove to his office at Slapsy Maxie's nightclub. To his amazement he soon heard his thugs were in lockup at the Wilshire station: rookies from another precinct had hauled them in after they made an illegal U-turn.

One phone call later, Detective Lieutenant Jack Swan, Wilshire station commander, released Cohen's men. Thoughtfully the officers returned their personal effects, which included two pistols, a tire iron, and a riding whip. It seemed the unsavory event had been swept away.

Hoping for a sale, that night an amateur photographer submitted photos to the *Los Angeles Times*. Seeing nothing of interest, the night editor passed. Undaunted, the enterprising teenager left the prints anyway.

Conversing with the editor, a reporter picked the photos off his colleague's desk. The crime beat veteran examined the prints of several men being frisked. He immediately identified them as the top tier of the Mickey Cohen mob. The shots were from the unintended bust that afternoon. Captured were the scowling mugs of Neddie Herbert, Frank Niccoli, Harold Meltzer, Dave Ogul, Jimmy Rist, Eli Lubin, and Lou Schwartz. The crime beat man decided to dial the private number of Mickey Cohen.

A short time later the amateur photographer sold the negatives to Cohen for $20. At four in the morning, the mobster appeared at the *Times* newsroom. Peeling five crisp, new one-hundred-dollar bills from his bankroll, Cohen told the supervising editor he wanted the prints for a joke he planned to play on his friends. His offer was refused. The *Los Angeles Times* broke the story with a banner headline in the morning edition. Illustrating the story were the fuzzy amateur shots.

What started as a carefully plotted scenario to punish Pearson and put him on notice escalated out of control. The newspapers jumped on the story. While Mickey and his men were satirized in a cartoon, portraying him as Snow White and his goons as the Seven Dwarfs, the grand jury called nearly 150 witnesses before returning indictments in the beating of Alfred M. Pearson.

The mobster and his men were charged with conspiracy to assault with a deadly weapon, conspiracy to commit robbery, and conspiracy to obstruct the due administration of the law. Three members of the LAPD — Captain Lorenson; Detective Lieutenant Swan; and Detective Sergeant Winfield S. Wolfe, the man "accused by brother officers of saying, 'Tear up your notes and don't talk about this case. It's too big for any of us'" — were indicted and suspended from the force until a jury decided their fate. Also charged with conspiracy to obstruct justice were Jerome Weber, the attorney Captain Lorenson retained for Mrs. Phillips, and the other man present at the Goodfellow's Grotto meeting, Burton Mold, aka Burt Burton, a high-rolling menswear manufacturer known as King of the Zoot Suit.

Mickey later claimed he called Mayor Bowron on his private line for help with the situation. The mayor of Los Angeles did not respond.

Positioned on a hill, high above the Sunset Strip, Lieutenant Willie Burns, head of the LAPD Gangster Squad, watched through a telescope as the seven thugs involved in the Pearson beating arrived one by one and entered Cohen's clothing shop. With all the "Dwarfs" cornered in the store, Burns and his men swooped down for a mass arrest.

Mickey welcomed the officers into his headquarters, although the city cops had no jurisdiction in the sheriff's territory of the Sunset Strip. Once inside Cohen's private office, behind the electronically operated, triple-layered, steel-clad door, the Gangster Squad was not pleased: the Seven Dwarfs were nowhere in sight. An hour and a half dedicated to tapping, inch by inch, on every wall and cranny and crawling under furniture proved fruitless. The lawmen couldn't unearth Mickey's men. In frustration, they escorted Cohen to headquarters.

The press was at the station. Lieutenant Burns needed Cohen's boys for his much-touted arrest and big photo op. Mickey recalled, "The lieutenant was so upset and befuddled . . . embarrassed because of the newspaper people that he had waiting . . . he took me off to the corner and pleaded with me to make some calls and to have these men make themselves available for this big pinch of his."

Where were the notorious Seven Dwarfs? Still at Mickey's private office, hiding inside a painstakingly designed soundproof room that had been built within the office walls. They could see out but couldn't be seen. Equipped with a short wave radio and well-stocked refrigerator, they remained there until it was safe to leave. Cohen said, "Later, I was given the story of how long each stayed in the hideout, and how they each . . . made their getaways."

Eventually, they all turned themselves in. Cohen personally paid the bail. Rist, Ogul, Lubin, and Schwartz were released on $25,000 each. Neddie Herbert and Frank Niccoli cost a rich $50,000 each, while the boss fetched the highest bounty, a steep $100,000. The total came to an exorbitant $300,000 (approximately $3.2 million today).

Undaunted, Mickey proclaimed with great irony, "I am as pure as the driven snow."

Hoping to be publicly identified as a veritable Robin Hood, Cohen took on the mission of burnishing his profile when he first rose to prominence. He began donating to various charitable causes. Every year he dispensed holiday cheer to hundreds of underprivileged families with bountiful Mickey Cohen gift baskets filled with turkeys, hams, and all the fixings. Mickey recalled, "For weeks before each Thanksgiving and Christmas, I would receive calls from captains in the different precincts . . . of persons that they considered in dire straits and in much need of help so that these families and their children could at least enjoy their holidays . . . For families who had small children I also made arrangements for . . . some toys and clothing that would add to a cheerful holiday." He added, "For the two or three weeks previous to each holiday, most of my time and that of the men . . . with my organization was taken up by making deliveries and visiting individually with most of these families."

Jim Richardson, city editor of Hearst's *Examiner*, recalled that Mickey was deeply disturbed after the Seven Dwarfs incident developed into a monumental affair. Cohen and attorney Sam Rummel visited Richardson at his home to discuss the situation.

"Mick," Richardson suggested, "I think a smart move would be this: pay whatever it takes to lift the plaster from the Phillips woman's home, then give it back to her."

A sympathetic chord was struck when Mickey bought back Mrs.

Sheepish-looking Mickey Cohen poses with Mrs. Elsie Phillips, who is ecstatic after the mobster bought back her house and gave her a generous cash gift. The poor widow was rumored to unwittingly be the front in the alleged Seven Dwarfs conspiracy. Summer 1949.

Phillips's house. The *Examiner* was in attendance as the handsomely tailored mobster presented the white-haired widow with the deed and a substantial cash gift. Given the exclusive story of the restoration of Mrs. Phillips's house, William Randolph Hearst personally called Richardson to congratulate him on the story. Ancient and ailing, the lord of San Simeon could still spot a hot headline. He lavishly praised Cohen's actions, telling his astounded editor, "This is a very kind and wonderful thing he did. I don't want you to refer to him as a hoodlum any more. A man who does a thing like this isn't a hoodlum. You can call him a gambler, but I wish you'd see that he gets a fair break."

★ ★ ★

In Mickey Cohen's world there was always a backstory, subplot, countless distracting diversions, and a hornet's nest of intrigue. Beside objectionable business tactics, a helpless widow, and lawsuits against powerful cops, rumors persisted that there was more to Alfred M. Pearson, electronics man, and his relationship to the mobster than news stories revealed. There were rumors that Pearson had worked on the wiretap in Cohen's house and

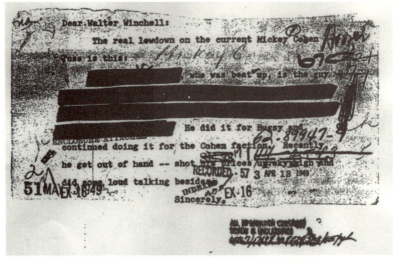

From Meyer Harris Cohen's FBI file: a never-before-published letter to top media figure Walter Winchell that sheds new light on the convoluted case of the beating of Alfred M. Pearson, the electronics expert at the center of the alleged Seven Dwarfs conspiracy. April 1949.

had blackmailed him with transcripts of the bug. An anonymous letter to columnist Walter Winchell about the case clearly illuminates Cohen's true motives in the assault of Pearson. It asserts that Pearson worked first with Siegel, and later worked for Cohen, electronically altering race information, but had gotten out of line.

The never-before-published letter, forwarded to the FBI on April 18, 1949, reads:

> Dear Walter Winchell:
>
> The real lowdown on the current Mickey Cohen fuss is this: [DELETED], who was beat up, is the guy [DELETED] . . . He did it for Bugsy and continues doing it for the Cohen faction. Recently, he got out of hand — shot his prices up sky high and did some loud talking besides.

The Pearson affair was inscrutable and covered in high jingo. As crime journalist and best-selling novelist Michael Connelly described the term, "You know what it means when a case has high jingo? Yeah, it means it's got command staff's fingers in the pie."

A great blow to Cohen, the Seven Dwarfs incident made it evident that his police and even political clout could not guarantee complete protection. The enormous publicity surrounding the event infuriated his eastern sponsors.

And the case wouldn't die. Many months later the Seven Dwarfs case would take a deadly, and very expensive, turn.

11

SMOG ALERT

"I have the damndest Gestapo you ever saw ..."
LOBBYIST ARTHUR H. SAMISH

Although representing Cohen gang member Harold Meltzer at the gun charge trial that began on May 5, 1949, attorney Sam Rummel's opening statement seemed to center on the plight of Mickey Cohen. "We will prove by testimony of witnesses from the stand that for a period of one and a half years before Meltzer's arrest, Lieutenant Rudy Wellpott and Sergeant E.V. Jackson kept up a constant extortion of Mickey Cohen.

"They [the police officers] would take their women to high-priced restaurants — the House of Murphy, the Brown Derby, Dave's Blue Room, Slapsie [sic] Maxie's and other places — would wine and dine them lavishly and when it came time to pay the check would say, 'Send it to Mickey Cohen.'

"We have witnesses from these places to prove that these shakedowns occurred. We will prove that this entire case is a frame-up because Cohen refused to contribute ten to twenty thousand dollars to what Wellpott and Jackson said was the campaign fund of Mayor Fletcher E. Bowron."

Called as a defense witness, in headline making testimony Cohen stated that the gun had been planted on Meltzer by LAPD vice officers Wellpott and Jackson because *he* — Mickey Cohen — was the target of a

The LAPD bugged the Mick and he bugged back. (L to R) Mobster Harold "Happy" Meltzer, Mickey Cohen, and wiretapper Jim Vaus, who worked for both Cohen and the cops, examine a tape recorder during Meltzer's gun charge trial. Vaus later became an attraction on the religious revival circuit, and Meltzer one of Cohen's great enemies. 1949.

shakedown by them. He asserted the cops were rogues, directly involved with the disreputable Brenda Allen, who were intent on breaking the law — and him.

Cohen said that he had showered the two cops with gifts and dinners, and in return they demanded significant payment to make the Meltzer complaint evaporate. Officers Wellpott and Jackson claimed the money they asked for was earmarked for Mayor Fletcher Bowron's reelection fund and was not extortion.

Rummel brought to the stand many defense witnesses, including Martin Pollard, a wealthy and prominent Cadillac dealer who managed campaign funds for Mayor Bowron. In testimony that was damning for the officers, Pollard testified that other than members of the campaign committee, no one was authorized to accept or solicit funds on behalf of the mayor.

On May 7, the courtroom was electrified when Rummel announced that he would produce recordings of compromising conversations between madam Brenda Allen and Sergeant Jackson that established their illicit business relationship and conversations between Cohen and Sergeant Jackson that would substantiate extortion of the mobster.

In light of the explosive courtroom drama involving Mickey Cohen and members of the LAPD, rumors circulated that Mayor Bowron and his city hall cronies were behind legal moves that stalled the Meltzer trial until after the upcoming mayoral election. By a slim margin, on May 31, 1949, Fletcher Bowron was reelected mayor of Los Angeles.

As the headlines shrieked, the L.A. County grand jury launched an investigation into the charges of LAPD officers consorting with call girls.

On June 16, 1949, Brenda Allen was brought from county jail to appear before the grand jury. Dressed like a schoolmarm, she wore an expensively tailored suit and a flower-strewn hat, her face shielded by both sunglasses and a veil. The shapely madam then posed for press photographers before she testified about the call girl ring she operated with police permission.

Allen swore that she paid $150 a week per girl for police protection and proceeded to inform the panel: "I paid for everything that I got, and I paid plenty. If they [the cops] got into this mess, it was their own business, not mine. Now it's everybody for himself."

On the day Brenda Allen began her testimony, the body of another sex crime victim was found. More than two years had passed since the remains of the Black Dahlia had been discovered. Also receding from memory were the brutal unsolved killings of Georgette Bauerdorf, Jeanne French, Mary Tate, Evelyn Winters, Rosenda Montgomery, Laura Trelstad, and Gladys Kern. The new victim was Louise Springer, a twenty-eight-year-old hairdresser. Disappearing not far from where the mutilated body parts of the Dahlia had been found, Springer's corpse was discovered in the back seat of her abandoned car. She had been choked to death, a fourteen-inch tree branch thrust through the lower part of her body.

The city was gripped by fear as the unprecedented wave of vicious sex murders continued. Blaring headlines, outraged citizens, a grand jury investigation, cuts in funding, an ongoing underworld war — and the smear arsenal unleashed by Mickey Cohen — confronted the LAPD. On June 28, 1949, LAPD Chief C.B. Horrall resigned, pleading illness. Leaves and transfers were taken throughout the force. For an interim term of one year, Mayor Bowron installed retired marine Major General William Worton as LAPD chief.

Cohen's risky gambit had worked spectacularly. The mobster could now gloat that he brought down the head of the LAPD. With control of the police commission, his goal was to approve the new chief. But the game of wits he was playing with the cops was treacherous.

Now, the Mick was involved in a war on two fronts.

Forced to step down as chief of the Mafia commission during the Bugsy Siegel debacle, Frank Costello was again heading the syndicate. Needing to show leadership, the underworld's most influential boss could no longer accept the chaos and bad publicity surrounding the Hollywood branch. A Jewish boss *was* controversial, although Costello had personally sponsored the profitable Mickey Cohen. Gangland's prime minister now turned to diplomacy: the little Jew and Dragna would have to work things out.

Mickey sensed it was time to call in favors. He would turn to lobbyist Arthur H. Samish, *the* man in the state capital. Wielding power from a fourth-floor suite in Sacramento's Hotel Senator, Samish had successfully mentored a state attorney general, state senators, assemblymen, mayors, and district attorneys. He could "push through laws or stop them cold."

A massive figure of outsized appetites, Samish was so powerful he had publicly proclaimed himself the "unelected governor of California." With a dossier on every individual of standing in California politics, Samish, fifty-two, preened, "I have the damndest Gestapo you ever saw . . . I can tell if a man wants a potato, a girl, or money."

He glibly declared that he was "the governor of the legislature and to hell with the governor of the state." When Governor Earl Warren was asked to comment, he concurred, "On matters that affect his clients, Artie unquestionably has more power than the governor."

Samish's long list of prominent clients included bus companies, railroads, chemical firms, racetracks, liquor purveyors, and cigarette manufacturers. Now, Mickey Cohen joined the impressive roll in Samish's sphere

"The Big Man" in California politics, lobbyist Artie Samish. Circa 1950s.

of influence. The Hollywood mobster understood, and deeply appreciated, his association with the man who handled politicians "like a fine master controls his dog." Calling the lobbyist "my godfather, my senior statesman," the time had come for Cohen to fully exploit Samish's legendary "know-how and know-who."

One of Samish's most prominent protégés was Fred N. Howser. A former L.A. County district attorney, Howser was the man who tried Bugsy Siegel for common bookmaking yet chose not to charge Cohen in the killing of Max Shaman. In January 1947, he was sworn in as California's attorney general. During his tenure as California's chief law enforcer, he performed many services that pleased the underworld. In July 1949, Howser made a bold move to ensure Mickey Cohen's safety. He assigned as his bodyguard Special Agent Harry Cooper from the California Department of Justice. Scheduled to testify before the grand jury about corruption in the LAPD, according to the attorney general there was information that Cohen had a price on his head and deserved the right of protection, as would any citizen.

Sergeant Darryl Murray of the LAPD Gangster Squad was also trailing Cohen. His detail had been given by Deputy Chief Thad Brown, who took the position that murder must be prevented in the city of Los Angeles, even if the intended victim was the region's most notorious criminal.

Out on the town: Special Agent Harry Cooper, the highly ranked state officer controversially appointed by the state attorney general to bodyguard Mickey Cohen, makes the Sunset Strip rounds with his mobster charge. Note Cooper's exquisitely tailored suit that had just been made for him at Cohen's men's shop. July 1949.

Los Angeles County Sheriff Eugene Biscailuz claimed no special precautions were taken to guard Cohen. But the Sunset Strip territory, which included Cohen's offices, clubs, and hangouts, was considered a safe haven for the mobster.

After a festive Russian dinner with Artie Samish, in the early morning hours of July 20, 1949, Cohen showed up at Sherry's restaurant as was his habit. As he was leaving the Sunset Strip hot spot, a team of assassins shot him and several others. Cohen and assigned bodyguard Special Agent Cooper, who was seriously wounded, were driven directly to the hospital. Screaming in pain, Cohen's other bodyguard, gangster Neddie Herbert, lay immobilized on the sidewalk in front of the restaurant for nearly forty-five minutes before ambulances arrived. A 30.06 deer slug had made a hole the size of a silver dollar in his back, and his legs were peppered with wounds. Dee David, a pretty young movie extra in the Cohen party, took three slugs; an older woman was nicked in the ear. Journalist Florabel Muir was hit in the fanny by a slug that ricocheted off a wall. But she was feeling no pain: the exclusive was hers. Competing newsmen had left the premises just minutes before the shootings.

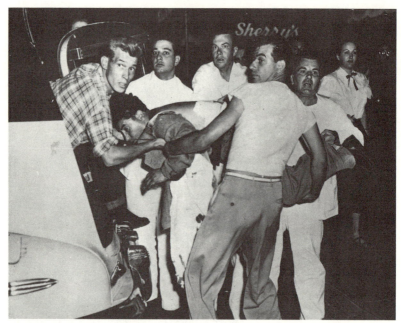

Ambush at Sherry's on the Sunset Strip: critically wounded Cohen lieutenant, Neddie Herbert, is carried to an ambulance after another unsuccessful attempt on Cohen's life. July 1949.

When sheriff's deputies finally appeared at the chaotic scene, they ignored Muir when she advised them the shots had come from a vacant lot across Sunset. Onto the biggest scoop of her career, the veteran reporter took matters in her own hands. She enlisted Barney Ruditsky to help search the area where she believed the gunmen had lain in wait. The armed ex-police detective and middle-aged newswoman, famous for her carrot-red hair, purple prose, and gangster intimates, poked around the dark, sloping lot. On a flight of cement steps they found spent shells and half-eaten sardine sandwiches. The assassins' shotguns were later discovered just south of the Strip.

The wounded were taken to Queen of Angels Hospital and placed under the care of Dr. Joseph Zeiler, the personal physician of Mickey Cohen. At the hospital, the death threats continued. In a wing roped off for victims of the ambush, city and county officers patrolled the floor, and a makeshift pressroom was set up to cover the story.

Mickey and Dee David recovered quickly. Cohen's longtime associate

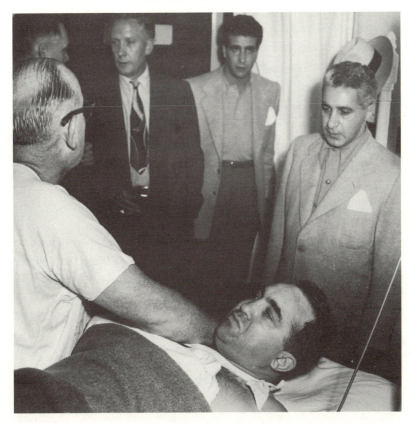

Survived again. At right, Johnny Stompanato and Frank Niccoli, with winged boss Mickey Cohen (on gurney) regroup in hospital after the botched attempt on Cohen's life at Sherry's restaurant on the Sunset Strip. July 1949.

Neddie Herbert hovered near death for a week before he expired. Critically wounded, Special Agent Cooper remained near death for more than ten days. The handsome state officer would eventually make a full recovery.

The next year, lawman Cooper married Dee David. Cohen had introduced them the night of the ambush.

L.A. was a city under siege, with a contaminated police force and an ongoing underworld war that now endangered innocent civilians. The ambush at Sherry's, the biggest outbreak of gangland violence in the city's history, terrified and enraged the citizens of Los Angeles.

Because of Mickey Cohen more political careers seemed in jeopardy. Governor Earl Warren issued a statement, while State Attorney General Howser called a press conference with Sheriff Biscailuz and LAPD Deputy Chief Thad Brown.

In a press release State Attorney General Howser announced, "We had specific information as to the source which might attempt to assassinate Cohen. The circumstances will testify to the authenticity of the information. But we are not at liberty to divulge any other details at this time."

From his hospital bed, Cohen posed for photographers and talked with the press. He claimed the attorney general was "the only guy who knows what is what."

Before the next day dawned, multiple suspects in the Sherry's incident were arrested. Cohen publicly dismissed them all as "not important." Before long, all were freed. And rumors circulated that LAPD vice squad cops were behind the lethal night at Sherry's. For once, Mickey Cohen had no comment.

★ ★ ★

While Cohen rehabilitated his wounded arm, the grand jury handed out indictments to the brass of the LAPD in the Brenda Allen–vice squad case. Former LAPD chief Horrall and two top aids were indicted for perjury. Cohen-baiters Lieutenant Rudy Wellpott and Sergeant E.V. Jackson were charged with perjury and bribery.

But in those dog days of August 1949, a host of enemies continued to pursue Cohen. Early in the month a crude bomb exploded near his home. On August 16, Mickey Cohen's name appeared on the front page of the *San Francisco Chronicle* with transcripts from the Brentwood bug. Made from April 1947 to May 1948, the transcripts of recordings were full of juicy tidbits, and Cohen's archenemies in the LAPD, Wellpott and Jackson, were publicly revealed to be behind the wiretapping. Reports confirmed Wellpott had, indeed, instituted the bug, and Jackson often sat in at the listening post.

When critics noted more than two years had passed before the transcripts were publicly divulged, Mayor Bowron defended the LAPD: "They didn't realize what they had." DA William Simpson told the press the wiretaps could hold the key to solving the Bugsy Siegel murder. A federal grand jury began scouring the tapes, looking for violations of federal statutes involving evasion of taxes, sales of narcotics and weapons, the Mann Act (transporting women across state lines for purposes of prostitution), and using the mail to defraud.

Claiming to know about the wiretap from the beginning, Mickey was coy and challenging. To DA Simpson, Cohen offered, "If he finds a clue to who done it to Bugsy in all that chatter, I'll eat it. Nobody wants to know who did that job more than I do."

Although the wiretaps consisted of nineteen wax recordings and miles of tape, very little of the transcripts was released to the public. As would be consistent with the acknowledged boss bookie, the 126-page dossier claimed much talk about gambling. Enormous deals, bigger than the Flamingo, and small start-ups were discussed. An assortment of people, from lawyers to boxers, bankers, businessmen, bondsmen, and underworld figures from prominent to marginal, appeared on the tapes, including many phone conversations with nationally known racketeers.

Attorneys Sam Rummel and Max Solomon visited the Brentwood house, as had Mickey's new neighbor Cleveland Mafia boss Anthony Milano, gambler Nick the Greek, and legitimate businessman Curly Robinson. Robinson spoke about the "half-million they could make if Burbank [Dincara Stock Farm] stayed open for 90 days" and tried to assuage Mickey's bitter complaints about his "new man," Captain Guasti, in the sheriff's office.

There were oblique asides about "Costello." In a hushed call to one "Inspector," Mickey complained that members of the LAPD were smearing his boy's pricey suits with red chalk. There was talk about shills and stars who were steerers. Chatter with the maid. Meaningless chitchat. And "business manager" Mike Howard perpetuated the great myth: "Everyone knows that Mickey has always worked alone."

There was palace intrigue: Howard warned LaVonne, "Neddie [Herbert] is not such a hot or smart guy . . . If Mickey doesn't look out, what he has worked [the town] for all his life will be taken away by Neddie, who came out here cold from New York."

After his dog tore up a flowerbed, Cohen was alleged to have compulsively repeated to the animal, "How could you do this?" — over and over and over.

And in a domestic spat, Mickey told LaVonne to go to hell while

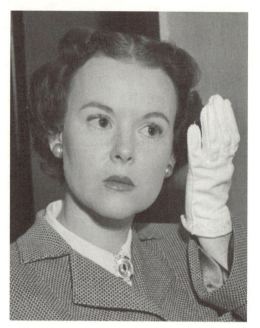

Courtroom debut: wholesome-looking LaVonne Cohen testified to her husband's innocence. 1949.

kissing his pet cockatiel. To this public allegation, the mob boss took great umbrage. Incredulous, he disclaimed, "How could I get my head in a cage to kiss a bird? Them cops are nuts. If I ever told LaVonne to go to hell, she'd crown me."

While the revelations turned out provocative tabloid fodder, the grand jury learned the taps did not constitute legal evidence. Another inquiry into police misconduct was started, and civil libertarians rushed to defend L.A.'s notorious mobster if he chose to pursue an invasion of privacy suit against the city of Los Angeles.

On August 30 at the dinner hour, two LAPD detectives, accompanied by a federal narcotics agent, showed up at the Moreno Drive house. The officers wanted to take Cohen to police headquarters to talk about guns and drugs they alleged were linked to his "business manager," Mike Howard. Entertaining a group of nationally prominent journalists in town to cover him, Cohen refused to leave his guests. He demanded the officers return in the morning, unless they produced a warrant. They couldn't, but they wouldn't leave. An argument started. Cohen exploded.

"Well then go fuck yourself!" he bellowed. "And tell the chief to fuck himself!" Declaring his rights, he screamed at the trespassers, "Get the hell of my property, you sons of bitches!"

Several days later, police arrested him. The charge: his swearing disturbed the peace. They stated Cohen called them names so graphic and foul the language was "unbecoming even to a gangster."

The case went to trial. The three newsmen who attended Cohen's dinner party testified they only heard their host impugn the ancestry of the cops. LaVonne, making her courtroom debut, defended her husband of nine years. Impeccably turned out, Mrs. Cohen closely resembled film star Donna Reed. She presented an attractive package to the jury, adding a wholesome quality to his public image. She swore that her husband had not used the profanities attributed to him and would never employ that kind of language in front of her.

His counsel, the distinguished Vernon Ferguson, admonished the prosecutors: "Mr. Cohen was the victim of a murderous assault last July ... This campaign of harassment has gone too far! The murderers are still at large. Instead, the police are harassing Cohen who is a sick man."

Attorney Sam Rummel took the stand as a defense witness. Utilizing his shameless courtroom ploys, the flamboyant lawyer testified that Mr. Cohen did not want to leave with the police, fearing they were the gunmen from the Sherry's ambush.

After deliberating for four hours, the jury chose to acquit.

Years later Mickey admitted, "The true story on the matter was that I had threatened to shoot both of the officers if they did not get off my property immediately, and if they wanted to see me to reach me at my office!"

And another bombshell revealed here for the first time: unknown to the jury and even the Cohens' personal friends, the mannerly and pristinely beautiful Mrs. LaVonne Cohen had an arrest record and aliases Simone King, Jean King, and Lani Butler. According to authorities, at fourteen she was sent to the Ventura School for Juvenile Girls, after allegations of immoral relationships with neighborhood men. In 1940, the year she married Mickey Cohen, while using the name Simone King, she was rousted by the L.A. County Sheriff's Department on charges of burglary and solicitation — while in the company of Lee Francis, Los Angeles's most illustrious madam. In the early days of World War II, LaVonne was arrested in

Honolulu for prostitution. By the end of the decade, Mickey Cohen, and his friends from the press, had neatly repackaged her as his pillar of respectability.

The grand jury had been occupied the entire summer of 1949 investigating the dozens of scandals and murders that blighted Los Angeles, including the operators of a well-known scandal sheet. On September 2, DA William Simpson disclosed to the press he had deposed *Hollywood Nite Life*'s Jimmy Tarantino and an electronics expert, Russell Mason, the day before.

Tarantino couldn't remember much. But the electronics specialist, questioned for more than two hours, could. Mason claimed to have met Tarantino at the publisher's Sunset Strip office in early 1948. And, in another small-world scenario, he went there to install a wiretap for Robert Mitchum's former business manager, Paul L. Behrmann, at the time employed by Tarantino as a salesman for *Hollywood Nite Life*.

According to Mason, Tarantino later approached him, offering an extravagant salary of $50,000 a year (nearly $450,000 today) to become Mickey Cohen's personal electronics man. Mason testified Tarantino derided the local cops, while praising the mobster's "actions, abilities, and smartness," and Tarantino told him that Cohen was aware a bug had been planted in his house.

After Mason rejected Cohen's extravagant offer, Tarantino chided, "You're foolish to turn this down. Mickey plans a real setup in this town, including a full-time soundman, a politician, and a newspaper."

A few days later, Mitchum's former manager, Paul L. Behrmann, offered the grand jury shocking new allegations. Out on bail and awaiting an appeal for a recent grand theft conviction, Behrmann was eager to stay out of San Quentin and had already turned informant. He had recently worked as a "paid investigator" for Warren Olney III's California Crime Commission, the group Governor Earl Warren had recently established to probe statewide racket activity. He was also a compensated source for Drew Pearson, the influential Washington political columnist. Admitting to the grand jury that he had worked for Jimmy Tarantino selling advertising for *Hollywood Nite Life*, Behrmann then made an explosive claim: Mickey Cohen was behind a major Hollywood sex-and-shakedown operation.

Notorious starlet Lila Leeds (with attorney Grant Cooper) is brought before a grand jury to testify about her alleged involvement in a high-end sex and extortion ring reportedly run by Mickey Cohen. A case was never made. September 1949.

Spinning a sordid story of well-heeled johns, prostitutes, and wild parties that were taped, Behrmann implicated a bevy of actress/models alleged to have been involved in the ring. Seven beautiful young women were named, including such exotics as the anonymous "Bootsie"; a twenty-four-year-old redhead who was the "assistant to Claude Marsan, French love teacher"; as well as the delectable starlet Lila Leeds and dancer Vicki Evans, the familiar figures from the Robert Mitchum marijuana scandal.

Divulging circumstances remarkably similar to those surrounding the extortion of Sir Charles Hubbard, Behrmann revealed the name of a Hollywood businessman victimized by the scheme. All parties named in Behrmann's testimony — including Mickey Cohen — were subpoenaed to appear before the grand jury.

When told of Behrmann's claims, Mickey responded with indignation: "Utterly ridiculous, stupid, and not worth answering. Anyone who knows me knows that I never mix in anything of the kind."

When the DA heard the story of the Mitchum reefer party — as retold by Lila Leeds — he announced Mitchum's and Leed's convictions should be "reinvestigated to determine whether extortion had engineered the case."

Then Behrmann went mute. Cited for contempt, he disappeared, only to reappear after a bench warrant was issued for his arrest. Still silent, he was remanded to jail by Judge Clement Nye.

With Behrmann unwilling to testify against Cohen, the grand jury was unable to pursue the dirty allegations. Mickey celebrated with a provocative new photo taken outside the hearing room. Blonde beauty Lila Leeds, and Vicki Evans, posed at his side.

12

Star-Crossed

*"Hollywood is like Egypt. Full of
crumbling pyramids."*
LEGENDARY PRODUCER DAVID O. SELZNICK

S ix months after the event, the fallout from the Pearson–Seven Dwarfs
case continued to devastate Mickey Cohen. On Labor Day weekend
1949, Frank Niccoli, one of the indicted Seven Dwarfs, was invited to the
Westchester tract house of Jimmy Frattiano. As they nursed Pabst Blue
Ribbons, the Weasel made Niccoli an offer he couldn't refuse. Italian to
Italian, Frattiano said that the Dragna family wanted him to join their
ranks. Pledged to Mickey, Niccoli refused the offer. In a matter of minutes,
men surrounded him. Pulling one end of the garrote, Frattiano remembered the victim's response as he strangled him. He wore an expression of
"surprised terror." Niccoli's body was tossed into a grave at a vineyard, east
of Los Angeles, in Cucamonga. To guarantee the remains would never be
found, Niccoli's corpse was buried with a bag of lime used to break down
the body. Cohen forfeited the $50,000 bond (nearly $450,000 today) when
his loyal friend failed to appear at the Pearson hearing.

Next to disappear was Dave Ogul, another Cohen associate out on bail
in the Pearson–Seven Dwarfs case. After leaving the men's shop on the
night of October 9, 1949, twenty-nine-year-old "Little Davy" simply

vanished. The Dwarfs' abandoned Cadillac was later found near the UCLA campus, but his body was never recovered. Harold Meltzer, the man Mickey had just defended in court, had delivered him to the Dragnas. Like Frank Niccoli, Ogul's body was buried in lime.

In the past days, Ogul, whom Mickey claimed was a headstrong punk he only used as fill-in, had been seen in Palm Springs with Jean Spangler, a dark beauty who had been a Florentine Gardens showgirl and recently worked as a bit actress. She mysteriously vanished just a few days before Ogul. Her disappearance was hot news: mired in salacious allegations of an illicit affair with new star Kirk Douglas, a vicious custody battle with her ex-husband, a cryptic note that possibly alluded to an illegal abortion, speculation of a connection to Mickey Cohen, and the confirmed connection with one of his missing Dwarfs. After an extensive investigation, Jean Spangler's disappearance became another of the high-profile cold cases belonging to the LAPD.

Opportunistic "sightings" of Ogul and Spangler, sometimes in the company of Frank Niccoli, were planted by Cohen's foes. Unable to prove Ogul dead, Cohen forfeited another $25,000 ($225,000 today) in bail.

The Dragnas' gruesome scheme had worked. Mickey Cohen was losing men, and his enemies had put a deep hole in his bank account. With four from his upper ranks murdered in just over a year, his operations were barely profitable. This, and the massive publicity surrounding him, did nothing to boost his reputation with the bosses in the East.

Because of Cohen's widespread activities, Los Angeles had become more dangerous and corrupt than Chicago during Capone's heyday. Governor Earl Warren released the findings of the California Crime Commission that had been instigated by his lethal escapades. The report ranked Mickey Cohen as the top leader of the West Coast underworld, with Jimmy Utley coming in second.

Newspaper publishers realized that mobsters continued to sell papers. Closing in on the truth, the story of New York's Frank Costello's "invasion" of Los Angeles began to appear in a local paper. The journalist promoting this theory mysteriously vanished on a fishing trip. And in the summer of L.A.'s nationally covered gangster scandals, even the most elusive figure in

They don't look like gangsters. Mickey Cohen at a hearing with four of his well-dressed Dwarfs. Front row: camera-shy Neddie Herbert, a circumspect Mickey Cohen protecting his hat, and Frank Niccoli smoking in court. Second row: Jimmy Rist in large dot tie, Eli Lubin in glasses. In the following months, both Herbert and Niccoli were executed. 1949.

the underworld was unveiled for the first time. Meyer Lansky was one of the Combination's founding partners and greatest strategists. His enormous power and importance was well known to investigators, but publicly he had managed to remain a shadowy figure for more than a quarter-century. Lansky's activities were clearly unmasked in a *New York Sun* cover story that described his long and notorious career.

Only Mickey's Cleveland mentors managed to stay out of the news.

As the decade of the 1940s wound down, movie attendance declined more dramatically, as the film business continued to face new, worrisome challenges. Now stripped by the federal government of their monopolistic theater chain ownership, and with four million TV sets in American homes and another eight million sets in the pipeline, film companies steeled themselves against the inevitable.

"Hollywood is like Egypt. Full of crumbling pyramids . . . It'll just keep on crumbling until finally the wind blows the last studio prop across the sands," producer David Selznick prophesized to Ben Hecht.

The careers of many of the greatest stars of the 1940s had come to an abrupt end. Rita Hayworth married playboy Prince Aly Khan and moved to Europe. Finished were the star-struck days of Veronica Lake, Judy Garland, Gene Tierney, Hedy Lamarr, Mickey Rooney, Errol Flynn, George Raft, Betty Grable, Tyrone Power, even Shirley Temple, and the great mogul Louis B. Mayer. Rumors circulated that Frank Sinatra's MGM contract would not be renewed and his voice was gone. In a show of support Mickey Cohen hosted a poorly attended testimonial banquet for the floundering crooner at the Beverly Hills Hotel.

In the waning months of the decade, director Billy Wilder filmed *Sunset Boulevard*, a picture that dared to unveil the dark side of the movie colony. A cautionary tale, it indelibly painted a devastating portrait of Hollywood and its denizens. Cast as an aging silent-film diva, lost in delusions of her magnificent past, was real life silent-film diva Gloria Swanson. No stranger to the vicissitudes of stardom, she had been Paramount's top drawing card twenty-five years before. While Swanson delivered a tour de force performance and received an Academy Award nomination, *Sunset Boulevard* was not the elusive comeback.

As the region's most celebrated mobster could attest: the dirty city of dreams was a treacherous place. But Mickey Cohen had no intention of joining the cast of Hollywood has-beens.

13

BUM-STEERED and BUM-RAPPED

*"Naturally, I was a little bit uncomfortable
in the hands of all those church people."*
MICKEY COHEN

The subject of countless intrigues and in the crosshairs of multiple enemies, after eight assassination attempts, Mickey Cohen was still standing. *Time* labeled him the "sad-eyed . . . Lucky Clay Pigeon of the Sunset Strip."

As 1949 came to an end he had been front-page news for more than a year. National magazines, including *Time* and *Life*, had featured him. His notoriety had even spread abroad. A household name, the thirty-six-year-old mobster received more fan mail than many movie stars. But the "Czar of Hollywood Gangland" was overexposed. The press gave him a much-needed rest.

"Puff Graham" were the words William Randolph Hearst used to promote Billy Graham, a new star. In the business of saving souls, tall, blond Graham, a thirty-year-old from North Carolina with all-American looks, was the antithesis of Mickey Cohen,

The Southern Baptist evangelist's first major crusade had begun in Los Angeles in the fall of 1949. Instantly catapulted out of obscurity by massive media attention, Billy Graham was soon preaching to crowds of eight thousand to ten thousand nightly from the Canvas Cathedral, a huge circus tent that covered nearly an entire downtown block, at Washington and Hill. Scheduled to run three weeks, the revival meetings were extended an additional four. Graham's Los Angeles crusade became the largest religious event ever held in the Southland, surpassing in scale even those of Aimee Semple McPherson, the wildly popular evangelist of the 1920s.

Graham's tent show included the cooperation of close to a thousand local churches, with total estimated attendance of 350,000. Nearly every day, the papers featured stories of Billy Graham and his notable converts. Among the newsworthy ones was an extremely valuable member of the Mickey Cohen outfit. Kneeling on the sawdust floor of the Canvas Cathedral, renouncing his old life of sin, was the mobster's electronics maven, Jim Vaus.

Vaus had worked for the cops, torn out the bug planted in Cohen's Brentwood home, and provided dozens of security devices for the gangster's protection. The technical wizard developed listening gadgets, recorders, tiny cameras, and other high-tech devices that were useful to Cohen. Most significantly, he was reputed to have provided a bonanza by electronically altering the race wire. Recently, Vaus had perjured himself in a case involving Cohen.

What Billy Graham was preaching was no revelation to Jim Vaus. The son of a Los Angeles minister, Vaus had been around that old-time religion his entire life. Before meeting Mickey, he had an unsavory past that included a term at McNeil Island Federal Penitentiary, and he had previously used "religious conversion" to shorten a prison stay. The claim that a known Cohen "henchman" had been born again at the Canvas Cathedral was news: the story, "Wiretapper Vaus Hits Sawdust Trail," appeared in the *Los Angeles Times* on November 8, 1949.

Invaluable publicity would come from saving Hollywood's ultimate sinner. Ambitious Billy Graham went on a personal crusade for Mickey Cohen's soul.

Cohen was very interested in much-needed "good" publicity. He recalled their initial meeting at the Brentwood house by saying: "Graham . . . had in his mind that he might convert me . . . Naturally, I was a little bit uncomfortable in the hands of all those church people." The phobic perfectionist was also concerned with making a proper impression in his

There's a new star in the heavens and he's desperate to save Mickey Cohen's soul: Southern Baptist evangelist Reverend Billy Graham makes his initial splash in L.A. and catches the attention of ailing press tycoon William Randolph Hearst by preaching fire, brimstone — and salvation. Fall 1949.

role as host. Uncertain about what to prepare for his pious guests, after much deliberation, he instructed the housekeeper to serve hot chocolate and cookies.

This encounter was not the end of the story. L.A.'s celebrity mobster and the Reverend Mr. Graham would meet again.

★ ★ ★

The new decade of the 1950s began with great uncertainty. China had fallen to the Communists. The Soviet Union had detonated an atomic bomb just a few months before the New Year. Now, the United States was saber rattling in Korea.

In Washington, a turf war had started between two freshmen senators. Joseph McCarthy, Republican from Wisconsin, and Estes Kefauver, Democrat from Tennessee, were squabbling over who would launch a nationwide probe into the sinister doings of the underworld.

Tall, thin, and exceptionally polite, Senator Estes Kefauver may have looked like a down-home boy in his old-fashioned spectacles and tweed suits, but the forty-six-year-old former attorney was a formidable presence. During his recent campaign, he employed the gimmick of sporting a coonskin cap, à la Davy Crockett, while plain-talking a populist platform to the voters of Tennessee. Brought up in a strict Baptist family, as an adult Kefauver easily moved into the secular world. He fancied pretty ladies and frequented Pimlico and Laurel, the Washington area racetracks, where he asked for courtesy treatment. Although the senator seemed to enjoy a day at the track, in 1949 he introduced bills banning the interstate shipment of slot machines and gambling information via the wire service.

But there was powerful opposition to the proposed crime investigation. In light of recent international events, well-oiled congressional critics glee-fully laughed off the notion of senators "chasing after crap-shooters."

In the early morning hours of February 6, 1950, Mickey Cohen smelled something burning. Although his habit was to stay in his own bedroom, he had been asleep in his wife's quarters when the security alarm awakened them.

Taking a shotgun from under the bed, he looked around carefully. All seemed well. But he still smelled an acrid odor. As he collapsed into bed, a mighty jolt rocked the house from side to side with such force the structure seemed to elevate. Time suspended as walls collapsed, windows blew, and the thick mirrored panels in LaVonne's bedroom shattered, propelling shards like shrapnel. In less than twenty seconds, it was over.

Was it a nightmare? Or the endgame earthquake every Californian feared?

This explosion was a special present designed to propel Mickey Cohen into permanent oblivion. Personally packed by Tom Dragna, it was a bomb containing thirty sticks of dynamite. To prevent another dud, the explosive had been topped off with two fuses.

As the smoke cleared, it was eerie. Miraculously, Mickey stepped out from the ashes. He was untouched. LaVonne and the housekeeper were stunned but unharmed. Even his beloved dog, Toughie, was safe. Mickey later revealed, "I was just so happy to see he [Toughie] was all right . . . everything else was . . . secondary, even though the front of the house was . . . blown apart."

Rolled into a crawl space under the house, the bomb landed beneath Mickey's cement-encased vault. The bank-sized safe deflected the explosion, sending the massive force downward and sideways. Digging a crater twenty

Saved by the safe: Mickey Cohen's bombed-out Brentwood house, which was quickly rebuilt. February 1950.

feet wide by six feet deep beneath the foundation, the detonation was heard ten miles away.

In the pre-dawn hours, cops, reporters, and television crews swarmed around quiet, sylvan Brentwood. Surveying the damage, Mickey coolly bantered with the press. Wearing pajamas, a robe, and an impassive expression, he obligingly posed. Surrounded by debris, flashbulbs exploded as he stood in his bombed-out dressing room, examining a closet full of tattered suits. Visibly shaken, LaVonne watched her husband in disbelief.

Broadcasting from Cohen's den, reporters took to the airwaves. They assured terrified Westside residents that another war had not broken out. The blast was merely the latest installment in the long-running underworld battle that had contaminated Los Angeles since 1946.

Before the end of the day, Governor Earl Warren declared the explosion was a "manifestation of gang warfare over spoils." Trying to hamstring Mickey and prevent a score-settling rampage, the LAPD placed a 24/7 detail on the mercurial Mr. Cohen. In turn, he hired a private security patrol. Tit for tat, members of the Gangster Squad flipped a man on Cohen's detail.

The beleaguered residents of affluent Brentwood had had enough. Windows were broken throughout the neighborhood, and a young girl was not just traumatized, but also slightly injured by shards of flying glass. A circus-like atmosphere prevailed in the once quiet streets, now overrun by police, press, Cohen associates, and the curious.

The Brentwood Terrace Property Owners Association went to Mayor Bowron, LAPD Interim Chief Worton, and the city council, demanding the mobster be forced to move. They pleaded, "The presence of Mickey Cohen in this neighborhood represents a continuous and increasing hazard to life and property."

L.A.'s Capone took action, appealing to his neighbors with a ghostwritten statement:

> On Monday morning, my home was bombed. Though this outrage con-
> stituted a great threat to my wife and my neighbors and has deprived
> me of the sense of security and sanctuary that every man feels when he
> steps across his home doorstep, it didn't make me nearly as unhappy as
> the action, today, of some of my neighbors . . . those who are trying to
> push me out of the community.
>
> Guided as I was by the kindly statements of those in the neighbor-
> hood who apparently took only into consideration the fact that Mrs.
> Cohen and I are going through a very rugged and painful period of our
> lives, I took it for granted that if I could expect no breaks from the mad
> beast who bombed me I would certainly have no reason to fear hurt
> from my neighbors, whom I have never molested in any way.
>
> In fact, I still have faith in them. I still feel that they will respond to
> the logic of the situation, and the human factors involved.
>
> I feel sure that they are aware that despite much adverse newspaper
> publicity not one single iota of proof has been brought forward that
> would show that I have done anything to draw the kind of savagery that
> occurred last Monday morning, and before.
>
> I am hopeful that some of the more well-informed are aware that I
> have done nothing in self-defense . . . though the opportunities were
> open to me . . . that would endanger my neighbors in any way. I have
> even sent away friends who would have stood by to help me. I didn't
> want to incur the possibility of wrong or unsavory appearances.

I have confidence that most clear-thinking people will realize that my position has been well misrepresented. In the words of some of the wild-eyed characters who have written about me for the public, you have been "bum-steered" and I have been "bum-rapped." Let's both stop being victimized. I am a gambler and a betting commissioner; no more, no less. I'm not a mobster, a gunman, or a thug. I leave such antics to Mr. George Raft and Mr. Humphrey Bogart, who make money at it, or to certain other local actors — bad actors — who make the penitentiary at it, ultimately. I am not in the dynamiting business, the shooting business, or in any of the other varied forms of homicide. I sell shirts and ties, and sometimes I make a bet or two.

That's being on the level with you.

I would like to go on living quietly among you . . . if for no other reason than that if I were to go elsewhere the same situation might arise, if there were enough intolerant people in the community. I have faith that the regular authorities will take steps to prevent any possible recurrence of Monday's incident. And I have faith that most of my neighbors will go along with me in this belief, as they will with me in my desire and determination to preserve my home.

And if for no other reason, I believe that my neighbors will stand by my right to live in Brentwood because to do otherwise would be to play into the hands of the fiends who lit that fuse last Monday morning . . . I don't think anyone in this little community of ours wants to give them that satisfaction.

Very sincerely,

Your neighbor,

Mickey Cohen

The Brentwood bombing garnered an onslaught of national coverage, highlighting the underworld's notoriety. The inept methods, which endangered innocent citizens, employed by the Dragna mob were unpopular with the eastern bosses, particularly in light of the proposed senate investigation. Pressure was put on the Dragnas, called the Mickey Mouse Mafia by the press, from both the law and the lawless.

Captain Lynn White of the LAPD Intelligence Bureau, the new name for the Gangster Squad, was assigned to bring in banana importer Jack Dragna for questioning. The mafioso lived in a neat, tiny Spanish-style bungalow at 3927 Hubert Avenue in the Crenshaw-Leimert Park area, a modest neighborhood far from the upscale enclaves off Sunset Boulevard. He wasn't present when officers raided the house, but Frank Paul Dragna, his twenty-five-year-old son, was held and questioned.

Charging false arrest, the younger Dragna slapped Captain White, and the city of Los Angeles, with a $300,000 civil suit. A war veteran who had lost an eye in battle, the mob boss's son claimed the incarceration had caused an infection in his damaged eye socket. For "attempting to embarrass me by filing the false arrest suit," Captain White countersued for $5,000.

A short, swarthy, slovenly dressed man of fifty-nine, Jack Dragna had always avoided the press. After the arrest of his son he sat down with reporters. In his heavy Sicilian accent, Dragna denied he was behind the attempts on his rival's life, declaring, "Mr. Mickey Cohen can stay alive as long as he wants. It doesn't bother me to have him around. He has nothing I want. I'm an old man and I look forward to raising my family and giving them a chance to have things easier than I ever did."

Meanwhile all parties were acquitted in the Pearson–Seven Dwarfs case. The disgraced LAPD brass and officers Wellpott and Jackson were acquitted in the Brenda Allen case, as well.

In national news, events were heating up. On May 10, 1950, the underworld steeled itself as the Senate finally passed Resolution 202, forming the Senate Committee to Investigate Organized Crime in Interstate Commerce. Estes Kefauver trumped Joseph McCarthy, winning the role as committee chairman. The Kefauver hearings would both shock and entertain the nation.

On the last weekend of June, the Cold War became white-hot. Full use of force had already been sanctioned to stop the invasion of communist North Korea into the south. In a mighty display of U.S. firepower, a thousand 122-millimeter PA howitzers exploded in a singular wall of flame above the 38th parallel, just inside the Democratic People's Republic of Korea. Again, the country was at war.

Disrespected don:
Los Angeles Mafia boss
Jack Dragna. 1950.

Subpoenas to appear before Senator Kefauver's committee began to be served. Nearly four hundred gangsters — powerful men who in most cases had managed to live their lives in undisturbed anonymity — panicked. "In fact 'Kefauveritis,' that mysterious ailment that struck crooks and politicians just before they were about to be subpoenaed, became a widely discussed national malady," noted Senator Kefauver. "It manifested itself in unexpected heart attacks, laryngitis, nervous breakdowns, appendicitis, and/or acute desire for privacy; the most pronounced symptom on the part of the victims was an irresistible compulsion to travel — far away from Kefauver."

Mickey Cohen, without question, was the most talked-about — and talkative — mobster of the period. That summer of 1950, he came down with a severe case of "Kefauveritis." With the police commission about to select a new LAPD chief, it seemed like a fine time for a road trip.

14

TSURIS

*"The rackets there, like the state itself,
were big and colorful."*
SENATOR ESTES KEFAUVER,
SPEAKING OF CALIFORNIA

By 1950, trumpeting that he was impervious to stress, Mickey bitterly groused that he was "going broke." He charged cops, Brentwood neighbors, bad publicity, and underworld competitors were conspiring to make his life unbearable.

Cohen got an urgent call from Frank Sinatra. The crooner insisted on dropping by his home, which had been quickly repaired after the bombing. Although Mickey was never interested in stars, Sinatra was an exception. He liked to gamble and would eagerly provide a hefty "loan" to Mickey whenever he saw him. Trying to discourage the visit, Cohen reminded him that the LAPD Gangster Squad was present around the clock, watching his house and taking the names of all visitors. But Sinatra kept pressing him, saying it was "important."

Finally Cohen agreed to meet Sinatra. The singer pleaded with the mobster to stop Johnny Stompanato, his handsome young associate, from seeing Ava Gardner, Sinatra's dazzling girlfriend. After eight years of speech classes to eliminate her thick Southern accent, the black-haired beauty was now poised to become one of MGM's most important stars. Irritated by what Sinatra considered "important," Mickey told him that he never interceded in personal affairs and that he should return to Nancy, his estranged wife.

Cohen again made headlines with the delivery of a custom-built bulletproof, bombproof 1950 Series 60S Fleetwood Cadillac. Built like a tank with puncture-proof Goodrich Silvertown Seal-O-Matic tires, the vehicle had eight-inch-thick carbon steel-plated doors that were lined with bulletproof fiberglass. The flat-bottomed automobile had been tested at Coachcraft of Hollywood, where the customizing had been done — and again at the LAPD gun range. Fast, and designed so that passengers could fire out through specially constructed hinged windows, nothing less than a bazooka could penetrate the vehicle.

California law read that armored cars were to be licensed only to bank couriers and law enforcement. Cohen's attorneys, Sam Rummel and Vernon Ferguson, went to court seeking permission for Mickey to be allowed to drive the automobile. The judge said he would license him, providing Cohen came before the court and revealed who gave permission for the bombproof Cadillac to be tested on the LAPD gun range. He declined the offer, and the costly Cadillac remained in storage until it was finally acquired, at a substantial loss, by a Texas car museum.

Dodging a subpoena from Kefauver and absenting himself from the city while the Los Angeles police commission selected a new chief, Mickey Cohen left L.A. He drove east with Toughie, his bulldog, and Johnny Stompanato.

In Albuquerque, police were called to his motel after complaints of noise in his room. In Phoenix, Cohen attended an art opening and told the press he was set to acquire several drugstores there but had been refused a license. Upon arrival in Chicago, Cohen and Stompanato were jailed overnight with a warning from the chief of detectives: "Get out of Chicago. You're not wanted." The next stop was Texas. Working on solid information from the LAPD that Cohen was there to set up a gambling syndicate, the Texas Rangers questioned him then put him on a plane back home.

Upon arrival back in the City of the Angels, Mickey told the press that he had been in Texas arranging legitimate oil deals. He complained bitterly, "If they do this to me in all the forty-eight states, where do they want me to go — Russia?"

Then he was struck by a combination of blows that left him badly shaken. The IRS started an audit for 1946, 1947, and 1948. Society woman Agnes Albro, a member of the five-person police commission entrusted with selecting the next LAPD chief, died suddenly, swinging the vote in the wrong direction. In a stunning tactical upset for Mickey, William H. Parker was named head law enforcement officer of the city of Los Angeles, beating out the favored candidate, Deputy Chief Thad Brown. A highly ambitious officer with a law degree, Bill Parker was not a Cohen ally. Lastly, the Kefauver committee subpoenaed Cohen to testify before a panel of U.S. senators about his criminal activities.

Senator Kefauver later observed the unique and tainted taste of the West Coast underworld: "Crime, vice, and corruption in California had a special flavor — exotic, overripe, and a little sickening. The rackets there, like the state itself, were big and colorful."

On November 17, 1950, at a packed hearing room in the federal building in downtown Los Angeles, Mickey Cohen met the senators. The day began badly when he arrived late for the 9 a.m. session. He refused to take responsibility for his tardiness, asserting that neither he, nor his lawyers, had been properly notified.

Dressed for the occasion like a pimp, the Mick was attired in a brown gabardine suit cut in his trademark zoot style, matching fedora, crisp white shirt with a fashionable swallowtail collar, and chocolate jacquard tie secured by a huge diamond-studded MC clip. A mezuzah and a St. Christopher medal dangled from his thick gold watch chain.

A buttoned-down Yalie, Kefauver remembered Hollywood's infamous mobster as a "Simian figure, with a pendulous lower lip, thinning hair, and spreading paunch . . . dressed in 'sharp' clothing, including a suit coat of exaggerated length, excessively padded in the shoulders, and a hat with a ludicrously broad brim."

Accompanied by a pair of second-string lawyers, Mickey anxiously awaited his turn. His friend, Barney Ruditsky, the former NYPD detective who was often his liaison with local authorities, testified about him, perpetuating the myth that pleased Cohen and his eastern bosses: "[He identified Cohen as] an outlaw without ties to a criminal syndicate." Next, newly appointed LAPD Chief William H. Parker haughtily offered the senators a scathing portrait of Mickey: "I would say he is essentially stupid. He is heavy-set and heavy-browed and quite ignorant."

After being sworn in, Cohen took his place at a counsel table across from the three members of the committee. They began with questions as to his name, age, birthplace, and business. Claiming his birth year was 1916 before finally settling on 1913, Cohen stated that he owned a men's clothing shop. There were a few questions about his boxing career, to which he replied, "I wasn't very good," and the bad old days in Cleveland and Chicago. Then chief counsel Rudy Halley got down to cases: the beating of Russell Brophy during the wire war and the killing of Max Shaman in Cohen's paint shop. Mickey's arrest record during 1945 was discussed. The questions went round and round about bookmaking on a national scale and the trio of bookie rivals, Gamson, Levinson, and Gibbons, murdered in 1946.

Then Senator Kefauver moved to the August 30, 1948, beating of gambler William Henry Petroff, for which Cohen, Jimmy Rist, Dave Ogul, and Joe and Fred Sica had been arrested. Allegations that Petroff had been taken against his will to a ranch in Malibu were discussed at length. Next, the killing of Cohen hoodlum Neddie Herbert was addressed.

Chief counsel Halley delved into the Hooky Rothman murder, the Sherry's massacre, the public pistol-whipping of Jimmy Utley — which Mickey calmly denied — and the convoluted and deadly Pearson–Seven Dwarfs case. His relationship with Joe Sica was brought up again. Mickey said they were "just kids hustling around . . . gambling and trying to do the best we could." Careful to distance himself from Sica, Cohen insisted that for the last six years there had been no business connection between them. Halley then introduced into evidence the FBI records of Cohen, Jimmy Rist, Joe Sica, Dave Ogul, and Eli Lubin.

Halley asked Mickey if he knew Eddie Borden. Cohen said he did, describing Borden as an editor for *Ring* magazine and a man who "would bet on anything." Hoping to open a federal kidnapping investigation, Halley questioned Cohen about the disappearance, and subsequent return, of Borden from Las Vegas on November 4, 1950. This line of questioning continued through the remainder of the morning. After a recess for lunch, chief counsel Halley resumed by asking Mickey about his current financial situation.

[Halley] I believe you testified that you are broke these days, is that right?

[Cohen] This is right, yes.

[Halley] You have had a fairly large amount of money come through your hands this year, haven't you?

[Cohen] Money came through my hands?

[Halley] Yes.

[Cohen] You mean that I have borrowed?

[Halley] Yes.

[Cohen] Yes, I borrowed some money.

[Halley] You borrowed quite a bit, haven't you?

[Cohen] Well, a fair amount of money, yes.

[Halley] How much?

[Cohen] I don't know, but my accountant was up here with the figures. Every time I borrow money I call him and tell him I borrow.

[Halley] It is about $60,000?

[Cohen] I don't know if that is the figure or not; it is possibly around there.

[Halley] What happened to that $60,000?

[Cohen] I paid off a $25,000 bond. For the last four years I have been constantly in courts and under harassment by the Los Angeles police department that is making it their business to see that I get broke.

[Halley] How did you spend the other $35,000?

[Cohen] On my living, and I had a colored maid.

[Halley] How else?

[Cohen] Lawyers' expenses, troubles.

[Halley] Is it all gone by now?

[Cohen] All excepting what I have in my pocket.

[Halley] You have nothing in the world except what you have in your pocket?

[Cohen] That is right.

[Halley] What do you have in your pocket?

[Cohen] $200 or $300, $285 or so. Yes, $285.

[Halley] That is all the money you have left in the world?

[Cohen] $286, I mean.

[Halley] How do you expect to live from now on?

[Cohen] I can get money.

In a packed courtroom in the L.A. federal building, Mickey Cohen carefully chooses his words when testifying before Senator Kefauver and his gang from Washington. November 17, 1950.

[Halley] You borrow it?

[Cohen] Yes.

[Halley] How much do you owe at this time, Mr. Cohen?

[Cohen] Well, Senator, I am under investigation by the Internal Revenue now for the last three or four years. There has been some talk about it.

[Senator Kefauver] Do you think telling how much you owe would incriminate you?

[Cohen] I don't know. I am under investigation by the Internal Revenue Bureau now. I want your answer, Senator.

[Kefauver] I am passing on objections, one way or the other. The question is, how much do you owe at the present time?

[Cohen] Is that a proper question to answer, if you are under investigation by the Internal Revenue?

[Kefauver] In my opinion, the fact that you owe some money doesn't make you guilty of any crime, but if you have another opinion about it you can consult your attorneys to see what you want to do.

[Cohen] I say about $300,000 [$2.4 million today].

Concerned as to how Mickey's testimony might affect the ongoing tax probe, his counsel sought to clarify immunity statutes. The testimony continued about Mickey borrowing fantastic sums of money — including $50,000 ($450,000 today), advanced without a collateral, interest, or payment schedule from Harold W. Brown, president of the legitimate Hollywood State Bank.

Questions about his interests in various illegal gambling casinos in the city and county of Los Angeles followed, among them Dincara Stock Farm in Burbank and the La Brea Social Club in Los Angeles.

Senator Kefauver probed deeper into the convoluted financial arrangements at Mickey's clothing shop, jewelry store, and tailoring shop. The senator noted allegations that Mickey had an interest in the Jim Dandy grocery store chain; denying this, Mickey conceded, "It is a rumor that goes around, and it is absolutely untrue." The next area of attention: the fight game. Acknowledging he once managed boxer Willie Joyce, had pieces of a few other fighters, and was well acquainted with Blinky Palermo, the acknowledged right-hand of boxing power Paul John "Frankie" Carbo, Mickey denied owning a piece of Ike Williams, a Carbo champion.

Halley asked Mickey about his ties with the Retail Clerks Union. He denied receiving money from the union. Next, Halley brought up the violence that pervaded Mickey's life.

[Halley] Going over your activities, it appears that you have been able to borrow $300,000 in the last five years; is that right?

[Cohen] Yes.

[Halley] And that you say you live quite extravagantly; that is probably right?

[Cohen] That is right, yes. Maybe too extravagantly. That is probably right.

[Halley] And that you have been surrounded by violence?

[Cohen] That is right.

[Halley] That six of your close friends have either been killed or disappeared?

[Cohen] Six? I don't know of six that have disappeared.

The names of dead men — Bugsy Siegel, Neddie Herbert, Hooky Rothman, Frank Niccoli, and Dave Ogul — were introduced into record, as well as Jimmy Rist, who in 1948 had been wounded in the attempt on Cohen's life at the men's clothing shop.

[Halley] And you have had five attempts on your life?

[Cohen] Five, I think, is the correct amount. I think five is right, yes.

Mickey became extremely agitated during questioning about the Pearson–Seven Dwarf case, when chief counsel Halley accused him of being a strong-arm man.

[Cohen] I don't like the way he is asking me these questions. He is asking me the questions like that is the truth.

[Kefauver] Just a minute, just a minute, please.

[Cohen] And there isn't one question that I have answered that isn't one hundred percent truth.

[Kefauver] Please don't argue with counsel. If you don't want to answer his questions, just say so. You answer them when he asks the questions the best you know how. Tell us what you know, and if you don't know anything about it then so state.

[Cohen] I say I haven't answered one question here that isn't to my knowledge one hundred percent the truth. This man would like to have you believe just one side.

[Kefauver] I have told you to answer the question if you know the answer and if you don't know the answer say you don't know.

[Halley] The question is whether or not your very close friends didn't beat up Pearson?

[Cohen] Is he going to answer those questions for me, Senator?

[Kefauver] Counsel, instruct him to answer the question or to say that he doesn't know the answer, and let's go ahead.

[Halley] The question is, didn't your very close friends beat up Pearson?

[Cohen] I say they didn't beat up Pearson, but that they were acquitted.

Redundant questioning by chief counsel Halley continued until Mickey again appealed to Senator Kefauver.

Halley then began questioning Mickey about top underworld figures, among them Frank Costello, Meyer Lansky, and Joe Adonis. Mickey categorically denied acquaintance with them, as well as a long list of others. Asked if he knew Dominick Farinacci, aka High Pockets, a Cleveland hoodlum who in recent years had resided in Los Angeles, Mickey replied in the affirmative.

When his old Cleveland mentor, Anthony Milano, was introduced as a subject, Cohen became noticeably uncomfortable.

[Halley] I think you said Anthony Milano is a bank president?

[Cohen] I am not speaking of him.

[Halley] He is one bank president, isn't he?

[Cohen] Yes.

[Halley] He spent six years in the federal penitentiary for counterfeiting, didn't he?

[Cohen] Do you want me to tell you about Anthony Milano so everybody can hear about it?

[Halley] I want to talk about bank presidents being honorable men.

[Cohen] Why, what did Mr. Brown [president of the legitimate Hollywood State Bank] do?

[Kefauver] Do you know whether Anthony Milano is president of a bank in Cleveland that you do business with?

[Cohen] No.

[Kefauver] Did you say you did business with him?

[Cohen] No. The man has loaned me some money.

[Kefauver] He loaned you money?

[Cohen] Personally, yes.

[Halley] That is what Brown did too?

[Cohen] Yes.

[Kefauver] Do you know whether he served time for counterfeiting, Anthony Milano?

Senator and Mrs. Estes Kefauver enjoy an evening at the extravagant Cohen-controlled Mocambo night-club on the Sunset Strip. 1952.

[Cohen] This man is a man of sixty years of age. I wouldn't have enough nerve to say to him, "Mr. Milano, have you been in the penitentiary for counterfeiting?"
[Kefauver] Do you know or don't you?
[Cohen] I don't know.

The topic moved to Mickey's unpaid "loans." Cohen said he intended to pay them, but after he was offered a partnership in a Texas oil business, the LAPD had made contact with authorities there and ruined his plans. Questioning continued about loans and lack of record-keeping. Mickey conceded he didn't "know how to keep no books," leaving those matters to Harry Sackman, his accountant.

When asked about Johnny Stompanato, Cohen stated that he was "a young fellow, a nice fellow. He is a good boy," whose "true age is 25 years old." Cohen admitted to borrowing substantial amounts of money from him and said that Stompanato worked at his Continental Café for a time as "the manager, the bartender, everything."

[Halley] Did he earn large sums of money? Was he a man of wealth?

[Cohen] I don't know that. I know he was able to get some money someplace; that is what he told me at the time.

[Halley] He borrowed very large sums of money from a rich man, did he not?

[Cohen] That is right, yes.

[Halley] Isn't it a fact that the government is now charging that he got that money by extortion?

[Cohen] I don't think so; I think it is not a fact.

[Halley] Perhaps I better read you the fact. This is a statement by the Revenue agent who made an examination of Mr. Stompanato.

[Cohen's counsel] Then it is a Revenue agent's form?

[Halley] I said it was a form we subpoenaed from your accountant. It is stated here: "The government intends to try to make a case showing Mr. Stompanato is a very wealthy man without too much business experience. That in 1948 and 1949 he . . . blackmailed . . . various persons for amounts in excess of $65,000."

[Cohen] That is a very funny question. He just had dinner with the fellow three nights ago . . . [Author's note: although his name wasn't disclosed at the hearing, the individual they are referring to is Sir Charles A. Hubbard.] I don't think he would have had dinner with the fellow three nights ago if he blackmailed him. It don't seem possible. On what grounds would Stompanato blackmail anybody?

[Halley] I am trying to find out how you and Stompanato succeeded in persuading people to loan you large sums of money.

[Cohen] I can only answer for myself. If you want Stompanato you can ask him.

Halley asked about the legitimacy of numerous loans. Senator Kefauver then asked about the contents of Mickey's personal phone book, which had fallen into the hands of the police. Kefauver noted that the phone book contained the names of many prominent mobsters, as well as top comic Joe E. Lewis and film star Eddie Cantor. "Friends of mine," Mickey told the senator. California's political kingmaker, lobbyist Arthur H. Samish, was the next topic. Mickey said he hadn't seen Samish since the night of the shooting outside of Sherry's restaurant. The committee produced phone records from his office that verified numerous calls had been made to Samish. Cohen shot back that the calls may have come from his office, but that didn't prove they were made by him. Mickey testified that Samish shopped at his clothing shop, but he had no business dealings with him. When asked about Frank Sinatra, Mickey admitted that he was "a good friend," but he denied helping the star promote a fight in San Francisco. After further questions into his gambling operations, the gangster was dismissed.

But that was not the end. Nervously mopping his brow, Mickey hurriedly exited the hearing room as flashbulbs detonated. Eager to critique his performance, a rabid press corps pushed toward him, shouting his name.

After the session concluded, Senator Kefauver issued a wrap-up statement about Mickey Cohen: "The Los Angeles Police Department does not go along with the theory that the little ex-pug has slipped and now is a second-rater in the crime world. Mickey, as a gambler and bookmaker, with far-flung interstate connections, an extortionist and all-round rackets boy, is decidedly important."

15

DEATH AND TAXES

"Sam Rummel was a cool-blooded businessman."
MICKEY COHEN

While the sparring with the senators had ended, Cohen's personal travails intensified, and two incidents greatly damaged his operations. Fresno drug dealer Abraham Davidian had been arrested on narcotics charges then turned informant. Cohen's longtime associates Joe and Fred Sica, and thirteen alleged confederates, were indicted for wholesaling narcotics. Although under close guard, Davidian was murdered the day before the trial. Stunning blonde starlet Barbara Payton, on screen with Cagney in *Kiss Tomorrow Goodbye,* appeared on page one of newspapers when she supplied the alibi for the suspect in the Davidian slaying. The case evaporated. The Sicas moved on, and Mickey Cohen was never implicated. But the multi-million dollar drug ring was decimated.

An ongoing investigation into Guarantee Finance, a massive book-making-loan syndicate that operated in county territory until it was shut down by state authorities in early 1949, was a source of great concern. "Confidential" books disclosed two mysterious, and unaccounted, entries made by accountant Harry Sackman, totaling $232,970. Authorities labeled the funds as "juice" — bribe money for authorities. Although Mickey's imprimatur enveloped the Guarantee operation, he had not been implicated.

As the case continued to unfold, several people close to him were indicted.

When asked at an anti-crime conference of mayors in Washington, D.C., Mayor Fletcher Bowron denied that Mickey Cohen was the underworld power of Los Angeles, dismissing him as a "disreputable little punk" and "small potatoes." Although many of his operations were in the city of Los Angeles, the mayor claimed no responsibility for Hollywood's celebrity mobster, taking the position that he operated solely outside city limits, in Los Angeles County.

The bad-mouthing by Mayor Bowron was what Mickey expected. "I didn't care if anyone I was backing took a stand against me, which is what he was supposed to do." He added, "There was no other way that you could do those things, if you understood politics."

As Mickey's empire appeared to crumble, L.A. was full of hoods and fixers from the East who tasted blood. Sidney Korshak, the powerful labor attorney from Chicago who had deep ties to the Capone outfit, now resided in Los Angeles. The influential lawyer was alleged to have informed on Cohen to the Feds. "Mickey was becoming an all-round pain in the ass, setting up crap games just to rob the players," a source revealed to author Gus Russo in *Supermob*, his account of Korshak's life. Gangster Flippy Sherer was also in L.A., overseeing interests for the Kid Cann mob of Minneapolis. And there was evidence Guy McAfee, former king of the L.A. rackets and now one of Las Vegas's most prominent citizens, had plans to expand operations he still maintained in Los Angeles.

After a lucrative career and spectacular courtroom success, attorney Sam Rummel had often been defined as the power behind the Mickey Cohen throne. Now publicly involved with Jimmy Utley and other less troublesome players, it seemed Rummel was cutting Mickey out. Years later, Cohen frostily called Rummel a "cool-blooded businessman."

Less than a month after Senator Kefauver's visit, forty-four-year-old Rummel spent a Sunday afternoon at the Brentwood Country Club, near Mickey's home. Late that night, he had a secret meeting with Captain Al Guasti, Captain Carl Pearson, and Deputy Sheriff Lawrence Schaffer, the men from the sheriff's department under indictment in the Guarantee Finance case.

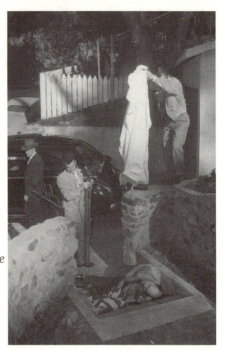

Sam Rummel, criminal mouthpiece and alleged power behind the Mickey Cohen throne, lies dead on the steps of his lavish Laurel Canyon palazzo. December 1950.

Scheduled to appear before the grand jury, Rummel was slated to testify about a conspiracy between county sheriffs and Guarantee Finance. With a complex corporate structure veiling the true workings of Guarantee, Mickey Cohen had yet to be linked to the bookmaking syndicate. Was his reputed role as the hidden face behind Guarantee to be revealed by Rummel at the hearing?

Around 1:30 a.m., December 11, 1950, Sam Rummel climbed the steep steps to his ostentatious palazzo at 2600 Laurel Canyon Boulevard. The boom of shotgun blasts pierced the silence. Sammy dropped backward onto the steps. Twelve-gauge slugs blew away part of his head. In a calculated move to muddy the trail of the true assassins, the death weapon, an old sawed-off shotgun that could be traced, had been casually left at the scene.

Mickey and LaVonne — accompanied by a bodyguard, six-foot-three, two-hundred-fifty-pound Sam Farkas — later visited the Rummel residence to offer the grieving widow comfort and condolences. Norma Rummel expressed great distress at their presence. The papers reported how the Cohens were shunned. The *L.A. Times* claimed that Mickey and Sammy had been on the outs.

The LAPD held jurisdiction in the area of the murder. Brought in for questioning at Rummel's mansion, Mickey went berserk when confronted by LAPD Chief Bill Parker. As the mobster screamed wild epithets at the new chief, Captain Jack Donahoe grabbed Mickey by the throat, lifted him off the floor, and dangled him like a puppet before his boss.

Claiming the lawyer's death posed a dire loss to him, Mickey offered a theory that Rummel's murder was another chilling plot to dethrone him. But not everyone was convinced by Cohen's tale of woe. On Parker's orders, he and members of his outfit, Joe Sica and Roger K. Leonard, FBI #2379765, were harshly grilled.

Rumors also circulated that members of the sheriff's department involved in the Guarantee Finance case were responsible, hoping to save themselves from conviction by sacrificing Rummel. Unable to indict an assassin or prove Cohen's involvement, the murder of Sam Rummel soon became another unsolved, high-profile case in the LAPD's abundantly stocked deep freeze.

Like Al Capone twenty years before, Mickey Cohen's most compelling enemy proved to be the IRS. His financial advisor, Harry Sackman, was not only under indictment in the Guarantee Finance case, he now had personal problems with the IRS. Cohen said, "My accountant, who I trusted implicitly for so many years, had formerly pulled me through three previous Internal Revenue investigations with a clean bill of health. Although I was warned by . . . one of the top persons connected with the Guarantee Finance situation that he, Sackman, would be forced into burying me to save himself, I couldn't accept this information."

On April 6, 1951, Mickey responded to a federal indictment for tax evasion declaring to the press, "I got less money than when I was selling papers." He professed, "I haven't beat the government out of five cents. I don't know what the hell to say. It's bad news." LaVonne, with whom he filed jointly, was also indicted.

The IRS charged that the couple had failed to accurately declare their income, owing over $300,000 (nearly $2.7 million today) in taxes for 1946, 1947, and 1948, with interest and penalties mounting.

From an FBI memo dated April 24, 1951:

MICKEY COHEN has advised a contact of the Phoenix Office that he desires to cooperate fully with FBI and would be willing to discuss any matter with Agency personnel.

But the FBI had a long history with him and were skeptical of his true motives:

These Agents report COHEN has held back information, has been evasive, misleading, two-faced and ingratiating. Los Angeles suggest that COHEN may pretend to act as an informant simply to try to obtain information from the Bureau, pointing out that he is well connected in nation-wide crime. Los Angeles recommends no effort be made to develop COHEN as a source of information or informant.

Because he couldn't prove they were dead, Mickey still owed $75,000 (nearly $800,000 today) in forfeited bail on Niccoli and Ogul, the two Dwarfs who had been murdered by the Dragnas. Deeply concerned about financing his defense, in May 1951 Cohen began raising cash by selling holdings like the Continental Café at 7823 Santa Monica Boulevard and book and screen rights to his life story as well as auctioning the contents of his home and Michael's Exclusive Haberdashery.

Donning his showman hat, Mickey's ballyhoo was spectacular. On the Sunset Strip, searchlights arced the night sky and a huge banner, bearing the gangster's photograph and the legend COHEN MUST QUIT hung from the storefront.

Giant ads ran in the newspapers:

THE YEAR'S MOST INTERESTING AUCTION EVENT
Furnishings from the home of Mr. and Mrs. Mickey Cohen
Nationally Prominent Personality
Expense was no object and every piece of furniture
was custom designed

Mickey's name attracted more than ten thousand spectators in the days when the contents of the Brentwood house were previewed. Police erected barriers to control the crowds around Moreno Drive.

Distressed Sale: to pay for his tax trials Mickey Cohen, wearing his promotional hat, sells all his visible assets. 1951.

Potential bidders and the curious were entranced by luxury novelties like a $20 ($180 today) corkscrew, Mickey's large collection of antique guns, and an assortment of bulletproof doors. Personally hawking the auction like a carnival huckster, Cohen posed with a long-barreled handgun, a vintage pistol, for *Newsweek* and television crews.

"If things were the other way around, I'd be bidding on these myself," he enthused. He signed countless autographs and proudly presented his quality wares: "Everything is made with wooden pegs. There ain't a nail in the joint."

Even Toughie's custom-made bed was on the block. Roused from his mahogany model of the finest dovetail construction, old Toughie was asleep in a cardboard box when the gavel went down. The tiny dog bed fetched a mere $35 ($300 today), while Mickey's matching model, along with a double dresser with secret compartments, went for $575 ($5,150 today), less than half the original cost. Custom electronics were items of interest: a specially devised radio fetched a fair price, and a huge nineteen-inch television went for $1,150 ($10,200 today).

Act Happy: LaVonne Cohen visits her husband (in prison denims) at the L.A. County Jail where he was remanded during his tax trial. 1951.

As the three-day spectacle wore on, Cohen became increasingly distressed; he couldn't believe his prized possessions were going for a pittance. But auctioneer Marvin Newman, who specialized in carriage trade sales, was elated: "It beats Jimmy Roosevelt's, Marlene Dietrich's, and even Rita Hayworth's. Mickey outdraws them all by thousands."

Federal Judge Benjamin Harrison was presiding when the tax trial commenced on June 3, 1951. As usual, the courtroom was packed. Journalists, photographers, film and television crews covered the proceedings. The government's case was hampered by the untimely death of its chief witness, Mickey's accountant Harry Sackman, a few days before the trial began. After a thorough investigation, the coroner concluded that sixty-one-year-old Sackman had died of natural causes, after suffering a heart attack.

Mickey was upbeat. "It's a pleasure walking into a courtroom with a clear conscience. It will turn out all right. Show me where I earned 50 cents that I didn't pay taxes on and I'll plead guilty."

Mickey Cohen and his wife LaVonne walking in opposite directions after she is included in the federal tax indictment. 1951.

When it came to LaVonne's inclusion in the indictment, Mickey gallantly asserted, "She doesn't know any more about it than a day-old baby." The government concurred; charges against Mrs. Cohen were dropped mid-trial.

A vivid cast of bad guys paraded through the proceedings. Cohen gang member Jimmy Rist was called by the prosecution, as was Allen Smiley, his close associate in the early years. Johnny Stompanato and his ex-wife, blonde actress Helen Gilbert, were also called to testify against Cohen.

A maitre d' spoke of a $600 tip (more than $5,000 today) from the defendant. Cohen's dentist was questioned. An Italian cobbler told of a weekly order for two to three pairs of custom-made elevator shoes, at no less than $65 ($530 today) per pair. Retired IRS agent Donald Bircher denied involvement in Cohen's accounting.

The excesses of the Brentwood house were extravagant even by Hollywood standards. Helen Franklin, interior decorator to the stars, said that she caught a "live one" in the free-spending mobster. A prominent furrier to the film colony testified that a $3,000 mink coat ($25,500 today) and $2,400 marten cape (nearly $20,000 today) were delivered to Mrs. Cohen. The prosecution questioned Harold W. Brown, former president of the legitimate Hollywood State Bank, about the huge loan he personally gave the mobster. Cohen enemy LAPD Lieutenant Rudy Wellpott admitted providing information about Mickey's spending habits to IRS agent Dan Goodyknoontz.

And fireworks erupted. During a recess, a prominent New York gambler called as a prosecution witness sat in the hallway talking to Goodyknoontz. When Mickey saw them, he exploded. A bailiff restrained him when he ran toward the federal official screaming, "[Dirty] double-crossing tramp . . . Who the hell do you think you are, trying to bulldoze this witness?"

After twelve drama-filled days, testimony concluded. It took four hours for the jury to deliver a verdict. Guilty on all four counts — three counts of evading taxes in the years 1946 through 1948 and the additional count of making a false statement to the IRS. His face turning red, Mickey rocked back and forth in his seat. This was his first felony conviction. "I'm not mad at anybody," he told the media. "I'm just a businessman trying to make a living."

On July 9, 1951, casually dressed in an open-collar sport shirt and blue Windbreaker, Mickey faced federal Judge Harrison for sentencing. The jurist was unusually sympathetic. Calling Mickey a "hard-luck problem child," he declared,

> You're not as bad as you're pictured. Perhaps more of us would be gamblers if we'd been as lucky as you . . . I think Mr. Cohen is a very personable individual. He's a good salesman — at least he's good at selling himself . . .
>
> Los Angeles must take part of the responsibility for what happened to him. He is a product of the melting pot of this city. He was permitted to operate here as a betting commissioner with what I think was a virtual acquiescence of law enforcement officers . . . His parents came from abroad. He had little education here and the environment produced Mr. Cohen.

*Brave young autograph
hunter consorts with the
underworld's celebrated
"Clay Pigeon" of the
Sunset Strip. 1951.*

Comparing the case to that of Al Capone, the chief prosecutor demanded the judge give him the maximum sentence.

Cohen "rocked on his heels like a fighter absorbing a jab" when Judge Harrison pronounced a harsh sentence of five years, levied a $10,000 fine for each of the four counts, and court costs amounting to $100,000 (approximately $830,000 today).

Led away in handcuffs, Mickey managed a faint smile.

The Brentwood house was sold, and he took a pauper's oath to avoid the significant fines. Glasser Brothers Bonds sued him over the forfeited bail for the dead men Niccoli and Ogul.

The LAPD, the L.A. County Sheriff's Department, the FBI, the Kefauver committee, and his underworld enemies had been unable to vanquish Mickey Cohen. Like with Capone, the white-collar workers of the Internal Revenue Service appeared to have ended the reign of the thirty-seven-year-old mobster.

16

JUDAS AND IAGO

*"If Mickey had kept his big mouth shut
and stayed out of the papers, he wouldn't
be in this mess."*
"HAPPY" HAROLD MELTZER, FAVORED
NEW MEMBER OF COHEN'S OUTFIT

If Bugsy Siegel had made his rise possible, Cohen blamed his fall on the combined efforts of Harold Meltzer and Jimmy Frattiano, the Weasel.

"Happy" Harold Meltzer, aka Herbie Fried, FBI #113017, had a dark history and deep underworld connections. He came to L.A. at the behest of Cohen lieutenant Neddie Herbert, his childhood friend. Born in 1905, Meltzer had served time for a drug conviction and was alleged to be a jewel thief, an assassin, as well as a major narcotics trafficker in Cuba, Mexico, Canada, Hawaii, Hong Kong, Italy, and Japan. Cohen later asserted that several sources had advised him that Meltzer was not just an "ingrate, but a well-known stool pigeon." Benny Siegel had warned Mickey about him.

Benjamin Siegel reputedly first smoked opium when he was a kid and had a long involvement in the drug trade. "The Siegel drug conspiracy had its inceptions in 1939 when at Meyer Lansky's request, [Siegel's mistress] Virginia Hill moved to Mexico and seduced a number of Mexico's top politicians, army officers, diplomats, and police officials," according to Douglas

Valentine, author of *The Strength of the Wolf.* Later Siegel and Hill formed a key relationship with Dr. Margaret Chung, attending physician to the celebrated Flying Tigers, the private airline General Claire Chennault formed to fly supplies to Chinese Nationalists in the opium-infused city of Kunming. Dr. Chung was said by authorities to be very important "in the narcotics trade in San Francisco."

In 1944, Meyer Lansky formed a cartel that funded a Mexican drug smuggling operation managed by Meltzer. Valentine wrote that Meltzer, "described as 'the man who most feared Bugsy's grab at Mexico,' based his operation in Laredo, directly across the border from Virginia Hill's nightclub, and moved drugs to the Dragna organization in California."

Harold Meltzer's operation prospered due to his connection to Salvatore Duhart, the Mexican counsel in Washington, along with funding and distribution from the syndicate and insatiable demand for product. Then things fell apart. "Happy" Harold began smoking opium and cavorting with a black prostitute. In a plan to dispense with Duhart's costly services, he put Los Angeles racketeer Max Cossman in charge of the Mexican end of the operation. But the gringos were soon taken. When containers were delivered to American distributors packed with coins, nails, and bullets — rather than brown powder — payment for the bogus goods was rejected.

"Even an appeal to 'Trigger Mike' Coppola to enforce payment failed, and Mexican suppliers kidnapped partner Cossman when Meltzer failed to send the promised payment," Alfred W. McCoy wrote in his book *The Politics of Heroin.* "Visiting New York in early 1947, Meltzer won a partial reprieve when . . . a dealer who had once worked for Waxey Gordon introduced him to Charlie 'The Jew' Yacknowsky [sic], a New Jersey waterfront boss, who interceded with the Jewish creditors."

In the summer of 1948, immediately after Charlie the Jew was murdered, Meltzer arrived in Los Angeles and joined up with Mickey Cohen. Quickly gaining the boss's favor, Meltzer was received into the top echelon of the gang. Meltzer immediately became privy to countless black secrets and was the recipient of many gifts and special privileges. Cohen screamed "setup" when LAPD officers Wellpott and Jackson arrested Meltzer on gun charges in January 1949. Cohen testified for him at the trial and again stood up for him later that year, when Meltzer was held as a suspect in the ice-pick murder of Charlie Yanowsky.

In March 1949, Meltzer was indicted as one of the notorious Seven Dwarfs, directly involved in the baroque scandal surrounding the beating of electronics expert Alfred M. Pearson. Heard on wiretaps planted at the residence of a beautiful party girl, Meltzer referred to Cohen as "that little jerk" and said, "If Mickey had kept his big mouth shut and stayed out of the papers, he wouldn't be in this mess."

When Siegel was alive, Cohen confirmed that he and Jack Dragna shared equal status as his lieutenants. Mickey claimed they never had "words or differences," adding, "as the years went by Dragna and my friendship progressed and he continued on in a sort of inactive way, but anything he wanted done he came to me for. I was the guest of honor at his daughter's wedding!"

But after Siegel was eliminated, Mickey disrespected the Dragnas.

When Meltzer heard that New York's Lucchese family put a contract on his life and that the contract belonged to Lucchese relative Jack Dragna, he hatched a wily scheme. Meltzer's plot was multi-fold. While saving himself, he planned to get rid of Cohen and, in league with the Dragnas, take control of his empire. Just like Frattiano, Meltzer continued to be actively involved in Cohen's operations while working with the Dragnas. The Judas of the intrigue incited the Dragnas about Cohen and kept them posted on the inner workings of his organization and whereabouts. Meltzer twice set up Cohen for assassination and served up two of his men to be killed.

Mickey later revealed, "The discord and resulting gang war was a matter of a bad apple getting into the barrel, a man who was in a position to play both ends from the middle, and who was able to knead and goad others into thinking things that were untrue."

Cohen later admitted to being so "completely high" on "Happy" Harold Meltzer that he did the unthinkable. He disrespected eastern masters by refusing to deliver Meltzer for assassination. For this supreme act of insubordination, the consequences were dire. Cohen recalled, "My refusal . . . brought disagreement between me and the other faction and alienated the good feelings that had formerly existed between us."

When Mickey discovered that he had supported a pair of double-crossers in his ranks, his rage knew no boundary. This time, it was the player that had been played.

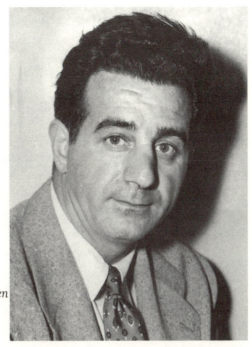

The Iago of the Mickey Cohen story: mobster Jimmy "The Weasel" Frattiano. 1951.

★ ★ ★

During 1950, Price Spivey, a Federal Bureau of Narcotics special investigator, focused his attention on the Mexican drug-smuggling operation of Harold Meltzer. Nearly finished with the investigation, Spivey suffered critical injuries when he was suspiciously "run off the road" outside Atlantic City. He recovered, and by March 1951 the case was complete. Harold Meltzer was indicted as a key figure in an international drug ring that imported heroin from Mexico, and opium from Turkey and Greece.

In a New York courtroom on June 15, 1951, less than a week after Cohen was convicted of income tax evasion, Meltzer pled guilty to drug trafficking charges. He was sentenced to five years in federal prison. Among the unindicted co-conspirators in the case were Meyer Lansky and Mickey Cohen.

★ ★ ★

Jimmy Frattiano, the Iago of the scenario, had "fingered" Cohen for assassination twice in 1948, delivered and helped murder Frank Niccoli, and had gotten close to Cohen's partner Joe Sica, when plans were afoot to execute him.

While the law neutralized Cohen and Meltzer, the vicious, ambitious Frattiano remained free and continued to prove himself in the underworld. Mickey was in county jail awaiting appeal on the tax conviction when Frattiano assassinated the Two Tonys — Trombino and Brancato — after they brazenly robbed the sports book at the Flamingo Hotel. Refusing to play by the rules, the pair was considered gangland outlaws, and their assassination was syndicate sanctioned. Cohen had originally brought the Two Tonys, small-time thugs with notorious reputations, from Kansas City to Los Angeles. They had been prime suspects in the Bugsy Siegel assassination, the Sherry's ambush, and the Rummel execution; now there was talk that Trombino and Brancato, broke and desperate, were willing to tell who killed Bugsy Siegel.

The media had a field day with the double hoodlum slaying that occurred on Ogden Drive, a fashionable residential street just off the Sunset Strip. LAPD Chief Parker "liked" Frattiano for the Two Tonys murders, but he was unable to make a solid case.

ACT III

THE
LONG
GOODBYE

17

SHIFTING WINDS

"I really have nothing.
I almost have to beg for money."
LAVONNE COHEN

While combat intensified in Korea and the Cold War with the Soviet Union persisted, the continuing Kefauver hearings, now televised, created a sensation, becoming the most highly rated programming in the brief history of the medium. The film business continued its free fall. Avoiding high-priced union labor, many productions moved from Hollywood to Europe. And a spectacular shooting, involving filmland insiders, toppled Hollywood's hoodlums from the headlines.

In the late afternoon of December 13, 1951, prominent producer Walter Wanger, fifty-seven, shot MCA talent agent Jennings Lang in the groin, in a Beverly Hills parking lot. Wanger, one of Sheriff Biscailuz's badge-carrying honorary deputies, was legally packing the .38 he used to shoot the agent. The producer was arrested at the scene, directly across from Beverly Hills city hall.

The urbane movie executive seemed to have lost his senses when he found out that his film star wife was engaged in an ongoing tryst with the jaunty thirty-six-year-old flesh-peddler, known for his manly attributes and special abilities with female clients. Mrs. Wanger — the black-haired beauty at the center of the triangle, known to filmgoers as Joan Bennett — often rendezvoused with the agent, allegedly to indulge their sexual appetites at exotic locales and, on a regular basis, at the Beverly Hills apartment of a junior agent.

Hollywood's moguls rallied round their brethren when Wanger was indicted for assault with a deadly weapon, a charge that carried a possible fourteen-year sentence. The call went out: "Get Giesler." The eminent attorney, Jerry Giesler, mounted a "temporary insanity" defense for the producer. While Lang recovered from the shooting and loss of a testicle, Wanger served his four-month sentence at the sheriff's Honor Rancho.

While the producer unwound in the comforts of the Honor Rancho, Mickey Cohen appealed his own conviction again, and again. All appeals failed. He offered to settle the debt for $200,000 (nearly $1.7 million today), but the IRS refused to make a deal. There were rounds of parties and dinners before the Mick left L.A. for McNeil Island Federal Penitentiary in 1952. Comic Redd Foxx cooked gumbo for him the night before he went away.

Ensconced at the medium security penitentiary in Puget Sound, Cohen adapted as operators do in prisons, but better. He was powerful: slicker and quicker.

He claimed to immediately institute a payroll for the prison staff, arrange a private cell for himself, as well as a cushy job in the officers' commissary. He ate whatever he desired, dining privately in the officers' dining room. All the tissues he needed were available, and freezers were stocked with his favorite ice cream. His housekeeper sent "care packages" filled with homemade treats. And the schedule was bent to accommodate his compulsion for showering several times a day. "Otherwise I would have probably flipped out, because at McNeil you normally showered twice a week," Cohen confessed.

In charge of the officers' commissary, his clothing was pressed just so and tailored to his liking. The commissary dispensed towels, soap, and other necessities needed to service his obsessive behavior. A special chest was built for his belongings. The huge piece of furniture arrived piece by piece from the prison woodshop and was placed under his bunk. The only thing missing was Toughie, his dog.

Tops in cops. (L to R) LAPD Chief William H. Parker, unidentified man, L.A. County Sheriff Eugene Biscailuz, Beverly Hills Police Chief Clifton Anderson. Circa 1950s.

"Working" for the federal government, he unloaded containers of war surplus and provisions, taken from Liberty ships preparing for dry dock. Crawling around inside the giant crates, Mickey would later marvel at the terrific swag he found. What he didn't want personally provided inventory for a lucrative business. He even found morphine, which he claimed to turn back to the Feds.

A progress report about him from McNeil Island noted, "[Cohen] had a compulsion to attract attention to himself and reacted hostilely to any kind of reprimand."

"I really have nothing. I almost have to beg for money," LaVonne confided to a journalist. The security and easy money Mickey had provided vanished. On her own for the first time in over a decade, she was forced to adapt. Her home, money, car, furs, and jewels, including a diamond ring so enormous and perfect it would have done the Countess di Frasso proud, were gone. She just had the dogs. While Mickey was at McNeil Island, she moved to a small apartment in West Los Angeles and got a job under an assumed name in the office of a Beverly Hills department store.

★ ★ ★

On the national scene, even the most prominent figures in the underworld felt the legal wrath that flowed from the Kefauver hearings. A federal law was passed banning the interstate transmission of wagers by wire, and the once untouchables finally proved vulnerable. The mightiest took wrist slaps or, like Mickey Cohen, worse. Frank Costello, suave and proud, was charged with contempt after walking out of Kefauver's humiliating televised interrogation. Convicted of the charge, he was sentenced to eighteen months. Costello was then convicted on tax charges. The IRS investigated Virginia Hill and high echelon mobster Longie Zwillman, and they convicted lobbyist Arthur Samish and several others. The wiliest of all, Meyer Lansky, would plead guilty to five counts of a twenty-one count gambling indictment. He was sentenced to three months jail time, with three years probation and a $2,500 fine (approximately $20,400 today). It was his first and last conviction.

Locally, Sheriff Eugene Biscailuz was twenty years into his run as top law enforcer in Los Angeles County. LAPD Chief William Parker needed to earn his stripes. His mandate was to get organized crime out of the city. Captain James Hamilton now headed the Gangster Squad. "They saw to it that word got out to other cities that Los Angeles was a 'hot town for alien hoods,'" wrote television star Jack Webb of *Dragnet* fame in his book about the LAPD, *The Badge*. "And locally, they followed the individual, rather than the crime. For the underworld it was aggravation all the time . . . Finally, the word went out, 'L.A. is closed.'"

But that was puff. Chicago was entrenched at a high level, working the labor and big business scene through attorney Sidney Korshak, their inscrutable golden boy, and his legion of Beverly Hills fronts. Mob royals like Sam Giancana of Chicago, New York boss Joe Bonnano, Lansky lieutenant Doc Stacher, and boxing czar Frankie Carbo spent time in the city. Cleveland remained an undeniable presence. Proving that the Dragna family had lost the war for control of Los Angeles, Mickey's sponsors, Cleveland's Milano family, now silently oversaw a territory that spanned several western states and California and reached into Mexico. Brought in by old Cleveland partners (Dalitz, Kleinman, Rothkopf, Tucker, et al.), they were purported to be secret investors at Vegas's new gambling resort, the Desert Inn, and other expansive ventures.

Mickey orchestrated his Southern California operations from the pen.

"The few big books still open are run by the Sicca [*sic*] mob. Many gamblers get their calls on Webster 11531, the 'Your Exchange Service,'" Jack Lait and Lee Mortimer reported in 1952.

> Cecilia Potts . . . is the official madam for the studios. They use her to get gals for VIPs. Another purveyor is Billie Bennett. She has a fine stable of working girls. Narcotics are plentiful here. The Los Angeles junk squad has the names of scores of addicts who cannot be touched because they are valuable cinematic properties and the studios are too powerful to buck . . . The overflowing Negro colony provides the background for a huge trade. Mexicans form a firm nucleus of addicts and traders.

In late 1952, Joe and Fred Sica were arrested at a gambling den running out of a downtown gas station at 1669 North Main. They were each given a year in county jail for felony bookmaking. Mickey's bodyguard, Sam Farkas, was arrested for robbery around the same time but had a solid alibi. Curly Robinson's legitimate statewide empire collapsed after the passage of bills outlawing slot and pinball machines.

The Dragnas were still present, but they hadn't struck it rich and were not without worries. The LAPD planted wiretaps above Jack Dragna's bed. Convicted on a morals charge after engaging in what was legally construed as "lewd acts" with a girlfriend, he served thirty days in county jail. Then the Feds neutralized him: he remained free on bond while fighting immigration improprieties that dated back twenty years. After Kefauver, Dragna family strategist Johnny Rosselli bought film rights to a religious story, *At the End of the Santa Fe Trail.*

Chief Parker couldn't boast L.A. was clean until all the jackals were defanged. "But before that happy day arrived, Intelligence along with other LAPD units had to perform two pieces of major surgery," Jack "Sergeant Friday" Webb observed. Mickey's archenemies, vicious turncoat Jimmy Frattiano and Squeaky Voice Utley, the self-proclaimed "Little Giant," were the players who were still free.

Unable to charge Frattiano with the Two Tonys murder, the LAPD had him under constant surveillance. "The episode [the Two Tonys case], with its incredible media coverage, established Jimmy's notoriety. In his own

Perp walk: Jimmy Utley (right), the underworld's "Little Giant," finally falls. Cohen's archenemy was taken down at his illegal abortion parlor in Long Beach. August 1955.

world, he had become feared and respected, exactly what he had sought most in his life. The public, too, had learned of his existence," noted Ovid Demaris in his book *The Last Mafioso*. In 1952, Jack Dragna made six new men and promoted Frattiano to the high-ranking position of captain.

Vowing to put Frattiano back in prison, LAPD's Captain Hamilton did everything possible to make good on this promise. In early 1954, Frattiano was convicted of extortion after threatening an oil developer. His second felony conviction sent him to San Quentin to serve a sentence of five to fifteen years.

Jimmy Utley proved to be more of a challenge. The LAPD Intelligence Unit, who labeled Utley "powerful and dangerous," initiated an elaborate sting. A French soldier of fortune was enlisted to frame Squeaky in a narcotics buy. Over a period of many months, the Frenchman won his confidence. Utley talked to and met with the sophisticated professional decoy countless times. All their conversations were bugged, but the cautious gangster never incriminated himself, or Jack Dragna.

Captain Hamilton didn't give up; Utley remained under constant surveillance.

Closely monitored, Jack Dragna began spending most of his time in San Diego. The most influential member of the Dragna family, Johnny Rosselli, was tiring of L.A. Seeing fewer problems and greener pastures in vibrant Las Vegas, he transferred back to the Chicago family and began overseeing their interests in the gambling mecca. Colorful Tony Cornero, sixty, died shooting craps at the Desert Inn in July of 1955. Both Harold Meltzer and Jimmy Frattiano remained in prison.

In August 1955, elusive Jimmy Utley was finally taken out of circulation. Authorities arrested him when they raided a storefront in Long Beach that proved to be one of his abortion shops. The Little Giant had acted as receptionist, cashier, nurse, and anesthetist in the $500,000-a-year ($4 million today) illegal abortion operation. Utley and abortionist Dr. Leonard Arons waived a jury trial and received ten-year sentences for conspiracy and illegal surgery.

Perhaps as a prelude to Mickey Cohen's imminent homecoming, the next month a prominent gambler, once a partner of Utley's in the defunct Venice bingo operations, escaped injury when his posh Pacific Palisades home was mysteriously shot up.

As film companies began flooding Rome, there were Hollywood-on-the-Tiber aspirations from an unlikely personage. Permanently exiled in Italy, Lucky Luciano was a bitter man who dreamt of New York and pastrami sandwiches. Aside from his mob business, the world's most notorious racketeer spent a great deal of time signing autographs. He was also busy "writing" a screenplay. It was a fantasy about an American underworld czar framed by a grandstanding prosecutor. After an unjust conviction, the innocent mob boss is deported to Italy, where his philanthropy and good deeds do not go unrecognized. Earning the admiration of the nation, he is finally able to return to the country that persecuted him. In a happy ending, the repatriated anti-hero is once again free to continue his lucrative criminal undertakings in the country he loves.

Charlie Lucky shopped a package deal: script, financing, and his blonde mistress in the female lead. The project was offered to acclaimed Italian producer Paolo Tamburella of *Shoeshine* fame. The Oscar winner passed.

On October 9, 1955, after three years, eight months, and sixteen days of incarceration, Mickey Cohen was released from McNeil Island Federal Penitentiary. Given a conditional release with significant time off for good behavior, he would be on probation until the next August.

He had many plans for the future. Like Luciano and Rosselli, he had Hollywood aspirations, too.

18

BRAVE NEW WORLD

"You can take it from me, that what is called the underworld is on the increase."
MICKEY COHEN

he land of perpetual summer, carnal delights, and blue-sky ennui still captured the imagination of dreamers everywhere. But L.A. had changed. Bigger and bolder than ever, freeways linked the suburban sprawl. Hollywood's old guard had lost their luster; a new and different breed was on the horizon. Among them was a high-haired, swivel-hipped young singer named Elvis Presley. *He* was considered dangerous.

Mickey Cohen, forty-two, was the last remnant of an era when gangsters talked out of the side of their mouths and boasted perfect manicures. He had captivated, corrupted, and terrorized Southern California. He had been shot at; bombed; probed by local, state, and federal authorities; reputedly driven out of business; and sent to prison.

Now back home in Angel City — he had changed too.

While incarcerated, Cohen had had much time to think. A new Mickey Cohen would appear on the day of his release. For the first time, he ran from reporters, who stood in a pounding rain awaiting the launch that transported him from McNeil Island back to the mainland. Howard Hertel, a reporter from Hearst's *Los Angeles Examiner*, had landed the exclusive.

Traveling by Cadillac with brother Harry and the newsman, Cohen's first stop was Portland, for talks about slot machines and policy wheels. Almost immediately, local authorities put him on a flight home. Flying into L.A., he chatted with Hertel, who still found him amiable and, more importantly, quotable. Welcoming him at the airport were LaVonne and the dogs.

A few days later, he called a press conference. Thirty-two photographers, twenty-two reporters, and TV crews covered the story. Looking trim and happy to be the center of attention, Mickey solemnly announced, "I'm through with the rackets."

But there were still prime pickings for a seasoned pro like him. As he told Ben Hecht, "You can take it from me, that what is called the underworld is on the increase."

On the day of his release, the *Los Angeles Herald* ran a piece stating that LaVonne had recently made several trips to Las Vegas. Speculating that Mickey might try to regroup in the desert boomtown, the article claimed that Vegas gamblers had placed a $45,000 ($360,000 today) price on his head. On October 12, 1955, the *Las Vegas Sun* went on record that Mickey Cohen wasn't welcome in the gambling town.

In his long career, he'd made many friends and countless enemies. On the outs with many of his sponsors, he had much to prove.

"He was very miserable," LaVonne later revealed. "For two months he sat around the apartment and wouldn't see anyone. He felt as though the whole world had let him down.

"He said I had changed, and he was certainly right. I had. When I'd been living with him I was like a puppet. Mickey pulled the strings and I moved when he wanted. Since he had been away I'd made a new life for myself among friends — decent, ordinary people."

Cal Meador, Mickey's probation officer, was convinced he had reformed. Working hard to keep him out of trouble, Meador had L.A.'s most notorious citizen doing social work. Mickey Cohen was the featured speaker at Volunteers of America and lectured at youth camps, proselytizing to juvenile delinquents that crime doesn't pay.

He began calling himself Michael Mickey Cohen. With new stationery and an updated wardrobe, he tested the waters. Showering three times a day, he now spent three or four hours on his ritualistic toilette. His clothing was changed five times each day.

Post-prison "legitimacy": Mickey Cohen, in gardener's smock bearing his new business's name, Michael's Greenhouse, polishes his merchandise. 1956.

Parker and the IRS observed his every turn. The FBI and sheriffs made periodic reports.

In early February 1956, Mickey was observed picking up George Bieber at the airport. One of Chicago's most influential mob lawyers, the pair drove to the El Mirador Hotel in Palm Springs and visited nearby Cabazon, a hamlet with a couple of legal poker parlors. A week later, Mickey was back in the desert, registered at the Palm Springs Hotel under the name

M. Weaver. Attorney Bieber and the gamblers from the Pacific Northwest conferred with him there. Palm Springs police arrested Cohen for not registering as an ex-con. He paid the fine but complained bitterly to the press.

On Valentine's Day, the *Los Angeles Times'* tabloid the *Mirror* published a story about Mickey and the lawyer from Chicago. The paper stated that police were disturbed by the Bieber connection and posed a question: "Is Cohen, through Bieber, making up with the group of Chicago gangsters, the remnants of the Al Capone syndicate? This meeting could mean Mickey Cohen is moving into the big time."

The next day Mickey established a new front: Michael's Greenhouse Inc., a warehouse at 1115 South Vermont Avenue, in the mid-Wilshire district. The day after that the "reformed" mob boss showed up on skid row. Addressing a captive audience of winos, Cohen announced that he'd "chucked the rackets for tropical foliage."

For five days he remained inside a room at the Ambassador Hotel, meeting with Jim Vaus, his electronics expert from the glory days. Vaus had become a full-time evangelist in 1950. Touring the country, his popular sermons combined a heavenly mix of electronic pyrotechnics, Mickey Cohen, and God. "Voice with a Helium Accent," "Sound Effects from Molecules of Steel," and "Confusion of Speech by Electronic Confusion of Mind" were a few of the items in Vaus's repertoire. His memoir, *Why I Quit Syndicated Crime*, which featured a foreword by Cohen, had just been made into a movie, *Wiretapper*. Produced by a church organization, the low-budget feature portrayed gangsters, redemption, and stock footage of Reverend Billy Graham. Authorities divined that "religious rackets" were to be a part of Cohen's future.

Then came a landmark death. "Throughout his career, [Jack] Dragna preferred to remain inconspicuous — somewhat the complete opposite of his contemporary, Mickey Cohen," the *Los Angeles Times* reported on February 24, 1956, the day after the body of the Mafia boss was found at the Saharan Motel, 7212 Sunset Boulevard.

Dragna, sixty-five, had checked into the seven-dollar-a-night motel on February 10 using the name Jack Baker. A maid discovered his pink pajama–clad body in bed. Dead for some time, his death was the result of an apparent heart attack.

Personal possessions found at the scene: a wallet containing his driver's license, bottles of assorted heart medications, two spare sets of false teeth, eyeglasses, $986.71 in cash, and a copy of the paperback *The Luciano Story*. In Dragna's suitcase was a newspaper clipping about the lawsuit filed by his son, charging three policemen with false arrest, and a small plastic statue of Jesus. A late model Cadillac parked nearby was registered to the address of nephew Louis Tom Dragna, 1429 Thelborn Street, in the eastern suburb West Covina.

At the time of his death, Jack Dragna remained free on bond, awaiting appeal in his federal immigration case.

Mickey's personal life became public when LaVonne filed for divorce on March 15. Citing mental cruelty, she told the *Herald Express* they wanted a "friendly divorce."

His "pretty red-haired" wife told the press, "It's just one of those unfortunate things. We haven't been able to make adjustments since he got back. It's not any more Mickey's fault than mine."

They reconciled a few months later.

She would later admit her vulnerability when it came to her husband: "It's easy for Mickey to get under your skin, you know. He has a certain charm about him. I can have words with him, and before it's all over I'm beginning to feel that everything is all right, and maybe I'm wrong."

In July 1956, he got some excellent publicity when a syndicated newspaper article appeared across the country, which included a photograph of him tending plants. "The man in a smock puttering with begonias is ex-mobster [Mickey Cohen] on parole until August 4."

"I didn't know a camellia from a coat hanger when I came in on this, but I'm learning . . . I just got my bellyful of the life I used to live," Mickey confided to John Beckler of the Associated Press. "It used to cost me two-three hundred bucks to walk out on the street with all the bites put on me . . . People all think I'm laying low until my parole is up in August. Well, today I'm satisfied sitting at home. I want a more relaxed way of life."

Mickey weighed in on the old days and his recent reconciliation:

"LaVonne married a dashing, colorful rough-tough hoodlum. When I came home she found me quite a bit different."

Beckler noted, "Whether the difference will be permanent is still anybody's guess. His parole officer, Cal Meador said, 'I'm a bit skeptical of all people. In twenty-six years I've handled the cases of about 50,000 men and women. But once in a while something so outstanding comes along, a feeling so deep and sincere, that skepticism has to take a back seat.

"'This, I think, is one of the cases. Mickey Cohen is becoming a very worthwhile individual.'"

On July 24, 1956, KFI Radio announced Mickey's death:

> Notorious Hollywood Mob Boss Mickey Cohen Has Been Murdered in
> a Remote Section of Griffith Park!

Eight minutes later the station issued a retraction.

In perfect health, Cohen filed lawsuits against KFI, its owner, three executives, and former mayor Fletcher Bowron. He charged that the announcement had caused LaVonne severe physical and mental shock and that he had suffered shame, humiliation, mortification, and invasion of privacy, and that his name had been used without his permission.

The frivolous suit was dismissed.

The LAPD hassled Mickey whenever they could. Leaving the Pantages Theater after viewing a closed circuit fight, he joined a crowd of hundreds across Hollywood Boulevard. Only Mickey Cohen was ticketed for jaywalking. Next, he was cited for jumping a red light. Even his traffic citations made news.

He was pulled over in the eastern suburb of Highland Park, an area with a largely Asian population, on July 30. Ben Tue Wong, alias Ben K. Wong, an ex-convict who served time at McNeil Island, was in his car. A chef at a restaurant frequented by the reformed mobster, Wong was well known in the narcotics trade.

Cohen's close associates Joe and Fred Sica were arrested in early August and charged with conspiracy to commit burglary and assault after allegedly threatening and savagely beating DaLonne Cooper, twenty-nine, and her

A girl on the Sunset scene, statu-esque movie extra Dee David, a.k.a. DaLonne Cooper, had quite an extensive history with Mickey and his men, and for a time a prominent lawman for a husband. She shot and wounded mobster Joe Sica during a business dispute. 1956.

current boyfriend, a handsome twenty-two-year-old heir. DaLonne Cooper, formerly known as Dee David, was the young woman wounded in the 1949 assassination attempt on Cohen at Sherry's Restaurant. She later married Special Agent Harry Cooper, the controversially appointed state officer assigned to bodyguard Cohen, who was critically wounded in the same ambush. Rumored to have been one of Johnny Stompanto's party girls, she had been a close friend of Cohen's.

No longer with her lawman spouse, she and her boyfriend had become reluctant witnesses in the case against the Sicas. Twenty-four-hour guards were placed around the pair, dictated by the unsolved murder of prosecution witness Abraham Davidian in the derailed 1949 narcotics case involving the Sica brothers.

On August 16, federal authorities claimed to have in their possession pornographic materials linked to Johnny Stompanato, Mickey Cohen, and a prominent, socially connected Chicago attorney. A nude girl, identified as a friend of Stompanato, was clearly photographed in sexually comprising positions with a man. The photographs were thought to have been part of a plot to blackmail an heir to the Woolworth fortune in Britain. When the victim refused to file a complaint, the investigation was suspended.

Mickey's probation ended that month. He quickly began to reinstate himself in the rackets. Some of his old illegal activities remained intact, but the pickings were not so rich and easy the second time around. He scammed, hustled, cajoled, and threatened. Nothing seemed too small or low for him; he actually pinched a penny or two. The chatter was that he had hidden a million dollars or more. If so, the problem was how to spend it. He had never repaid the original tax debt, and as a result the IRS remained very interested in every dollar he expended.

His old mainstay, the loans hustle, was back. Easy marks were shaken for dining-out money, and illicit cash was laundered through nonexistent loans. Long before the tax conviction, he never bought anything for himself; all major purchases were made for him. Although he had sold the exclusive rights to his story in 1951, Mickey now solicited loans for a forthcoming book and movie based on his life.

His old fight managers, Eddie Borden and Harry Rudolph, alias Babe McCoy, the three hundred pounder in charge of the Olympic Auditorium, were linked with him in a statewide boxing probe. The Chicago and Oregon connections continued. A chain letter, alleged to be associated with legitimate charities, boasted his name. There were plans for a business in Chinatown and talk of a restaurant in Beverly Hills, or perhaps the Miracle Mile. Companies eager to have a well-known name representing muscle put him on payroll. According to journalist Ed Reid, "Mickey . . . made rough pitches to café operators in an effort to induce them to obtain their linen services through Model [Linen Service]."

The coffers at Cohen's plant business grew quickly. Expenditures increased even more rapidly.

A free man for nearly a year and living singly, in September 1956, Mickey moved to a fashionable address, 10599 Wilshire Boulevard in Westwood. His new home was the Del Capri, a small residential hotel that serviced a mid-level movie crowd.

Observed leaving Billy Gray's Band Box on October 4, Mickey was in the company of two Italian underworld figures and George Miller, a gambler who owned the tout sheet *Post and Paddock*. Miller, who had a history of loaning him hefty sums, was brutally beaten in the parking lot.

A few days later, Cohen told columnist Joe Hyams that going straight was costing him financially, but there were no regrets. The journalist announced that Mickey was writing an autobiography with the aid of his religious connections: *The Poison Has Left Me.*

For the past year he had been driving a modest used car lent to him by Reverend Vaus. A new Cadillac, a flashy El Dorado, was purchased on October 12. Registered to family members, the car was actually owned by a finance company.

To complete his new life, he acquired a bulldog, Mickey Jr., and a new look: jodhpurs, riding boots, tailor-made zip jackets emblazoned MC, and driving caps that resembled large inverted mushrooms. For court appearances, clubbing, and more formal occasions, he now appeared in fashionably conservative, custom-tailored single-breasted suits made of a wrinkle-proof wool blend.

Cruising the Sunset Strip — in style — it seemed like old times.

19

SACRIFICIAL LAMB

*"I'm sincerely interested in anything
that's the correct thing in life."*
MICKEY COHEN

While hula-hooped hips gyrated in perpetual motion, L.A. continued
to morph. The Sunset Strip was tarnished; in the beatnik era, the
Crescendo and Mocambo showcased watered-down bebop and folk singers,
while legendary Ciro's had become a tourist trap. Shakedowns and smut
were mainstream: *Confidential* and *Playboy* magazines appeared on news-
stands everywhere. Marilyn Monroe and her platinum clones proved that
sex still sold. And the success of wide-screen Technicolor epics *The Robe*
and *The Ten Commandments* proved that religion, properly hyped, could
engage huge audiences.

The real-life soap opera of Mickey Cohen continued to play out publicly.
In January 1957, LaVonne filed for divorce, again. Asking for four hundred
dollars per month in alimony, his wife of sixteen years claimed he was
hiding assets.

The Sica brothers' assault trial began the same month. Featuring a
colorful cast of Hollywood's greatest offenders, the court case was major
news and put Mickey Cohen back on page one. The state's case was based
on an incident where Joe and Fred Sica allegedly beat DaLonne Cooper
and her male companion over control of Activeaire, a company that dealt

Caught by a camera: the elusive Fred Sica. 1956.

in electric hand-drying equipment used in public facilities. The Sicas claimed Cooper, their former business partner, had maneuvered them out of the Activeaire company, in favor of her boyfriend.

In court, DaLonne Cooper admitted that Fred Sica had acquired the franchise and advanced her money to get the business started. She also testified that after the beating, Freddie Sica threatened her, "You get that business turned over to me, or I'll kill you."

The *Los Angeles Times* reported, "Shortly before noon, Mickey Cohen, ex-mobster under subpoena by the defense, upset Miss Cooper, who was under guard in an anteroom.

"Miss Cooper went into near hysterics after Cohen assertedly stood outside the door and yelled extremely uncomplimentary references to her background. Cohen subsided when a sheriff's deputy was placed on guard outside the door, and detectives stood nearby with pencils poised to write down any further comments by Cohen.

"'Wait'll I get on the stand,' Cohen said. 'Then they can't stop me.'"

Under oath, Mickey besmirched the reputation of DaLonne Cooper, informing the jury that since the late 1940s the statuesque bottle-blonde had been on close terms with him, the Sicas, and many other notorious ex-convicts and police figures and that her career choice was disreputable.

Joe Sica testified that *he* was the injured party, claiming Miss Cooper shot off a revolver, wounding him.

The jury chose to acquit the brothers. Control of Activeaire had already been returned to Fred Sica.

To the public, no one embodied the dark imagery of the underworld more completely than Mickey Cohen. Hoping to annex his marquee name, Mickey began receiving substantial "brotherly love gifts" from his former wiretapper, Reverend Vaus, and other old friends now involved in big-time religion.

On April 1, 1957, Mickey permanently closed his greenhouse and set off for New York. Evangelist W.C. Jones, who at the time sat on the board of directors of Billy Graham's ministry, paid his ticket and expenses. After checking into a lavish suite at the Waldorf-Astoria, he met with Reverend Graham. A press conference was called the next morning.

Attired in custom-tailored white pajamas monogrammed MICKEY, Hollywood's celebrity mobster smiled for photographers as he poured coffee from room service. He regaled reporters with the story of how he had flown to New York just to see Graham, now the country's most prominent religious figure, and that they had prayed and read the Bible together. Mickey informed them, "I am very high on the Christian way of life . . . I'm sincerely interested in anything that's the correct thing in life. Billy has guided me in many things. He's my friend . . . But it's hard for me to say if I'll be converted."

Reverend Vaus declared, "Michael is making a sincere investigation of the claims of Christ to play a bigger role in his life."

In a story entitled "Mickey Cohen Prays with Billy Graham," the *Cleveland Plain Dealer* observed, "He [Cohen] said he has known Graham since 1949 and plans to attend the evangelist's New York crusade in May.

"Cohen was raised in the Jewish faith, but he said he was 'never a very religious person.'" The *Plain Dealer* laid claim to the mobster at the end of the article: "He is a former Cleveland resident."

Before his appearance at Madison Square Garden, Mickey accepted an invitation to appear on the *Mike Wallace Interview* show. Shocking and provocative, the nationally televised program dealt in controversy and sensationalism. Wallace asked the tough questions; his interviews made both his guests and audiences squirm. The loquacious, star-crossed mobster was perfectly cast for the show.

ABC brought Mickey, accompanied by Fred Sica, back to New York. Putting him up at the luxurious Hampshire House on Central Park South, the prized guest was provided with first-class treatment. He was given a limo, four-star dining, and a blowout party in his suite. A red leather box with an engraved silver plaque was presented to him in commemoration of his appearance.

The show was broadcast live from New York on May 19, 1957. Photographed in tight close-up, Mickey evoked a film noir villain, his flat broad face dramatically filling the screen. At forty-three, dapper but again paunchy, he began by telling Wallace that he had had a "bellyful of the rackets." And the old bromides, intended to give a veneer of respectability, were replayed. "I've never mixed with prostitution. And I've never mixed with narcotics."

When asked about syndicate leader Frank Costello, who had survived a recent assassination attempt, Cohen responded in his pleasant but gravelly baritone that the underworld chief was "a fine, wonderful man."

When Wallace brought up the subject of Billy Graham and talk of Mickey's conversion to Christianity, Mickey said he had no intention of becoming a convert. "I don't find everything or anything in Christ."

Wallace probed further: "You've killed at least one man; how many more?"

Eyes piercing and steady, Mickey calmly responded, "I don't know if you'd call these . . . uhm . . . them killings . . . It was either my life or their life . . . I never killed a guy who in my way of life didn't deserve it."

Wallace broached another topic that had been discussed during the show's pre-interview. Coaxed along by the host, Mickey began slowly, "I have a police chief in Los Angeles, California . . ."

With those words, he began a diatribe, foul and vitriolic, that blasted LAPD Chief William Parker: "A sadistic degenerate . . . known alcoholic . . . known degenerate . . . a sadistic degenerate of the worst type."

He disparaged Parker in the "roughest rawest language ever broadcast publicly." Captain James Hamilton, former mayor Bowron, and ex–LAPD chief Horrall were also part of Mickey's tirade. The explosive performance was the type of fiery spectacle Wallace's show embodied.

Minutes after the show ended police appeared at the ABC stage. A female viewer called in, stating she believed to have seen the outline of a gun in Cohen's jacket. They patted him down and searched his dressing room. They found nothing. In a patented move, Mickey insisted that he needed police aid. He reported a contract and telegram missing from his dressing room.

Immediately after the program, Wallace wired Chief Parker: "Tonight on my program . . . Mickey Cohen made certain remarks to which you may take exception. In the interest of fair reporting, I would like to invite you to be my guest on next Sunday's program to rebut what was said and otherwise set the record straight."

Reacting quickly from L.A., the outraged city officials demanded that New York DA Frank Hogan take action against Mickey for slander. The FCC began a study of the controversial broadcast.

Television sensation Jack Webb was one of Chief William Parker's staunchest supporters. Webb and Captain Hamilton, who worked as his consultant on *Dragnet*, were visiting New York the night of the Wallace broadcast. The news services reported their reaction to the show: "Hamilton was mad but calm, the usually cool Webb was steaming: 'Parker has put in thirty years of service, and Jim has a fine record and reputation.'"

For the mobster, it was just one more controversy. Two nights after his implosion on the Wallace program, Mickey Cohen attended Billy Graham's revival at Madison Square Garden. The farm boy from North Carolina had packed the house: an audience of 17,500 New Yorkers showed up to hear the famous evangelist. They were soon worked into a pitched frenzy, responding to a sermon that placed special emphasis on killing and adultery. Graham preached, "Hate is as bad as murder and that means all of us here tonight are murderers."

"Saving" Mickey Cohen did not happen. If there was a pact for the Hollywood mobster to accept Christ that night, Mickey welshed, remaining a wayward but committed Jew; he merely stepped onstage and waved to the audience.

Graham responded to the slight: "I have for a long time hoped and prayed Mickey Cohen would give his life to Christ and use his influence to turn the tide of crime and juvenile delinquency in this country. I have not given up hope."

When Mickey later spoke about the Graham connection, his response

Mickey Cohen and Billy Graham Pray and Read Bible Together

By David Lyle

Mickey Cohen, the celebrated former West Coast gambler, read the Bible and prayed with Billy Graham, the evangelist, at lunch yesterday.

"I'm sincerely interested in anything that's the correct thing in life," Mr. Cohen said later in his suite in the Waldorf-Astoria.

"And I believe he is sincerely interested in spiritual things and leading a new life," said Mr. Graham, who was reached by telephone in his suite in the Hotel Statler in Buffalo, where he had flown after the luncheon to attend a meeting of the National Association of Evangelicals.

Served Prison Term

Cohen, the dapper little man who was once known as the czar of Los Angeles gambling, was released from prison in 1955 after serving nearly four years for evading $150,000 in Federal income taxes. He has been investigated by a half-dozen government committees, shot at ten times and bombed once. "He certainly needs the prayers of Christian people everywhere," remarked Mr. Graham.

The ex-gambler, who checked in at the hotel under his little-used real name of Michael Cohen, now operates a nursery—"Michael's Greenhouses, Inc., It's the biggest on the coast." He said he flew here yesterday especially to see Mr. Graham, whom he has known since 1949. "I've talked to Mr. Cohen on a number of occasions," Mr. Graham explained. "My first contact with him was in 1949,

and on every occasion we talked about spiritual matters and about the possibility of receiving Christ as his Saviour. Today we had Bible reading and prayer together." The meeting took place in Mr. Cohen's suite at the hotel, with an assistant to Mr. Graham also in attendance.

"Billy has guided me in many things," Mr. Cohen explained. "He's my friend. I expect to be here for Billy's rally in May (in Madison Square Garden). He's invited me for it and I think I will be here for it."

Mr. Graham confirmed the invitation. "I've invited him, as I've invited everybody else."

Mr. Cohen, who expects to see Mr. Graham again today in Buffalo, said he doesn't belong to any church at the moment. "I was raised in the Jewish religion," he said. "But I was never a very religious person."

He met Mr. Graham through Jim Vaus, a man who worked for the ex-gambler in Los Angeles for years, then turned to religion and became an evangelist.

Mr. Vaus, his former boss explained, "had to do with telephones and recording." Mr. Vaus "watched out that I didn't have any bugs (tapped wires) in my place," said Mr. Cohen.

Mickey Cohen

Billy Graham

Mickey Cohen and world-famous evangelist Reverend Billy Graham make news together. April 1957.

was diplomatic but firm. "I've known Billy a long time. Our agreement from the beginning was that he wouldn't try to convert me. But he certainly has helped me to see the sense of living a right life.

"I was born a Jew and raised a Jew . . . I have no intention of changing my religion."

It was later reported that the evangelist's publicist had paid Mickey $10,000 (approximately $80,000 today) for his appearance at the Garden. More rumors abounded of a $50,000 ($400,000 today) offer made by Graham's organization to engage Cohen for a speaking tour on the religious circuit.

"The evangelist denied the story indignantly," wrote journalist Ed Reid. "He said he never paid anyone to attend a meeting or to admit to conversion, and that he felt this would be blasphemous."

The religious folk had learned the hard way that getting close to Mickey Cohen was as safe as touching uranium. But the convicted felon got what he wanted: money, ink, and a luxurious paid vacation that provided cover to meet with eastern associates.

★ ★ ★

When his return flight to Los Angeles stopped in Chicago, Mickey was asked to deplane. He was brought before a federal grand jury investigating the activities of Chicago boss Paul "The Waiter" Ricco. Attorney George Bieber was photographed huddling with a tense-looking Cohen before the Angeleno testified about Ricco, who was having tax and immigration problems.

Before flying out of Chicago, Mickey sent a telegram to Chief Parker:

> Sorry to have to announce that the telegram you requested on arrival of Mickey Cohen from Chicago Police Department . . . be disregarded, as plane Cohen was on had to turn back on account of motor trouble . . . I advise you to further check on Cohen's arrival as I most certainly would not want such as honorable and highly regarded a police chief to be disappointed.
>
> Please advise your great admirer and adviser, Mr. Jack Webb of this development, and discuss with him what your next move should be.

Back in L.A., Mickey was arrested for another traffic violation. He growled, "I didn't hold up no traffic. They're rousting me. Those cops followed me for a mile-and-a-half, waiting to get me." Attired in riding clothes, Mickey posed sullenly after posting fifty dollars bail. He shouted to reporters, who were tracking every salvo in his war of words, "I'm going to fight this! They can't get away with stuff like this!"

Mickey next announced that he planned to sue Chief Parker. A lawyer representing him issued a facetious statement that joked, "Mickey was considering a suit charging alienation of affections against some members of the police department, allegedly because some officers once had 'looked upon Cohen with love and affection.'"

Cohen contended the LAPD chief had damaged his business: "Parker sent cops to numerous of my clients to try to get them to stop doing business with me. He asked clients to say I had scammed and muscled them into taking my plants."

Coached by his coterie of eminent attorneys, the semi-literate mobster then delivered a startling dissertation on civil rights and free speech: "Parker in my opinion shares the purview of Alexander Hamilton: 'the people are the great beast.' . . . Obviously Parker has a hatred of constitutional guarantees."

Claiming Parker was "a totalitarian-minded man . . . who was 100% for bugging your bedroom," Mickey challenged the chief to sue him.

Parker told the United Press that he was reluctant to get into a public argument. "I have received the Purple Heart and I have been decorated by three governments," he said. "I do not feel I must defend myself against a man of the character of Cohen."

A week after Cohen's appearance on the Wallace show, there was an unprecedented televised retraction by the network. ABC vice president Oliver Treyz stated that remarks made by Cohen on the program "in no way represented the network's attitudes or beliefs." He said that ABC "deeply regrets the wholly unjustified statements," noting that Philip Morris cigarettes, the program's sponsor, joined the network in the retraction.

Mickey's response was quick. "Any retractions by those spineless persons in regard to the television show I appeared on with Mike Wallace on the ABC network does not go for me!"

Although New York DA Hogan said no criminal action could be taken against Mickey, Parker and Hamilton sued the network and its sponsors, but not Mickey Cohen, in Los Angeles civil court. Charging that the mobster's remarks had impugned their "honesty, integrity, citizenship, morality, character, and decency," the police officers sued for a total of $3.2 million in damages.

Working with the team of ABC lawyers, Cohen set forth a strategy for the defense. Years later he said, "The only defense against libel is the truth, and believe me, I had Parker right by the fucking nuts."

William Henry Parker was born in 1903. A native of Lead, Montana, he was seeped in the frontier traditions of good men, outlaws, and Indians. His grandfather, and namesake, had been a legendary peace officer of the Old West and late in life went to Washington, as a member of Congress. Young Bill had been an altar boy at St. Ambrose Roman Catholic Church in Deadwood before migrating to Los Angeles as a young man. After spending his early days in the city driving a downtown cab, he became a member of the LAPD in 1927. Unusually ambitious, he studied law at night and married a policewoman, Helen Schultz. After getting his law degree he remained with the LAPD, due to the lack of opportunity during the Great Depression.

A product of the corrupt years of the LAPD during the administration of Mayor Frank Shaw, he served as a top aide to shady Chief James E. Davis. Parker certainly witnessed, at close range, the dirty dealings that made the force one of the most lawless in the country. Mickey Cohen claimed he had done more than just watch.

After the political scandal and "the purge" of the LAPD in 1938, Parker appeared to be an outsider within the ranks. His calculating personality and personal ambition did not ingratiate him with fellow officers. Although he consistently received top exam scores, promotions passed him by. He found it difficult to rise as high and quickly as he desired. After serving in the Army during World War II, he organized the police systems in post-war Germany, Normandy, and Sardinia. In the late 1940s, Parker returned to the LAPD: the force was again in shambles, now disgraced by Mickey Cohen.

In the summer of 1950, underdog Parker beat out the presumed winner for LAPD chief, popular Deputy Chief Thad Brown. Immediately after becoming chief, assassination plots against Parker were foiled. He then withstood enormous flak surrounding an incident where an officer shot and killed an unarmed college honor student during a routine traffic stop. The new chief was even left unscathed following the momentous "Bloody Christmas" scandal of 1951, where a group of drunken cops brutally beat seven young, mainly Latino, men until their holding cell ran red with blood.

In the intervening years, Chief Parker assiduously cleaned house, turning the LAPD into the "Blue Religion" — a tight unit run with military precision that was considered the toughest force in the country. From top mob figures down to street-corner bookies, Parker's mantra was an all-out war on the underworld. "But for all of our hoodlum-obsessed activities, Parker was most fearful that they would somehow infiltrate the LAPD," noted his protégé, Daryl F. Gates.

Chief Parker's techniques were hardly clean. He used paid informants and sanctioned entrapment. Vince Kelly, a wiretapper who moonlighted for Howard Hughes, planted illegal bugs, while Officer Roger Otis, a big bare-knuckled intimidator, planted the fear of the LAPD. It has never been

Smug LAPD Chief William Parker (front) and jubilant Captain James Hamilton (back right) display their juicy settlement checks from ABC after Mickey Cohen badmouthed them on national television. 1957.

proven if Parker had been a bagman for disgraced Mayor Shaw — as Mickey Cohen alleged — but other unseemly behavior couldn't be completely hidden.

Daryl Gates, who would himself head the force beginning in 1979, was a rookie when he became Parker's driver in 1950. Gates later remembered those years in his autobiography, *Chief*:

> After trying to absorb Parker's brilliance by day, I would, too often by night, drive him home drunk.
>
> And I mean loaded. He drank until his words slurred and stairs became a hazard. He would repeat the same thought over and over and over until he became a terrible bore . . . Those who knew of his weakness

for bourbon deluxe call him Whiskey Bill. And most of the department knew. So did the press . . . Luckily, in those days personal peccadilloes weren't written about.

As to the degenerate claim, teetotaler Cohen found a woman in Miami willing to testify that a drunken Parker, while at a convention, had pinched her buttocks so violently that she needed medical attention.

The *Los Angeles Times* revealed that constitutional rights would be the core defense position in the Parker-Hamilton lawsuit. On September 10, 1957, the paper noted, "The defense of ABC, Paramount Theaters, Inc., Philip Morris cigarettes and N.W. Ayer & Son is based on fair comment and criticism of a public official."

But this time Mickey would get his comeuppance.

Parker and Hamilton were officers of the law. They had clout and prestige. The network powers were not about to have the mercurial Hollywood gang boss drag them into a nasty, and heavily publicized, trial.

The suits were quietly settled out of court. Chief Parker was awarded $45,975.09 ($370,000 today). Captain Hamilton received $22,987.55 ($180,000 today). Former mayor Bowron also sued and made a settlement. When the suits didn't go before a jury, Mickey felt betrayed. He had finally been shown that you couldn't fight city hall — at least not all the time.

The ugly public battle he picked with the chief intensified his post-prison difficulties. William H. Parker was now his most tenacious foe.

20

INK JUNKY

*"I could feel the subtle way
in which he manipulated me."*
JOURNALIST AL ARONOWITZ

In less than a decade, he seemed to have boxed himself into a corner. Mickey Cohen, former underworld kingpin, was now blatantly selling a straight-life charade, offering something for everyone — his rehabilitation, his life story, and the concept of his religious conversion. But law enforcement agencies noted that, miraculously, he had staged a comeback: back in big-time gambling, he was doing very well. Cohen traveled often around the country; many old connections remained viable and new alliances were forged. As before, he was involved in a full line of criminal activities. The dirty secrets he collected? They guaranteed loans and kept people compliant.

"Mickey had the inside dope on everybody in Hollywood simply because one of Mickey's sidelines was blackmail . . . he was one of my best 'sources,'" observed former *New York Post* reporter Al Aronowitz. "The whole time I knew Mickey, I could feel the subtle way in which he manipulated me. It was as if I could feel his hands on my shoulders, gently but firmly steering me exactly where he wanted me to go."

The media carefully referred to him now as ex-mobster or reformed criminal boss — but they didn't stop writing about him. His every move remained news as his addiction to the coverage grew. Bad or worse, the content no longer seemed to matter. When it came to money and ink, Mickey Cohen was insatiable.

He had become living theater: an ominous mix of comic opera and Grand Guignol. The charismatic, sought-after "gambling czar" of the prior decade was now unusually cast as a treacherous buffoon. The label was his own making: brazen publicity stunts and outrageous antics had made him laughable. One TV newsman labeled him "a horsefly on the rump of community decency."

But he still had plenty of defenders. "It was easy for Mickey to seduce me. The truth is I fell for him hard," Al Aronowitz admitted. "He was a showman. Oh, I know he killed people and he was a Yiddish *momser* and he was just plain no good . . . But mostly I liked Mickey because he was fun."

After the recent debacle in New York, his forthcoming book was out of the hands of the evangelists. The project was passed on to his old acquaintance Ben Hecht. Starting the endeavor from scratch, the mobster continued promoting the book angle to anyone who would nibble.

Syndicated columnist Walter Winchell: "Mickey Cohen's bizarre quest for publicity (which has amazed even the underworld) is easily understood when you hear Ben Hecht is writing his biography with a view toward the big movie money."

But the likelihood of a rich Hollywood sale was not guaranteed. While the public was still fascinated by him, both he and Hecht were pariahs at the studios. Because of his ties to the Irgun, the once-heralded screenwriter had been blackballed in the film business and his books banned in England. The garrulous ex-con, never a true showbiz insider like Bugsy Siegel, was shunned for his erratic behavior, predilection for blackmail, and the undisputable fact that anyone getting close to him might end up dead. Producer Nick Nayfack, nephew of brothers Nick and Joe Schenck, Hollywood's most prominent moguls (respectively, heads of MGM and 20th Century Fox) took a serious interest in the project.

Many of Cohen's former rivals were gone, but there was still much competition in his usual trade. His archenemy, "Happy" Harold Meltzer, was out of prison and working with the Dragna family. Freelancer Jack "The Enforcer" Whalen was a rising power on the scene. Surrounding himself with a loyal and faithful crew, Mickey's aides and associates catered to his every whim as he worked with Hecht on the book project and continued his grab at underworld dominance.

Fred Sica donned an apron while cooking for Cohen's dinner parties and obligingly walked Mickey Jr., remaining in the boss's good graces. Cohen would reward Sica on his birthday with a gold Lucien Piccard watch inscribed: *To Fred from Mickey — I Luve's Yuh.* Phil Packard, aka Philip H. Packer, an ex-con well into his fifties, was another constant companion. Packard, from Chicago, seemed to have taken the senior advisory role once held by Mike Howard, the victim of an untimely passing — said to be a suicide. Wholesale appliance dealer George Seymour Pellar; Roger K. Leonard, present since the late 1940s gang war; Ellis "Itchy" Mandel, a Chicagoan involved with the Stagehand's Union; Max Tannenbaum of New York; William K. Howard, a pal from McNeil Island; and longtime associate Johnny Stompanato were all in loyal attendance. Bail bondsman Abe Phillips was a constant and devoted presence.

Mickey moved back to affluent Brentwood. Under the name "Mr. Jones," he now lived in a small, newly erected garden court apartment building that was advertised as "ultra-luxury." Located at 705 South Barrington Avenue, he inhabited Apartment C. A 500-gallon hot water heater and giant air conditioning unit were added to the building, expressly to meet the needs of the high-maintenance tenant.

While his one-bedroom, two-bath apartment was not large, consisting of approximately 850 square feet, it featured all sorts of material luxuries. It was soundproofed and an "ultra-thick" carpeting of the highest quality wool covered the floors. Cohen could find comfort in a "king-size king bed," do business on six phones, select channels on three televisions (one of which was the latest technology, a color set), and listen to records like "Mack the Knife" by Bobby Darin, his new friend, on custom stereo equipment. He could recline on one of his two white leather specially designed semi-circular sofas and offer guests a drink from a well-stocked wet bar illuminated by a glowing blue light. The gleaming black-and-white kitchen featured stainless-steel cabinets and every convenience a professional chef could desire.

Like at the Brentwood house, there was a built-in soda fountain that dispensed soft drinks and ice and a special freezer for ice cream.

Floor-to-ceiling draperies opened and closed by remote control. The marble fireplace had a hearth designed as seating and inlaid with a mosaic MC. Two oil paintings of his dog graced the walls. The well-groomed bulldog had a specially designed sleeping nook, his own set of dishes, an assortment of red leather collars and leashes that were the most expensive available, and a pink plush rabbit.

Of course, the pièce de résistance was Cohen's carefully designed closet. Dean Tavoularis, future Oscar-winning production designer of *The Godfather* and *Apocalypse Now*, attended gatherings at the Brentwood apartment in the company of a Cohen lawyer. "It was extraordinary. I had never seen anything like it," Tavoularis said, recalling the layout. "Everything was perfectly arranged, in boxes and built-in drawers, and each suit was partitioned off, behind glass panels."

Tavoularis found his host cordial and intriguing. "He kept his cash tightly wound — like a roll of film. Before a large party for his mother at the Ambassador Hotel, he went around handing out twenties to the waiters. When he'd bring a group back to the apartment, the first thing he did was pick up the phone and say, 'Parker, I'm home!'"

Long-suffering LaVonne, whose color photo was prominently placed in the new apartment, voiced complaints: "After eighteen years with him, I don't have anything . . . I see him wearing little pieces of jewelry now and then that I've seen before. He carries a big roll, but I have to beg him for money to live on. I'm still trying to figure out what makes this man so different or interesting."

His new front, an ice cream shop, was located near his apartment. After a thorough renovation, the Carousal Ice Cream Parlor, at 11719 San Vicente Boulevard, was stocked with Mickey's favorite ice creams and Toblerone Swiss chocolate. The Carousal opened like a Hollywood premiere, with members of the press in attendance. Broadway columnist Walter Winchell, in Hollywood doing the narrative on *The Untouchables*, the hugely popular new series set in the underworld, officiated at the opening. Although some appreciated the quality ice cream, the majority of Brentwood's residents were appalled to see that Mickey Cohen was not just residing in the community again, he was now openly doing business there. It was common to see his confederates gathered in the tiny store at three in the morning.

"I was living in Malibu," actress Barbara Bain, future star of the iconic *Mission Impossible* television series, recalled. "On my way into town, I noticed a new ice cream shop on San Vincente. I went in, my baby daughter in my arms, and saw Mickey Cohen sitting there . . . slumped back from the edge of the chair, like a boxer in his corner, legs splayed out. He was wearing a bright rust sports jacket with loud white topstitching all over it. As we approached, he shouted [to the counterman], 'Rum raisin.' Immediately having second thoughts, I rushed out and never stopped there again."

But everything wasn't just Hollywood dreams, pampered pets, and expensive ice cream. Mickey Cohen's true nature was becoming increasingly apparent.

In the eyes of attorney Paul Caruso, who handled Cohen's legal matters upon his prison release, "Mickey was always a perfect gentleman when he came to my home. He doesn't drink or smoke, of course, and he didn't swear once. In time Mickey and I had a gradual cooling off, and I began to see that he was not really soft-spoken at all.

"He is dangerous and the fact that I was his attorney was damaging me with other clients. By the time we parted company he owed me $7,900 [$64,000 today] and he refused to pay."

The young lawyer had guts. He dunned the gangster. Mickey challenged the attorney to come over and collect the money. When he did, Caruso claimed Mickey pulled a .38 on him. In a quick move, he grabbed Mickey's sister, who was standing in a small office with them. Using her as a human shield, Caruso backed out to his car with the armed mobster in pursuit. After the harrowing escape, he reported the episode to the LAPD. The police came, but Mickey was gone — and nothing happened.

At two in the morning the attorney received a call. He recognized the voice of a Cohen hoodlum: "Listen, Caruso. You got the little guy mad at you. He don't like you and it's gonna cost you a grand to square the beef."

Caruso refused to be extorted: "Mickey lives on the theory that people are afraid to talk. I'm sure he thought I'd never say a word to anybody."

Mickey was involved in another skirmish at a favorite Hollywood restaurant, Villa Capri, 6735 Yucca Street. Attending an after-party for Sammy Davis Jr., with Sinatra, Shirley MacLaine, and comic-innovator Ernie Kovacs, a waiter accidentally spilled coffee on Cohen. According to the server, he apologized, but "the little guy, I didn't know it was Cohen then, snarled, 'That's no excuse.'" Then the phobic gang boss punched him.

The waiter hit back, bloodying Mickey's nose before "two big lugs" threw him down and sat on him. Shortly after the brawl, a criminal complaint was filed. Mickey was charged with disturbing the peace and battery. Thoroughly schooled in his constitutional rights, Cohen claimed police harassment. The waiter then filed a civil action for $50,000 (more than $320,000 today).

The case went to trial a few months later. Despite character witnesses like Robert Mitchum and Sammy Davis Jr. supporting Mickey, the jury found Cohen guilty of assault. Municipal judge Gerald C. Kepple imposed a $500 fine, a ninety-day suspended sentence, and placed him on two-years' probation. He also lost the civil case.

But the waiter proved no winner. A short time later, he was arrested, allegedly holding wholesale amounts of marijuana and pills.

Next on the agenda was a trip to La Paz, Mexico. Mickey traveled with Ben Hecht; Chicago attorney George Bieber, who according to Hecht was Mickey's "head man in his battery of barristers"; producer Nick Nayfack; comic Billy Gray; and his bodyguards. The FBI followed Cohen there, noting that he was "investigating the possibility of investing in a hotel with gambling provisions, as well as to work with Ben Hecht."

Cohen told Hecht his stories while the group was deep-sea fishing. Hecht observed the mobster on the fishing boat: "Mickey, in his white flannels, rope-soled shoes and three layers of stylish sweaters, reminds me . . . of an orphan on an outing. He sits gingerly in a cockpit chair and regards the rushing water . . . Mickey has reeled off the details [of his life], as if he were reciting a tale that belonged to someone else. He speaks of his crime and cruelties without any atonement."

Finally Mickey told Hecht, "I'm amazed over what I've been tellin' you . . . I got ashamed a number of times over what I was sayin'. I kept wantin' to tell you lies, but I didn't. I kept saying to myself that was me and that's

Federal drug agent Chappell won his bout with the former professional boxer, but after two trials, Mickey Cohen was not convicted of assaulting the federal officer. 1958.

what I did."

Cohen added, "Of course, I'm older and I couldn't do half the things I did — for no other reason. But aside from that, it ain't in my heart anymore . . . I'm a different man than the wild hot Jew kid who started stickin' up joints in Cleveland, who lived from heist to heist in Chicago and Los Angeles. Why, there was nothin' he wouldn't do if there was money in it. Or if the right people asked him to do it."

Upon his return from Mexico, Mickey was warned: informants had made allegations to authorities of his involvement in drug trafficking. On March 26, 1958, he drove downtown to the federal building and, unannounced, marched into the office of Howard W. Chappell, the regional head of the Federal Narcotics Bureau. Without provocation, the ex-boxer, five-three in his stocking feet and nearly forty-five years old, shot a left to Chappell's mouth. Tall and nearly two hundred pounds, the drug agent rose from behind his desk and gave the mobster a devastating working over.

Mickey later claimed the drug agent gave him the worst beating he'd ever taken. At his arraignment a few days later, his face was still bruised and swollen, and he sported a prominent black eye.

Indicted for assaulting a federal officer, the case was brought to trial twice. In closing arguments at the second trial, the prosecution contended Cohen had been a professional boxer and knew how to use his fists. Rising legal star Melvin Belli represented the mobster. He countered, "Is this not the man known as 'Black Canvas Cohen' because he lost so many fights?"

The jury deadlocked again. Cohen was not retried on the charges.

21

THE OSCAR

*"It's the first time in my life I've ever seen
a dead man convicted of his own murder."*
MICKEY COHEN

A product of the American heartland, John R. Stompanato, Jr., was born on October 9, 1925, and grew up in a two-story clapboard house in Woodstock, Illinois. His father made a comfortable living as the town barber and dabbled in real estate. His mother died during his delivery, but he developed a close bond with the stepmother who raised him. After his freshman year at the local high school, he was sent to board at Kemper Military School in Missouri. At the strict all-male school, he had disciplinary problems but graduated at seventeen. Joining the marines in 1943, he saw enemy fire in the Peleliu and Okinawa campaigns. Mustered out in 1946, Johnny claimed to have run nightclubs in Tientsin, China, but in actuality, he may have worked there as a minor bureaucrat employed by the U.S. government.

Married three times, his first wife was Sarah Utich, an older Turkish woman. Returning to Woodstock after the war, he briefly took a job as a bread salesman. His wife bore him a son, John Stompanato III, but the marriage didn't last. By 1948, at age twenty-two, he was in the film capital.

Once in Hollywood, the dark wavy-haired veteran, tall and classically handsome, quickly connected with Mickey Cohen. How the association began is unknown. Stompanato once claimed to have met him while shopping at Cohen's Sunset Strip men's shop. Others said he came to the mobster's attention while working in a Cohen-controlled nightclub. An out-of-state connection, perhaps from Chicago, is another possibility.

What is certain: Johnny Stompanato first appeared in the mobster's world during the gang war for control of Los Angeles. Mickey's boys were "panicked and skeptical" about someone not "tried and tested." But the boss liked him — and reassured them. Stompanato ran Mickey's Continental Café, held a piece of Cohen's Courtley's jewelry shop partnership, and quickly became a fixture in the midnight world of the Sunset Strip. Although often incorrectly described as Cohen's bodyguard, Stompanato avoided violent encounters and, in Mickey's view, lacked a "vicious nature." A lover, not a fighter, he adopted seductive aliases John Valentine, John Steele, and John Holliday. His bedroom prowess quickly became legendary, and Oscar, his nickname, referred to the Academy Award–winning size of his phallus. Involved with legions of lonely widows, beautiful showgirls, and hungry bit-players, there were whispers he also romanced top stars, like Ava Gardner and Janet Leigh.

Early on Stompanato was featured in some prominent newspaper stories. At the scene of the Sherry's shooting, in July 1949, he identified himself to reporters as Johnny Valentine, jeweler. He received more publicity that night when he appeared in a photo supporting distraught LaVonne Cohen, en route to see her wounded husband. Johnny made the papers again when he accompanied Mickey on the summer road trip of 1950 and during the Kefauver investigation that November. The next month, he was brought up in the nasty custody battle between aging movie star Franchot Tone and his former wife, Jean Wallace, a lovely actress.

The *Los Angeles Times* reported in the December 9, 1950, edition "[Regarding] 'partying' by Jean Wallace. The names Lawrence Tierney, much-arrested actor, and Johnny Stompanato, henchman of Mickey Cohen, were among several brought into the questioning concerning drinking parties. Miss Wallace said she once invited Johnny to stay for dinner when he called at her home, identifying himself as Johnny Valentine. 'He made me think he was one of Mr. Cohen's bookies,' she said. When asked if Johnny had found an apartment for her, she replied she had been looking

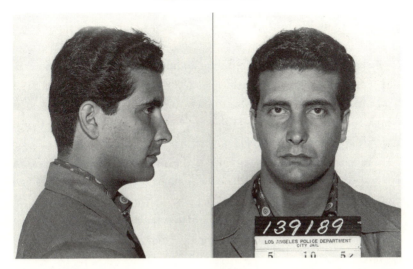

Johnny Stompanato's LAPD mugshot. Although he was a Cohen associate for a decade, he had a slim arrest record and no convictions. 1952.

for one and Johnny helped her."

By the time he was called as a prosecution witness at Mickey's 1951 tax trial, he turned camera-shy, covering his face with a handkerchief as he exited the courtroom.

His criminal record was slim. In 1949 he was rousted for being on the Sunset Strip after curfew. When arrested, he was holding a gun and $5,000 ($45,000 today) in cash. Prominent attorney and former judge Joseph Scott represented him in the case. Although convicted, he won his appeal, and the case was eventually dismissed. In 1952 he was rousted for suspicion of armed robbery. The DA was unable to make a case.

According to the John Stompanato FBI file, #257318A:

> The Los Angeles Police Department has characterized STOMPANATO a notorious pimp in the Los Angeles area. He was regarded by the police as the procurer of girls for Mickey Cohen's out-of-town contacts. STOMPANATO was the subject of a Bureau White Slave Traffic Act case in 1956. Information developed that STOMPANATO was sending girls from Los Angeles to Las Vegas, Nevada. Prosecution was declined by the United States Attorney.

Reportedly one of the boss's trusted "banks," he was reputed to be a key steerer to illegal abortion parlors alleged to be running under the aegis of Mickey Cohen. A United Press article alluded that blackmail and extortion was an important piece of business: "Stompanato had once borrowed $85,000 [more than $760,000 today] from Sir Charles A. Hubbard, a British millionaire who served three months in jail here [Hollywood] on a charge of possession of marijuana."

"Handsome Johnny was one of the most successful 'wolves' in Hollywood," noted Beverly Hills Police Chief Clifton Anderson. "We had considerable information on him. We knew he had obtained large sums of money from individuals who were afraid to complain to the police, and we were aware that he had accepted money from a number of his women friends."

In his syndicated "New York Confidential" column, Lee Mortimer wrote:

The Stompanato–Mickey Cohen blackmail angles (first revealed here) will explode into a new and bigger page one story involving dozens of Hollywood, Broadway, and political figures who have been paying off in fear for years. The ring is operated out of Chicago by the Fischetti-Capone mob and the glamour boy and gal affiliates employ gigolos of the Stompanato type, babes and homos, while sleazy, slimy little hoods such as Cohen are the front men who do the dirty.

Not long after his arrival in Hollywood, Stompanato took a second bride. He became the fourth of seven husbands of Helen Gilbert, a blonde working actress. The three-month-long marriage ended in 1949. In divorce court, Miss Gilbert declared, "Johnny had no means. I did what I could to support him."

After Mickey went to prison in 1951, Stompanato ran a pet shop, bred lovebirds in a home aviary, and sold used cars and furniture. He wed Helene Stanley, another beautiful B-movie veteran. The union lasted from 1953 to 1955. At divorce proceedings she charged, "He'd stay out all night two or three times a week, then he'd say, 'You ought to be happy that I came home at all. I don't take you anyplace because you bore me.'" The actress testified he tried to strangle her mother when she mislaid his handkerchiefs.

There was press speculation of a possible fourth marriage to a Mrs. Rosemary Trimble. The theory was based on slim evidence of a joint bank account and a ring inscribed, "From Here To Eternity — Rosemary and Johnny." Mrs. Trimble, the wife of a West Los Angeles physician, admitted knowing him during his marriage to Helene Stanley but denied anything more than a social connection.

Fleecing well-heeled women was Stompanato's specialty. But he was believed to dabble in bisexuality for financial gain. "Stompanato on occasion was in the company of wealthy homosexuals," an FBI memo noted. "One informant stated that he would 'go with either men or women for sexual purposes for a price.'"

By 1955, at age thirty, he was living at 11720 Bellagio Road. Despite the exclusive Bel-Air address, Johnny was not ensconced in a mansion. His domicile was a furnished one-bedroom apartment in a small two-story building built around a pool. There, Stompanato tried to fit in. But he immediately became the object of great curiosity as the building's resident "celebrity." Word spread: not only was the masculine, deep-voiced neighbor a Mickey Cohen associate, he was "the best fuck in Hollywood."

Among his neighbors was Rosaline George. "Despite his extreme good looks, I did not find him particularly attractive," she noted. "His manner could be crude and abrupt . . . He treated most women as objects . . . unless he was planning to seduce them.

"Nice and polite, if he wanted to impress you," she observed. "But for him it was a man's world."

Assortments of women were constantly in and out of Johnny's immaculate apartment. One frequent visitor was a slim, well-dressed woman in her forties. He would cruelly describe her as "The Dog." A dignified widow, Mrs. Doris Cornell, gave him $8,100 (approximately $65,000 today) for the formation of a new business, the Myrtlewood Gift Shop. The tiny store, near the UCLA campus on Glendon Avenue in Westwood Village, dealt exclusively in knickknacks made of myrtle wood — and whatever Mickey Cohen had to offer.

Several married tenants, and a pretty blonde co-worker of Rosaline George's, experienced his intimate company. There was even gossip that mother-and-daughter neighbors had both surrendered to Johnny's highly touted seduction.

"But one day all that stopped," remembered Rosaline George.

It seemed Stompanato began to concentrate on just one woman.

★ ★ ★

The sexual predator had set his sights on a female who had romantically devastated countless men. The dream girl of millions, Lana Turner was one of Hollywood's most glamorous and highly paid stars.

Born Julia Turner in Wallace, Idaho, on February 8, 1921, she was the daughter of an itinerant with a betting fever and a hairdresser. Her father deserted the family when she was very young, and her mother was often forced to place her only child in foster homes. When she was ten, her father was murdered in a gambling scrape. The girl's Depression-era childhood was filled with trauma, poverty, and disappointments.

Mildred Turner and her adolescent daughter made their way to Hollywood in 1935. Enrolled at Hollywood High for just two months, the beautiful fourteen-year-old was spotted by Billy Wilkerson, Bugsy Siegel's friend and the owner of the influential film trade paper the *Hollywood Reporter*. She was sipping a Coke at a soda shop across from the school when asked by the prominent Hollywood figure, "Would you like to be in movies?" The teenager responded, "I don't know. I'll have to ask my mother."

Six months after arriving in the film capital broke and without promise, a Hollywood dream came true. Turner immediately signed an exclusive contract with Mervyn LeRoy, an important producer and director. At sixteen, she created a sensation in LeRoy's *They Won't Forget*. She was now nationally celebrated as the "Sweater Girl," and her contract was sold to MGM, the most prominent studio in Hollywood. Renamed Lana Turner, she was never a struggling extra girl or forced to suffer the degradations of the casting couch, a common practice in the film industry. A platinum-blonde money-machine, the young star was coddled and protected from the press and scandal by the all-powerful studio.

Turner quickly became the quintessential spoiled movie star. A "wild nightclub queen," she had two husbands, an illegal abortion, a child, and dozens of celebrated paramours, among them Frank Sinatra, Howard Hughes, and movie star Tyrone Power, before she was twenty-five.

Her first husband was renowned clarinetist and bandleader Artie Shaw, whom she met on a Metro soundstage. On her nineteenth birthday,

Screen legend Lana Turner and her lover Johnny Stompanato arrive with unexpected (and unwanted by Lana) fanfare from a stormy vacation in Acapulco. Her daughter Cheryl Crane and the tipped-off press greet them. 1958.

in 1940, Turner became the third of Shaw's eight wives. The marriage lasted less than a year. Shaw claimed he wanted someone who could share his intellectual pursuits.

Her second husband was Stephen Crane III. They wed in 1942. A mysterious young man from small-town America, he made the Sunset Strip scene and ran high-stakes gin-rummy games out of his apartment. The couple frequently socialized with Bugsy Siegel's mistress Virginia Hill. By the time Crane met the luscious young star, Hill had already given him money to have plastic surgery done on his nose and chin to improve his appearance. Turner remembered Hill as a "fun gal." Mickey Cohen hosted a wedding breakfast for Turner and Crane at the Streets of Paris, a Hollywood Boulevard restaurant he held an interest in.

But Bugsy Siegel was decidedly the most intriguing figure in this social orbit. "A great dancer," Turner gushed about the glamorous mobster. Her flirtatious comment did not go unnoticed. When stories of a secret affair between Siegel and Turner surfaced, the studio became intolerant of their young diva's reckless behavior. MGM's Louis B. Mayer was furious when she refused to behave. But he had his own underworld associations and little control over self-indulgent Lana. Instead, he capitalized on the Siegel gossip, casting her in *Johnny Eager*. In the film she starred as a politician's daughter in love with a handsome underworld boss. Robert Taylor, her leading man, resembled Siegel.

In 1943 Lana and Steve Crane had a daughter, Cheryl. But the marriage ended the following year. Hollywood columnist Hedda Hopper took the star's side, calling Crane a "brash and tragic example of the sexy promoters Lana is so susceptible to."

Because of Cheryl, Steve Crane remained a constant presence in the Turner ménage — but he continued to run with the gangland crowd. In 1946, he was the greeter at Lucey's, Jimmy Utley's popular restaurant, where he witnessed Cohen savagely beat his adversary. By 1948, Crane was engaged to the ubiquitous Turner look-alike Lila Leeds. When the blonde starlet and Robert Mitchum were arrested for marijuana possession that year, Crane mysteriously left for Europe. He stayed away from Los Angeles for several years. Curiously, he returned only when Mickey Cohen was in prison.

While on the continent, he ingratiated himself with the hedonistic international set of wealthy playboys and pleasure-seeking heiresses by trading on his Lana Turner connection. Daughter Cheryl Crane noted in her book, *Detour*, "To help support himself and his love of baccarat and chemin de fer at the casino in Monte Carlo, Dad took up smuggling."

In 1946, Turner hit her stride, starring in *The Postman Always Rings Twice*. A noir tale of lust and murder, the picture made her more popular than ever. In her mid-twenties, Turner's career seemed invulnerable. She began refusing scripts, deciding to take a break after ten years of nonstop work. Two years later, socialite Bob Topping, an older, bloated heir with a weak chin, proposed by dropping a fifteen-carat diamond ring into her martini. Lana's third wedding, and the groom's fifth, was a small but elaborate affair at Billy Wilkerson's Sunset Boulevard mansion.

The reception, for sixty world-famous celebrities, featured a ham embossed with "I Love You" and a prime rib announcing, "She Loves Him." A European village was fashioned of exotic foods: colored potatoes carved into cottages, mounds of caviar replicated black hills, a wishing well of woven carrots, and a stream with live goldfish. Finishing off the spectacular spread was a massive ice sculpture of the bride and groom locked in an embrace.

Topping told *Life* magazine, "This is forever." The newlyweds embarked on a sybaritic life of multiple residences, travel, and indulgence — occasionally residing in Turner's four-acre Holmby Hills estate with daughter Cheryl.

But the marriage lasted only a few years.

With new management at MGM, Turner's career began to suffer. Unlike Louis B. Mayer, the new studio chief, Dore Schary, did not cater to her. With trouble at the lot and her personal life in disarray, Turner's drinking increased. She attempted a suicide that was neatly covered up by studio fixers.

In 1952, Turner delivered a strong supporting performance in *The Bad and the Beautiful* and married again. Her fourth husband was actor Lex Barker, a handsome Princeton man whose cinematic claim to fame was playing Tarzan. But the great star's downward trajectory continued throughout the marriage. The servant circle that met daily in Beverly Glen Park gossiped: Lana was a tramp. She and her mother were drunks. And her daughter, Cheryl, was not just mixed up — she was locked up in her room. When Cheryl told her mother that Barker was sexually abusing her, the troubled marriage ended.

By 1956, Lana Turner was at low ebb. At thirty-five, time and heavy drinking had started to compromise her once glorious looks. MGM canceled her contract. Deeply in debt, and with serious IRS problems, she was forced to sell the Holmby Hills estate. Her daughter, now thirteen, ran away to skid row.

During this period, using the name John Steele, Stompanato began calling her private number. Telling her they had a mutual friend — Ava Gardner — he began a relentless pursuit. Stompanato was gentle and attentive. His dark looks and manly physique attracted Lana. He lavished her with extraordinary floral arrangements — from Cohen's Michael's Greenhouse Inc. — and dazzled her with a beautiful engraved watch, and a matching set of jewelry in a leaf design that included a gold and diamond brooch, two bracelets, and a ring.

Turner recalled in her autobiography, *Lana*, "When I asked him, 'Do you happen to have a money tree?' He replied, 'No, only the leaves.' He clearly knew how to court a woman."

When she asked Stompanato what he did for a living, she was led to believe he was involved in record production.

Turner was quickly hooked. Mickey recalled that she sometimes called Stompanato five times in an hour. From the beginning, Johnny developed a close relationship with her adolescent daughter. With an advance from

Cohen, he bought Cheryl an expensive horse. Johnny was an expert rider, and the pair often rode together. Occasionally Mickey would join them. In the summer of 1957, with Lana away on location, Cheryl worked in Johnny's Westwood shop.

Complaining about his own financial woes, Cohen refused to stake him money to keep up with Lana Turner's extravagant lifestyle. Neighbor Rosaline George noted, "Was Johnny broke? Apparently he was remiss in timely payments of his rent." He seemed desperate to sell a large unset diamond. He borrowed cars to transport the star, preferring the Georges' flashy new T-Bird. Once after taking Turner out in the borrowed car, Stompanato screamed wildly at the Georges: they had left the tank empty, and he and the screen goddess had run out of gas.

George noted, "One Sunday, Johnny got my then husband, a young attorney-at-law, to help sell some of his stock [from the Westwood shop] out of our car on Sunset Boulevard, in West L.A. My husband thought it was a funny adventure . . . It seemed Johnny was forever scrounging for new angles to make a buck."

Turner had recently signed with MCA. Lew Wasserman, the powerful agency head, was poised to revive the great star's career. She eschewed her bombshell image by playing the mother of a teenage girl in the highly anticipated film version of the bestseller *Peyton Place*.

Associated Press's Hollywood correspondent James Bacon revealed to this author, "I knew she was living with him [Stompanato] and others did, too." Lana Turner was a monumental film entity with a major picture about to be seen in movie theaters around the world. Now was not a time for scandal. Hollywood closed ranks around their precious commodity. The affair remained a secret to the public, which angered Stompanato. Like Mickey Cohen, he had Hollywood dreams — and a script. Stompanato's reveries included becoming a producer and costarring in a film with Turner.

In 1958 the star flew to London to work on the film *Another Time, Another Place*. Stompanato complained to actress Corrine Calvet that Turner was driving him crazy with out-of-control phone calls and tears: "She begged me to close the store and come with her, but you don't fool around with my investors." But he soon joined her on location in England. All went smoothly for a while. Then they began arguing, and Stompanato became violent. Turner, who once couldn't get enough of him, now claimed she couldn't get rid of him. In a heated encounter, her good-looking costar, newcomer Sean Connery, decked Stompanato in one punch. After that, Scotland Yard was contacted; Johnny was evicted from England.

Filming wrapped. When Turner arrived in Acapulco for a holiday, Johnny was with her. They stayed in the Mexican resort for a couple of months, but the sojourn was fraught with arguments and violence. During the personal turmoil, great news came from Hollywood. Turner's work in *Peyton Place* had garnered her an Academy Award nomination for Best Actress. She would also have the honor of being a presenter at the Oscar ceremony.

Along with newsmen and photographers, daughter Cheryl was waiting at the airport when Lana and Johnny returned to Los Angeles. The details of their flight had been leaked to the press. Turner wrote, "Somehow the newspapers anticipated my arrival . . . sure enough, the photographers were there.

"They snapped me with Cheryl and John, who seemed to be basking in the limelight. He made it appear as though we were a happy couple who had just returned from a marvelous vacation."

The shots were telling. In one, Turner displayed a broad but forced-looking smile. In others, her features appeared tight with tension. Johnny and Cheryl looked relaxed as they beamed at each other, her hand at his waist. When questioned by reporters, Turner denied a romance, but the *Los Angeles Examiner* revealed she had vacationed with Stompanato: "Turner Returns from Vacation with Mob Figure."

Impressed by her nomination, and looking forward to escorting his famous lover to the Oscar ceremony, Johnny was on good behavior. When she told him he wouldn't be attending the Oscar festivities with her, Stompanato became furious.

On March 26, 1958, Turner attended the Academy Awards ceremony accompanied by Cheryl, her mother, and a publicist. Although Joanne Woodward received the Oscar for Best Actress for her performance in *The Three Faces of Eve*, for Lana Turner it was a glorious evening. Her elusive comeback seemed assured.

After the gala, Stompanato broke into her bungalow at the Bel-Air Hotel. With Cheryl in the adjoining room, he allegedly threatened and brutally assaulted Turner.

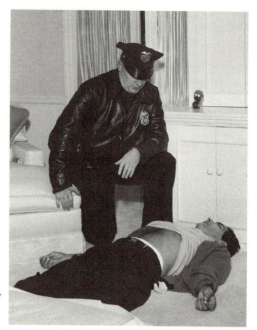

No blood at the crime scene!
Dead at age thirty-two,
Johnny Stompanato's corpse
lies in Lana Turner's pristine
bedroom. 1958.

"I received a telephone call from Mrs. Turner, mother of the actress, informing me that her daughter had become terribly frightened of this hoodlum," Beverly Hills Police Chief Clifton Anderson noted. "When she asked me what should be done, I advised her that her daughter should come in and report to the police immediately. This was never done."

On April 4, 1958, a rainy Good Friday night, it was reported that Johnny Stompanato's body could be found in the pink bedroom of Lana Turner's palatial Bedford Drive rental. The Hollywood fixers went into containment mode. The first call that stormy night: "Get Giesler." Representing Lana Turner and Cheryl Crane, the famous criminal attorney, Jerry Giesler, immediately took control of the crime scene. Mickey Cohen also took prompt action. Arriving at Turner's house as the coroner's men were wheeling out Stompanato's body, he then marched into the office of Beverly Hills Police Chief Clifton Anderson, demanding answers as to what had happened to Stompanato.

Simultaneously, Johnny's apartment was expertly burglarized. Beverly Hills Police Chief Anderson later admitted, "At the time I was unaware of the existence of some startling material which the late playboy had cached in a small wooden box and passed for safekeeping to a third party because

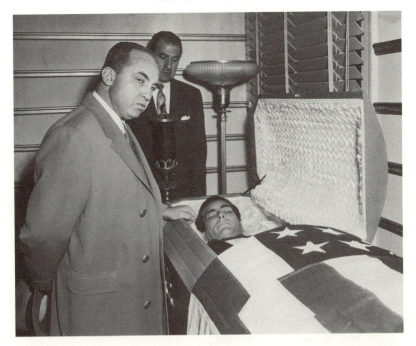

The Mick views the body of Johnny Stompanato. (The man in the back is the mortician.) A former Marine, Stompanato was given a military funeral by the government with full honors. 1958.

he did not trust his underworld associates." The missing container reputedly held sexually explicit negatives of Lana Turner — and other famous women — that Stompanato had secretly taken with a tiny Minox camera.

As soon as the story of Stompanato's death appeared, salacious rumors began circulating: Lana killed him, Cheryl and Johnny were having an affair, Mickey Cohen was paid by Hollywood powers to have Stompanato killed, someone other than Cohen was paid to kill him.

At first Lana was denounced by newspapers and from pulpits across the country. But when tales of Johnny Stompanato's sordid past as a Cohen associate, alleged gigolo and blackmailer came to light, public opinion shifted toward Turner. Mickey Cohen did his best to stop Turner from becoming a figure of sympathy. While the star remained in seclusion, and Cheryl Crane sat in juvenile hall suspected of killing Stompanato in defense of her mother, Cohen held a press conference in his apartment. He delivered Lana's love letters to Johnny exclusively to Agness Underwood, editor of Hearst's *Los Angeles Herald-Express*.

Cohen bitterly complained to the editor about Lana's shabby treatment of her dead lover: "It's the first time in my life I've ever seen a dead man convicted of his own murder . . . Here was a boy who met a horrible accident in a woman's house. She started to claim he was an unwelcome guest. I was sorry for Lana at first, but I'm not sorry now. If Lana had acted decently, got in touch with Johnny's family, and maybe offered to pay some of the funeral expenses, then Carmen [Stompanato, Johnny's brother] and I would have burned the letters."

Lana's love letters made scorching copy in papers around the globe. The first Turner missive, dated September 19, 1957, was postmarked Copenhagen.

From an undated letter from London:

My beloved love — just this morning your precious exciting letter arrived . . . every line warms me and makes me ache and miss you each tiny moment. It's beautiful — yet terrible.

But just so is deep love. Oh darling, darling, the letter I wrote you last might was so much in the same vein I've just received — so you see we certainly are in tune — all the way — I'll close now, love . . . *Cuidado y baci, baci, baci* — Hold me, dear lover, *mi macho* — *ciau, ciau, Papito* — love you. Lanita.

Another letter from London:

Daddy Darling . . . how very lonely I am — and only for you. I don't really give a damn about any others. I miss you and need you so . . . Dearest love, whatever will I do over here without you? Exist? Yes, but nothing, nothing else. I'm not so sure now I can make it. I miss you, want you, and ache for you "All the Way" — so there!!!!!

I have your dear letter here with me and I read and re-read it until it's almost worn thru! I savor every little word and meaning. Beloved, I do love you terribly, the very same "mutual" love that you felt.

I'm your woman and I need you, my man! To love and be loved by — don't ever, ever doubt or forget that!

My Romance, hah! It's a hell of a lot more than that! That's for sure

The personal effects of Johnny Stompanato. Note the scripts; like everyone else in L.A., he had Hollywood dreams. 1958.

. . . There's so much to say, but it's easier when you're holding me all thru the night. Then we can either whisper, or shout or scream our love for each other, to each other. Phones are great, yes, but I need to touch you, to feel your tenderness and your strength. To hold you in my arms, so, so close — to cuddle you sweetly — and then to be completely smothered in your arms and kisses, oh, so many, many kisses!! *Quando, Papito? Quando? Quando? Quando?*

In all, more than a score of Turner's steamy letters gave the world a vicarious thrill and the Hearst tabloids a heavy circulation bump. Lana's feckless raptures became men's room talk from Sunset Boulevard to Main Street to the Champs-Elysées.

And Mickey had more: drafts of notes from Stompanato to Turner, which in comparison were extremely subdued, and a few outpourings of innocent correspondence to Johnny from the teenage girl alleged to have shoved an eight-inch kitchen knife into his solar plexus. The most explicit article in Mickey Cohen's collection: a packet of Turner's pubic hair that was photographed and published in Hearst papers.

Mickey began promoting to the press the incendiary theory that Stompanato had been asleep when the blade pierced his aorta and kidney. And crime scene photos seemed to back up the premise. Curiously blood-less, the bedroom where Stompanato was said to have been killed — as well as the victim's body and clothes — appeared pristine, suggesting that the scene was staged and he had been slain in a location other than Turner's immaculate bedroom. The face of his corpse wore a flaccid expression, suggesting someone who had been drugged. No toxicology tests were performed.

Mickey had more ammunition when he met with Walter Winchell at the Mocambo. Turning over Stompanato's passport, he groused: "I love the kid [Cheryl Crane] and I like Steve [Crane, her father] but I hate Lana." Winchell warned against mob vengeance, telling him, "Respectable people in all forty-eight states are on Lana's and Cheryl's side." Cohen dismissed talk of underworld reprisals.

A week after Johnny Stompanato's death, the international media and hundreds of spectators stood in line outside downtown's hall of records, hoping to gain entrance into the coroner's inquest. Cheryl Crane wrote, "Mickey Cohen, who was scheduled to be the first witness, bustled in five minutes late, sending an electric reaction through the jammed and swelter-ing courtroom. Intending to shock, he wore a cartoon gray gangster suit and gray felt hat and he chewed gum."

When questioned about identifying his former associate's body at the morgue, Cohen took no chances: "I refuse to identify John Stompanato Jr. on the grounds I may be accused of his murder."

Observers were perplexed. A seasoned and circumspect participant of

After more than twenty years on the silver screen, Lana Turner dramatically emotes during the coroner's inquest into Stompanato's death.

the nuances of life and crime, Mickey was wary of being set up for Stompanato's murder. When asked the question a second time, Hollywood's most talented "actor" repeated his lines. The mobster was then dismissed. Picking up his hat, the underworld celebrity donned it and stomped out.

Mickey's scene-stealing turn lasted all of two minutes.

The next sixty-two minutes belonged to Lana Turner. She gave the performance of her life. Her emotionally charged testimony, replete with anguished tears and clenched fists, reached a crescendo when she described Stompanato walking toward her in the bedroom, carrying a jacket and shirt on a hanger, and looking "as if he intended to strike me." At that moment, her daughter ran into the room holding a knife. "I saw them come together and I thought, oh, my God, she is hitting him in the stomach. Then he swung halfway round and fell. He began making the most horrible noises in his throat and gasping. Cheryl began sobbing and ran out of the room."

After the courtroom theatrics, the case was closed. Cheryl Crane was found to have committed a justifiable homicide in defense of her mother.

The Turner family was eager to forget Johnny Stompanato, Mickey Cohen, and that long Good Friday. The explicit film taken of Turner was located and destroyed in front of her by attorney Louis Blau. Soon back at work, the public loved the blonde star in *Imitation of Life* — another mother-daughter weeper in which she had gross points. The screen legend's second career would last well into the next decade.

But to many, the Stompanato case would remain Hollywood's most sensational whodunit.

22

BOMBSHELLS AND BOBBY

"He never seemed to have grown up.
I had the feeling life was just a game to him."

LIZ RENAY, COMMENTING ON MICKEY COHEN

L aVonne, forty-one, was granted her divorce from Mickey Cohen on June 18, 1958. Accompanied by Doris Saks, her sister, both women smiled broadly when greeted by the press. Shedding light on the reality of her marriage, LaVonne was no longer tight-lipped: "No matter what happened away from home, he was continually berating me — seemed to take pleasure in it — and humiliating me. I was under a doctor's care during most of my marriage."

Mickey's former sister-in-law supported her: "I've seen him berate and belittle her and tell her how stupid she was in front of me, my husband, and other guests. He made her nervous and highly emotional — in tears."

The judge questioned the one-dollar-per-year settlement, with no share in community property. LaVonne accepted the terms.

"My lawyer said there's no use fooling myself. I can't get anything except what he wants to give," she told journalist Dean Jennings.

Not long after her divorce became final, LaVonne and immense Sam Farkas — Mickey's former bodyguard — eloped to Las Vegas. Claiming he was now in the steel business, the groom said he was reformed. Farkas, FBI #462422, owned a Wilshire Boulevard carpet store where another

Jubilant LaVonne gets a divorce decree from Mickey Cohen, her husband of eighteen years. 1958.

LaVonne's new husband, bodyguard and bookmaker Sam Farkas, with Mickey. The trio remained friendly.

Ladies' man? Beautiful Barbara Darnell, twenty-three, kisses L.A.'s Capone. Mickey seems to find the experience distasteful. 1958.

Cohen associate, Stumpy Zevon, was a fixture. "She married a bookmaker, a Mickey Cohen — second class. She liked them," a Cohen attorney told this author.

The press took note of LaVonne's quick remarriage. The implication? Hollywood's most famous tough guy was a cuckold. "Cohen always liked to have a young, pretty girl around when he dropped in at nightclubs — probably to create the illusion that he was interested in women," bookmaker George Redston observed.

Mickey began a dating frenzy. His much-publicized female companions were usually young beauties working the showbiz fringe. Some were "party girls," the polite term for high-priced call girls or unemployed actresses willing to entertain visiting mobsters, Teamster's big shots, sports stars, politicians, and other celebrities. Not to be outdone by his ex-wife, Mickey had already been showcased in the company of exotic dancer Arlene Stevens, "movie girl" Ann Sterling, and lovely Barbara Darnell, and he was prominently featured in *Life* magazine sharing an ice cream sundae with glamorous Liz Renay.

A Marilyn Monroe look-alike contest winner, Renay was born Pearl Elizabeth Dobbins in Mesa, Arizona. A self-styled poet and artist, her parents were evangelistic zealots. Breaking away from her religious upbringing, she quickly married and divorced three husbands and had

Glamorous Liz Renay and Mickey strike a pose. They were later entwined in criminal problems together. 1959.

countless affairs. By the late fall of 1957, she was the mother of two adolescent children and had worked as a waitress, a movie extra, a fashion model, a showgirl, a stripper, and a mob courier. On the periphery of the New York underworld's most inside scene, she was well acquainted with numerous top mobsters. Her boyfriend was Anthony Coppola, the right-hand man and bodyguard to the notoriously violent Albert Anastasia. After having assassinated his boss, Anastasia now headed one of the New York's Five Families, originally named the Manganos.

At this time, the New York underworld was in upheaval. In May 1957 there had been an attempt on the life of Frank Costello, the nation's top mobster and head of the Mafia commission. He survived the shooting, the bullet barely grazing his head, but rival Mafia boss Vito Genovese had not intended it to be just a warning. Albert Anastasia, the force who for decades had provided Costello's muscle, was assassinated in the barbershop of Manhattan's Park Sheraton Hotel on October 25, 1957. Wanting to avoid the aftermath of the Anastasia assassination, it seemed like a perfect time for Liz Renay to try her luck in Hollywood. An introduction to Mickey Cohen was arranged.

Renay spent her first weeks in the film capital being wined and dined by Cohen, their dates documented by TV cameras and newspapers. While their relationship grew warm, it remained strictly platonic. The stunning blonde observed of Mickey: "He never seemed to have grown up. I had the feeling life was just a game to him."

In her memoir, *My Face for the World to See*, Renay wrote that Cohen told her his hand-washing compulsion dated back to his newsboy days: "'One day I started to hand a lady her change and she said, "My what dirty hands you have, little boy. Why don't you go wash them?" I was so embarrassed I hung my head and ran to the fountain to wash. Before I knew it, my hands were black again.'"

After that he returned to the fountain every few minutes, not realizing that each time he touched a paper, ink would rub off on his hands. The demeaning encounter became a defining moment, and the hand-scrubbing compulsion never died.

With misty eyes, Cohen confided more. The root of his publicity obsession also dated to those childhood days when he was a newsboy. He told Renay that appearing on the front page was the ultimate achievement. He then revealed his youthful vow that one day he would be in the headlines himself.

Perusing album after neatly arranged album and endless stacks of clippings, Renay observed his dream had certainly been fulfilled. Mickey's response was self-effacing, declaring the publicity "kid's stuff" that had nothing to do with the present.

While working on Mickey's biography, Ben Hecht broached the subject of sex. "To tell the truth, I don't go for it much," Mickey said. "Girls very often like me and seem attracted to me, and I find them also attractive, at times. It's talkin' to them that's the hard part."

When Hecht visited Mexico with the mobster, Mickey reluctantly accompanied his friends to a brothel. Observing as Cohen carefully avoided the prostitutes, Hecht noted his phobic behavior. "Mickey wouldn't sit down in the whore house parlor. He was afraid the chairs were contaminated."

"He would kiss his dog, but not a girl," a Cohen attorney confided to this author. "Why? Girls are dirty!" Like his other complexes, the fear of germs, and women, harkened back to his youth and the devastating bout of gonorrhea.

While Mickey Cohen was not a lady's man, he played the role to the hilt. When the papers began describing Liz Renay as his girlfriend, they became the subject of numerous stories. Never missing an opening, Mickey decided to push the notion further. He gave an interview holding a photo of her. The next editions shrieked: IF LIZ SAYS WE'RE ENGAGED, THEN WE'RE ENGAGED.

The wily provocateur was a master at getting what he wanted. From Renay, it was playboy publicity and a favor: two checks made out to him (to be immediately reimbursed) totaling $5,500 and inscribed as "loans." She became a pawn in the old scheme he used to launder dirty money.

These checks would come back to haunt them both.

Mickey signed an exclusive deal with Curtis Publishing for a four-part biographical series. Writer Dean Jennings went to Los Angeles, where he spent six weeks closely observing his subject. With more than 3 million subscribers, Curtis's hugely circulated weekly, the *Saturday Evening Post*, began the series "Mickey Cohen: The Private Life of a Hood" in September 1958.

As the first installment arrived in homes across the country, Lee Mortimer declared in Winchell's "Along Broadway" column: "Top hoods telling Mickey (The Louse) Cohen that if he doesn't shut his trap and keep out of the papers, he'll get only one more story — on the obit page."

The *Post* series gave Cohen a self-serving platform, but it also provided its readers with never-before-revealed information.

> Living up to the legend of Mickey Cohen has to be a tour de force when the power and the big money have gone, when you have to manufacture your own news to stay alive in print, and when you owe a million dollars in taxes and personal debts you can never repay . . .
>
> But now it is twilight . . . And in this extremity Mickey is hopping around blindly like a beheaded chicken, trying to identify the villains who done him wrong . . . It has never occurred to him that the man who administered the coup de grace was Mickey Cohen himself.

For better or worse, Cohen apparently didn't need prompting when speaking to the journalist.

On taxes, he declared, "Internal Revenue is making us a nation of cheats. Always snooping. You can't expect Mickey Cohen to go around like a three-dollar-a-day bum. Why should I give them what little money I have when they'll only give it away to some foreign country?"

On Chief Parker: "I know that today I'm not a mobster or a gangster. If I were in the rackets now, I'd run around in a cheap car and I'd stay out of the nightclubs and I wouldn't get any publicity at all. But I can't live that way. Me driving a big car is what's aggravating Police Chief Parker. I do this because this is me."

On his California Highway Patrol Badge: "I bought it. It cost me a hundred." And he boldly talked of "partners" — prominent ones: "These people are still powerful in Los Angeles. They own big homes, big cars, and have plenty of money in the bank. They owe much of this to me, and they're still grateful. My credit with them is unlimited, and there is no problem getting money."

Reporter Jennings fearlessly provided explicit information about members of Cohen's outfit and his high living, and, for the first time, his curious compulsions were divulged. Indeed, the most devastating blow to Cohen's fragile ego was this observation: "Now mobsters don't consider him important enough to kill."

★ ★ ★

"Mickey, anxious for publicity from any corner, gave a magazine interview . . . when Ben [Hecht] was writing the book," wrote journalist Sidney Zion about the *Post* articles. "The piece tore the little dandy apart, and he lost his biographer in the bundle."

The *Post* series proved damaging, but Mickey refused to accept responsibility for his self-destructive behavior. Used to controlling and manipulating the news — planting puff pieces and staging photo ops, feeding the press versions of stories he devised — Cohen blamed Jennings for outing him on a grand scale.

Payback? Of course.

A month after the series appeared, Cohen filed a libel action against Curtis Publishing Company for one million dollars.

Cohen withdrew the lawsuit less than two months later.

★ ★ ★

In March 1959, Mickey flew to Washington, D.C. He had been subpoenaed to testify before Senator John L. McClelland's high-profile committee investigating labor racketeering and criminal corruption and infiltration of businesses by the mob. Officially called the United States Senate Select Committee on Improper Activities in Labor and Management, the McClelland hearings were intended to be Kefauver redux. With a special focus on the Teamsters union, the committee was first active from 1957 to 1960. Unlike his testimony before the Kefauver committee, this time Mickey Cohen's appearance was televised.

The committee's chief counsel was Robert F. Kennedy. Born in 1925, the Harvard-educated attorney was a scion of one of the most prominent Irish-Catholic families in the country. John F. "Honey Fitz" Fitzgerald, his maternal grandfather, had been the mayor of Boston. His father, Joseph P. Kennedy Sr., the driven son of a saloon-keeper, made fortunes in stock speculation, Hollywood studios, real estate, and allegedly high-end bootlegging. A power in Democratic politics, Joe Kennedy was appointed the first head of the Securities and Exchange Commission by President Franklin Roosevelt, where he served briefly; afterward he became a highly controversial ambassador to Great Britain.

For all the great achievements, there was much talk that Joe Kennedy's practices and connections were often less than savory. In the late 1920s, silent-film legend Gloria Swanson became his secret lover and business associate. She wrote in her autobiography, *Swanson on Swanson*, "Joseph Kennedy had taken over my entire life, and I trusted him implicitly to make the most of it . . . When Joseph Kennedy left California, he claimed to have cleared millions in motion pictures, and to have made me financially independent . . . the second part of the claim, the part about me, was not true." Left in extreme financial peril after their business partnership failed, Swanson's accountant told her more unfortunate news: it was *she* who had paid for extravagant gifts that Kennedy gave to her and others.

More of Joe Kennedy's dealings raised red flags. Mobster Frank Costello was a name that often was rumored to be as a behind-the-scenes associate. Soon after Prohibition ended, Joe Kennedy acquired the hugely lucrative American distribution rights to Gordon's Gin and Dewar's Scotch. Among his real estate interests were shares in Miami's Hialeah Racetrack, alleged to be an underworld stronghold.

Bobby Kennedy, now in his early thirties, had plans to establish his name. He would do so through nationally televised racket hearings that

New Orleans racketeer Carlos Marcello, left, and his brother Vincent, center, and Mickey Cohen, right, await the start of the Senate rackets committee in Washington. Cohen, who says he is reformed, invoked the Fifth Amendment sixty-eight times and refused to answer questions about the shakedown of an L.A. cigarette machine operator. March 24, 1959.

included appearances by Teamsters boss Jimmy Hoffa, New Orleans mafioso Carlos Marcello, and Hollywood's Mickey Cohen. Older brother John F. Kennedy, junior senator from Massachusetts, sat on the McClelland committee, but the hero of the headline-making hearings would be Chief Counsel Robert F. Kennedy.

Capitol Hill, March 24, 1959: RFK, the privileged son from the tree-lined boulevards of Brookline, Bronxville, and Palm Beach, faced off with the brazen Sunset Strip mob boss, who still maintained a tight grip on the streets of Los Angeles.

After diminutive New Orleans Mafia leader Carlos Marcello finished his testimony, another tough little man followed, in the person of gum-chomping Mickey Cohen. Bobby Kennedy aggressively pressed and prodded the West Coast gang boss, grilling him about muscling in on L.A. and Orange County labor rackets and his specific role in a feud between two cigarette vending machine companies.

Cohen, the courtroom veteran, repeatedly invoked the Fifth Amendment of the Constitution. Time after time Mickey answered each question, "I respectfully decline to answer on the grounds it may tend to incriminate me."

With the intention of getting a rise from the mercurial Mr. Cohen, Kennedy posed the query, "What does it mean to have someone's lights put out?"

Always seeking what came naturally, a laugh, and with it the audience's empathy, Cohen replied, "Lookit, I dunno what you're talking about, I'm not an electrician . . . I got nuthin' to do with electricity."

Incensed by Cohen's mockery, Robert Kennedy leaped toward the notorious Angeleno as if to strike him. Senator McClelland quickly grabbed his counsel by the sleeve, forcing him to cool down. But Kennedy could not countenance being derided by the contemptuous California mobster.

By the time the hearings were over, Bobby Kennedy had become a national figure. He had also created a personal enemies list: Jimmy Hoffa, Carlos Marcello, and Mickey Cohen.

In nearly ten years as Los Angeles's chief of police, William H. Parker had been unable to neutralize Cohen. In 1959, none other than the leader of the Soviet Union, Premier Nikita Khrushchev, would taunt Chief Parker about Los Angeles's "gangster" problem.

At the height of the Cold War between the United States and the Soviet Union, Khrushchev made a trip to the U.S. that culminated in the Communist dictator's visit to Hollywood. He was feted at a "stars-only" luncheon on a Fox soundstage that was attended by two hundred luminaries, among them Marilyn Monroe, Elizabeth Taylor, Gary Cooper, Judy Garland, Kim Novak, and Frank Sinatra. At the luncheon, Khrushchev announced that his great wish was to visit Disneyland. Chief Parker took aside Ambassador Henry Cabot Lodge Jr., the dictator's official guide, and informed him, "I want you, as a representative of the president, to know that I will not be responsible for Chairman Khrushchev's safety if we go to Disneyland."

At the end of the extravagant affair came the requisite speeches.

Khrushchev arose and with the aid of a translator gave a forty-five-minute diatribe, which ended with a direct attack on Chief Parker. "[I] was told that I could not go to Disneyland," he announced. "I asked, 'Why not? . . . Have gangsters taken hold of the place? Your policemen are so tough they can lift a bull by the horns. Surely they can restore order if there are any gangsters around.'"

The fact that even the head of the Soviet Union had heard of Los Angeles's underworld was more than Chief Parker could bear. In a final effort to rid Los Angeles of Mickey Cohen, Chief Parker and Bobby Kennedy joined forces.

"By then, the feds had decided the only way to get Cohen was to prove 'conspicuous consumption,'" Daryl Gates, Parker's protégé, concluded. "If they could show he spent far more money than the income he accounted for, they'd have him. Painstakingly, using our contacts around the city, they documented where he dined and how much he spent."

Mickey tried to settle his outstanding tax debt for a second time, but he was rebuffed. He became aware the IRS was closing in on him when a grand jury began investigating his finances, again. And Liz Renay became a central figure in the new tax probe. Federal authorities then charged her with five counts of perjury, claiming she lied about the two checks she had written to Cohen as loans.

Cohen's friends and associates — savvy, powerful men — informed Renay that the case had been blown into a major political issue with intense pressure coming directly from Bobby Kennedy. The consequences could be disastrous for the Mick.

Before she was brought to trial, Liz Renay accepted a plea. In federal judge John D. Martin Sr., she found a sympathetic arbitrator. Although her associations were unsavory, she had no prior convictions. Pleading guilty to one count of perjury in July 1959, Liz Renay received a suspended sentence and probation. Later she was sent to jail to serve a three-year sentence, after breaking the terms of her probation.

Unfazed, nothing stopped Mickey. In the "romance department" he become involved with someone who seemed more than just a photo op. The thorniest yellow rose ever to come out of the Lone Star State, pistol-packin' Candy

Mickey's bodacious blonde fiancée, porn legend and exotic dancer Candy Barr, teaches Joan Collins how to strip on a 20th Century Fox soundstage. 1959.

Barr was already notorious when she met him.

Born Juanita Dale Slusher in 1935, this brash young woman seemed ready-made to be a mobster's girlfriend. A dirt-poor, down-home girl from a Texas whistle-stop, she had the requisite hardscrabble childhood. Her birth mother died in a car accident when she was nine, and her father remarried, making her one of an extended family of eleven children. By the time she ran away to Dallas at age thirteen, Juanita had matured into a striking beauty. There may have been allegations of childhood abuse, but that didn't appear to have soured her on sex. She quickly married and divorced a safecracker then became involved in prostitution. What she lacked in proper education, she made up for in carnal knowledge.

In 1951, the bodacious brunette teenager entered the world of explicit pornography. Like a netherworld Lana Turner, she immediately caused a sensation. As the star of the contraband stag movie *Smart Alec*, her uninhibited performance, angelic face, and show-stopping body made the eight-millimeter short the most popular blue movie of the next two decades. The nameless tartlet from the grainy black-and-white flick personified wanton sexuality, fueling the erotic desires of millions of men.

After working as a cocktail waitress and a cigarette girl, the underage siren bleached her hair platinum and put her bountiful assets to work in the lowest rung of legitimate entertainment. Using the stage name Candy Barr, she became an institution in the Dallas demimonde, stripping at the Colony Club and hanging out with sordid characters like strip club owner Jack Ruby at his Vegas Club.

In short order, the petite green-eyed blonde became one of the highest-paid exotic dancers in the country. Costumed in her trademark cowboy hat and boots, spangled vest and shorts, with a holster holding a pair of pistols slung from her hips, she headlined clubs from New Orleans to Vegas, earning two thousand dollars a week. In 1959 she was peeling down to pasties and G-string at Chuck Landis's Largo on the Sunset Strip and facing a fifteen-year sentence for marijuana possession in Texas.

"A victim . . . vulnerable, bright but not smart," Grammy-winning recording artist Nino Tempo said of her. "Very needy, completely, completely insecure. She didn't know the difference between right and wrong, up or down. She had a nickel-plated revolver on her dresser — and was desperately looking for a man she could trust."

Candy's manager, Joe DeCarlo, introduced her around town. After two years of legal wrangling in the marijuana case, she was hoping for a last-ditch appeal. Mickey Cohen gallantly stepped in, spending more than $15,000 ($110,000 today) on an all-star cast of attorneys; he hired civil liberties advocate A.L. Wirin, Melvin "King of Torts" Belli, and appellate expert Julius Lucius Eccles to handle aspects of her case.

Together, Candy Barr and Mickey Cohen proved to be Hollywood's most outrageous couple. She loved displaying her incredible body, and

Mickey never shied away from exposure. The press ate it up. Soon, there were reports the great exhibitionists were engaged. Photographed with Candy, Mickey beamed.

Employed by 20th Century Fox as a technical adviser, she tutored Joan Collins in the art of striptease for the film *Seven Thieves*. In April 1959, Candy accompanied Mickey to the Saints and Sinners testimonial banquet for Milton Berle and entertained his old Cleveland friends, including Teamsters official and Hoffa confidant Louis "Babe" Triscaro, at the Largo.

And there were allegations that Mickey began using Candy Barr as a female Johnny Stompanato. In June 1959, the FBI noted in their voluminous Meyer Harris Cohen file that Alfred Bloomingdale, department store heir and founder of Diners Club credit card, had been the mark in a sexual shakedown — "badger game." Mickey was thought to be behind the blackmail scheme, but he was never interviewed about the allegations. According to an FBI memo in the Meyer Harris Cohen file: "Mr. Bloomingdale had been most anxious for no prosecution in this matter and had so advised the Police Department as he did not desire the unfavorable publicity."

The Los Angeles County DA's bureau of investigation filed reports that Kennedy brother-in-law and Rat Pack actor Peter Lawford "was [raising] funds to aid Cohen's associate, Candy Barr, in jail on narcotics charges. Lawford was 'desperately attempting' to obtain compromising sound tapes of 'parties' he had attended in Barr's dressing room."

But Candy Barr was to be a short-lived entity in Hollywood. As she awaited appeals, Mickey had her hair dyed brown, gave her cash and a new identity, and sent her to Mexico. Then things became skewed. Dark, good-looking bodybuilder Jack Sahakian, a top Hollywood hairdresser, joined her there. She married Sahakian on November 25, 1959. A few days later Candy lost her final appeal in the U.S. Supreme Court. Mrs. Sahakian entered a Texas prison to begin serving a fifteen-year sentence for possession of a marijuana cigarette on December 4, 1959.

But Mickey already had his fill of the voluptuous paramour. No well-mannered LaVonne, boisterous, untamed Candy — who had shot her first husband and slugged Mickey in the face — proved too rowdy for him. He had already announced his engagement to a statuesque twenty-two-year-old brunette, a stripper who used the stage name Miss Beverly Hills. "She's a real lady. Her morals and concept of life are really high," he proudly said of his new fiancée.

The engagement didn't last long. By late November he moved on to even fresher flesh. Eighteen-year-old Bardot ringer Claretta Hashagen, professionally known as Sandy Hagen, was a showbiz hopeful with a poodle, a parakeet, and a husband when she met Hollywood's mobster.

The sophisticated blonde teenager and forty-six-year-old Mickey Cohen had known each other for just a week when another headline-making event linked them forever.

23

END GAMES

"People were the keys to the truth in the Cohen trial."

JOURNALIST ED REID

O pening in the fall of 1959, Rondelli's was a small Italian restaurant in the Valley, at 13359 Ventura Boulevard in Sherman Oaks. Mickey Cohen and his outfit called it home. The boss loved to sit in a booth with Mickey Jr. in his lap. He would tie a linen napkin around the dog's neck and feed him linguini. His boys roared at the sight of the pasta-eating bulldog.

Rondelli's quickly became a hotspot, with celebrities turning out for the tasty, home-cooked food. Liberace liked the place, and so did attorney Melvin Belli. Errol Flynn, squiring his fifteen-year-old girlfriend, Beverly Aadland, came, too. The swashbuckling screen legend, now a bloated, drug-addled has-been, spun fantastic yarns with the legendary mobster. Private eye Fred Otash recalled, "There I sat with two of the world's heavy-weights, each in his own class."

But on the night of December 2, 1959, the good times at Rondelli's ended when Big Jack "The Enforcer" Whalen was stopped cold, with a bullet between his eyes.

A product of Los Angeles, John Frederick Whalen was his given name. Fred Whalen, his father, was a prosperous pool shark, con man, and bookmaker who had been around since L.A.'s old days of the white-shoe racketeers. Wanting a straight life for his son, Freddie the Thief, as the senior Whalen was called, sent his boy to Hollywood's exclusive Black-Foxe Military Institute, along with the sons of filmland's elite.

An excellent polo player, young Whalen reached the position of commander there and grew into a strong, handsome young man. Jack Whalen was full of charm and enthusiasm — but there was violence at his core. During World War II, he enlisted in the air force. At the top of his class in officer's training school, he served as a flight instructor. But upon leaving the service, he eschewed the privileged career path laid before him as a Black-Foxe graduate. Instead, he followed in his father's footsteps. Flyboy Jack Whalen became a professional tough guy, freelance bookie, and strong-arm debt collector. He quickly gained a top following and married a local social figure. Doing well, Whalen bought a house and two planes.

"Then Mickey Cohen and the Mafia syndicate came into his life," noted his one-time partner, George Redston.

Mickey worked all his tricks to bring the competitor in line. It seemed like a one-sided battle since the mobster had a crew of armed killers on his payroll, as well as a number of cops, while the Enforcer was known to be an army of one. But nothing in the playbook seemed to stop Big Jack. When Cohen's men threatened his agents or welshed on bets, Whalen slapped them around. Behind the bluster was a dirty secret: Whalen was an informant for LAPD Detective Jerry Wooters, an original member of the Gangster Squad, and he used his police connection to bully anyone not subscribing to *his* program.

Finally, in 1959, Mickey sent out the heavyweights. Whalen and Fred Sica went at it. With one punch Jack Whalen put Freddie in the hospital. Soon after the incident, Whalen saw Sica walking Cohen's dog. Pulling his car to the curb, he taunted him outrageously in front of a witness. Freddie just stood there, mutely seething. The boss vowed vengeance: Jack Whalen was added to the list of Mickey Cohen's obsessions.

Friends warned Whalen, "Don't fuck with that little Jew!" But the Enforcer didn't seem to care. Whalen held the opinion that *he* was the tough guy in town, and he believed the LAPD cop would protect him.

Rumors began circulating about personal run-ins between Whalen and Cohen. In the most devastating version, Big Jack found the diminutive mobster hiding in a back room of a restaurant and confronted him. Cornered, Whalen tore off Mick's trousers, fished out his bankroll, and peeled off money to pay an outstanding debt. Then he flung the roll and shredded pants in Cohen's face. As he walked out, Whalen barked, "Lay off me, and stop blackmailing my friends — or else."

Among Mickey Cohen's underworld sponsors, doubts had begun to surface about his muscle and legendary organizational skills. It was imperative to finally get Whalen under control.

The FBI noted in their Meyer Harris Cohen file: "COHEN apparently was taking orders from someone on the East Coast by the name of RAYMOND."

The FBI believed that the mysterious "Raymond" was Raymond Patriarca Sr. of Providence, Rhode Island. The Mafia boss of New England, Patriarca was alleged to be both a secret owner of the Dunes Hotel in Las Vegas and a prominent Cohen backer.

The Whalen situation had festered long enough. Mickey raised a war chest. An intrigue, worthy of Machiavelli, was hatched. The scenario had lots of twists and turns and overtones of the successful plotline used as far back as the Max Shaman killing. Three men would provide key performances in the Cohen-directed drama, and a fourth player would take the fall.

The setup: Cohen's handsome Italian boy, George Piscatelle, alias George Perry, owed a bookie. Perry disputed the debt, and Jack Whalen had been brought in to settle the matter. A Johnny Stompanato stand-in, Georgie Perry had a provocative backstory: police operatives had recently tailed him to a Van Nuys motel in the company of Marilyn Monroe. LAPD officer Gary Wean claimed to have heard bedroom recordings of the pair, which he assumed were for extortion purposes.

On December 2, 1959, Whalen received a call from "Sam," a friend of Perry's. "Mickey's pretty hot at you and he's plenty mad. He would like to talk to you." A date was made. Whalen agreed to appear at Rondelli's before midnight. He called Jerry Wooters for backup, but the LAPD officer was now living under a shadow. He had recently been demoted to a uniform job, on the four-to-twelve shift at the Lincoln Heights jail, after allegations surfaced that he was shaking down bookies. When Whalen reached him, Wooters said he was on active duty and couldn't join him. But he strongly

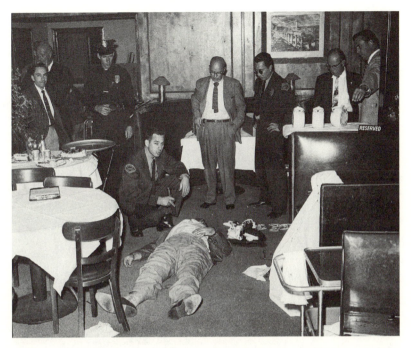

Another Cohen enemy ends up in the morgue. The police and coroner inspect the body of Jack F. Whalen, shot dead in a busy restaurant, a known Cohen hangout, on December 3, 1959.

warned Whalen, who had legal problems: do not take a gun to the showdown.

Arriving at Rondelli's around 11:30, Jack Whalen entered the restaurant from the kitchen, immediately slugged a man in a phone booth, and shouted threats at another. As he leaned over the table Mickey Cohen occupied with four men and his date, Sandy Hagen, Whalen was shot twice with a tiny .38 belly gun. The entire scene lasted a few minutes.

The shooting happened in the presence of many restaurant patrons, but by the time police arrived, the restaurant was nearly deserted. Mickey was nowhere in sight; his boys and his date were gone. The LAPD found no murder weapon, no suspects, and no evidence — except Big Jack Whalen lying dead, his brains spilled on the floor.

Then a man appeared with his dog. He announced, "I'm Mickey Cohen," and explained that he'd been in the bathroom washing his hands. He said he and Miss Hagen had come to Rondelli's for a midnight snack.

The Mick's latest girlfriend, teenager Sandy Hagen, and the mobster engage in a heated discussion. She was with Cohen at the scene when Jack Whalen was murdered. 1960.

Seated alone, with Mickey Jr. on his lap, he'd been feeding his dog — when *it* happened. He told police that shots rang out almost as soon as the fight broke out. Everything had happened so fast, he ducked under the table and "didn't see a thing." He denied killing Whalen.

Deputy Chief Thad Brown took Cohen to the Van Nuys station, where he was booked on suspicion of murder. In a grandstanding move, Chief Bill Parker then personally took over the case. Released the afternoon of the following day, headlines reported the city's most notorious mobster *had not been charged* with the slaying of Jack Whalen.

For the citizens of Los Angeles, thoughts harkened back to dark times passed. It seemed that in the final days of the sixth decade of the century, nothing had changed when it came to Mickey Cohen.

★ ★ ★

A woman came forward and described a member of the Cohen party as the shooter. Her memory soon faded. Then someone took the fall. Walking into Chief Parker's office, trailed by a television crew and accompanied by a pair of lawyers, Sam LoCigno, a Cohen associate from Cleveland, stated he had killed Jack Whalen in self-defense. The next act called for the case to evaporate or, at worst, for LoCigno to receive a light sentence for manslaughter.

In March 1960, LoCigno went on trial for the murder of Jack Whalen. Mickey and his friends corroborated on a final version of how the victim died; all repeated the same story in court. The jury came back with a shocking verdict: a conviction of first-degree murder. Sam LoCigno, thirty-three, was sentenced to life in prison without possibility of parole.

In San Quentin for a few months, LoCigno changed his story. Recanting to the prison chaplain, Sam admitted to taking the blame for $50,000 (nearly $325,000 today), legal assistance, and assurances that he would receive, at worst, a manslaughter conviction and short sentence.

He was returned to L.A. and housed in the county jail. There he met with members of the DA's office and told his new story. He informed interrogators he was just the fall guy; another member of the Cohen party was Whalen's real killer. He never named the assassin, but LoCigno directed authorities to the murder gun, which had been thrown off a mountain near Mulholland and Beverly Drive. The rusted Smith & Wesson .38 revolver was traced to an Arizona gun store where "Kallman de Leonard" had bought it. The proprietor of the store identified the purchaser as Cohen hoodlum, and erstwhile movie producer, Roger K. Leonard.

The saga turned more ominous. LoCigno had an unexpected caller at the jail, Mickey Cohen. Used to bending laws, the mobster didn't seem to care that it was illegal for a convicted felon to visit prisoners. Apparently neither did anyone else. In hushed tones, he talked to Sam and visited again and again. During the course of Cohen's visits, LoCigno was beaten up.

Sam realized he must revert to the version Mickey approved. LoCigno now denied the story that Whalen had been slain by someone else. His lawyer went back to court, offering a guilty plea in exchange for a manslaughter conviction. The offer was rejected, but the first-degree murder conviction would eventually be overturned. Granted a retrial, LoCigno was now charged with voluntary manslaughter.

With the start of a new decade, Hollywood's old guard, led by the ring-a-ding-dinging Frankie Sinatra, put on a new face. Young, bland, and blonde,

Sandra Dee and Troy Donahue were box office stars. And 1960 was a presidential election year: incumbent Vice President Richard M. Nixon versus Senator John F. Kennedy of Massachusetts.

Mickey had experienced some rough days since Jack Whalen's murder. Rondelli's never reopened after the killing. Another link to his past, the Garden of Allah on the Sunset Strip, was bulldozed to make way for a bank. All the nasty publicity, rumblings from the IRS, the tapped phones, and Chief Parker with his constant surveillance continued, and there were reports that Freddie "The Thief" Whalen was out to avenge his son's death. But the party never stopped for Mickey Cohen.

The mobster could be seen nightly on the Sunset Strip at the Rounders, Schwab's Drugstore, Gaiety Deli, the Cloisters, or Dino's Lodge (Dean Martin's restaurant used for the exterior of the TV series *77 Sunset Strip*), and Cohen's associates were fixtures at the Beverly Hills Health Club, 1125 South Beverly Drive. Every Monday, at five-sharp, Mickey appeared at the barbershop there, then on to the weekly Friars Club meeting at the Band Box on Fairfax. On La Cienega, at the Slate Brothers' club, he roared with laughter when acid-tongued funny man Don Rickles dared to put him down. He sat, his eyes glazed, at the Crescendo while narcissistic comic Lenny Bruce yammered on about *his* civil liberties. On La Brea Avenue, Panza's Lazy Susan restaurant and Pink's famous hot dog stand were part of his route. Mickey Cohen remained a regular at the Formosa, the Largo, Frank Sennes's Ciro's and Moulin Rouge, once Earl Carroll's showplace at Sunset and Vine, Tommy Tucker's Play Room on Washington Boulevard, and the Apple Pan burger joint.

He still maintained suites for out-of-town guests at the Chateau Marmont and rooms at the Park Sunset Hotel, 8462 Sunset, and at the Del Capri. He loved the action at the Gingham Pup, the hot dog–shaped stand at the kiddie park, at San Vincente and La Cienega. He made the scene at P.J.'s, the "in" spot for the trendy young set, and held court, across from city hall, in the Red Garter Room at the Cedar Bar. A favorite dinner haunt was chi-chi Puccini's, a new restaurant at 224 South Beverly Drive, in Beverly Hills. Servicing the Rat Pack and their A-list friends like Marilyn Monroe, investors included Frank Sinatra and Peter Lawford, the hard-partying Kennedy in-law.

His pet, beloved Mickey Jr., died in July 1960. Newspapers reported a

The press came to the pet cemetery: did the mobster's prized bulldog Mickey Jr. meet with foul play? 1960.

car hit the bulldog. Girlfriend Sandy Hagen and talent manager Joe DeCarlo, followed by reporters and photographers, joined a sorrowful Mickey Cohen at the pet cemetery when his bulldog was interred after an elaborate funeral. There were questions if the dog's death was really an accident — or an act of revenge by Freddy Whalen.

On September 17, 1960, everything changed for L.A.'s celebrity mobster. As a result of a three-year investigation, Mickey Cohen received a new indictment from the IRS. He was charged with thirteen federal counts of income tax evasion. Arrested at his Barrington apartment, he was set free on bail arranged by Abe Phillips. He immediately flew to New York. Cohen was seen outside of Manhattan's Warwick Hotel consorting with top mobster Joe "Stretch" Stracci, who had managed the syndicate's Havana operations. Another high-placed New York underworld figure, Charlie "The Blade" Tourine, was spotted in the elevator at the hotel.

Beating out incumbent Vice President Richard Nixon after a tight election, alleged to have been fixed by underworld patrons in Chicago, in

January 1961, John Fitzgerald Kennedy was sworn in as the thirty-fifth president of the United States. His brother Bobby was appointed to the post of attorney general. First on RFK's agenda was an all-out war on the underworld. His personal enemies, Jimmy Hoffa, Carlos Marcello, and Mickey Cohen, were to receive particular focus. Special assistants from his office were sent to Los Angeles to help put Cohen behind bars.

Commencing on May 2, 1961, Mickey's second tax trial lasted forty-one days. The prosecution called 194 witnesses and provided nearly a thousand exhibits to prove that Cohen had evaded taxes during the years 1956–58 and that he owed the government more than $400,000 ($3.1 million today) — plus interest and penalties.

Half of the Los Angeles IRS office worked on the case, and collateral support came from seventeen other tax districts. It was revealed that Treasury agents tried to locate Cohen's assets, not just in Los Angeles but also in Independence, California; Cambridge, Massachusetts; Tucson; El Paso; New Orleans; Miami; and St. Louis. Prosecuting the case was Assistant U.S. Attorney Thomas R. Sheridan, who was one of Robert Kennedy's top men. Jack Dahlstrum, a former marine who had passed the bar just three years before, handled Mickey's defense.

The majority of the witnesses were subpoenaed. "Paper evidence seemed to do the job in this case but people were the keys to the truth in the Cohen trial, with nightmares often plaguing the witnesses forced to testify against Mickey," noted journalist Ed Reid. "Many witnesses were called; a few took the Fifth Amendment."

The first thing the government proved: when Mickey Cohen talked, people listened — *very carefully*. The jurors learned details of Mickey's profligate lifestyle. They were shown examples of extraordinary items, like the fabulous 12 1/2 carat diamond ring that had been the community property of Mickey and LaVonne before the earlier tax trial — and was still part of his holdings.

Testimony showed that most of the "loans" given to Mickey were provided with the hope and anticipation of rewards from the sale of his book and a movie. Dr. Leonard Krause, a psychiatrist who claimed he wanted to study Mickey's obsessive-compulsive disorder, invested more than

$25,000 in the projects. So did retired Nashville shoe manufacturer Max Feigenbaum. Jukebox distributor Aubrey V. Stembler invested $15,000, while businesswoman Ruth Fisher, of Los Angeles, invested $7,500. Carhop Jesse Belle Heavilon loaned him $3,000, which was repaid, and another $7,000 that wasn't. And Ben Hecht made an appearance.

Two of the biggest stars in Hollywood were paraded before the jury. Mickey's plan to play himself in the proposed Mickey Cohen movie was brought out by the prosecution, although Jerry Lewis revealed the mobster had asked him to play the role. Lewis testified that he passed, but pledged $5,000, and suggested Robert Mitchum, tall, handsome, and goyish, for the lead. The comic/director explained to the jury that any part in which he became involved "should deal with levity — for some strange reason that's what people expect from me. It would be difficult for me to apply myself to this concept."

Next up was Red Skelton, another comedy legend. Lewis kibitzed with Skelton as he got down from the stand: "Let's see how funny you're going to be. Let's see if you get a laugh." Skelton told a familiar story of a seemingly one-sided, but steady, relationship with the mobster — and the fact that hefty loans were involved.

Charles Schneider, a tree surgeon from Cincinnati, testified to paying Cohen $2,350 ($17,500 today) to promote the singing career of his twelve-year-old daughter. Pleased with the results, Schneider explained that the mobster arranged a private audition at Skelton's home and introduced them to Frank Sinatra, Danny Thomas, Bobby Darin, Ginger Rogers, Walter Winchell, Edward G. Robinson, and other luminaries. Due to Mickey's efforts, the youngster appeared on several television shows.

Liz Renay and Candy Barr, brought in from their respective prisons, testified about Mickey Cohen — and his money. Stripper Miss Beverly Hills provided evidence of a Cadillac and a four-carat engagement ring given to her by her one-time fiancé, Mickey Cohen.

Welterweight champion Don Jordan appeared, and Lillian Weiner, the gangster's gray-haired sister, and her college student son, testified. The relatives were grilled about the finances of Mickey's various businesses and assorted bank accounts.

When the spectacle ended after the fortieth day, federal Judge George H. Boldt spent more than two hours on instructions. The jury was given a thirty-nine-page index of exhibits introduced during the trial and sequestered in a downtown hotel. After twenty-two and a half hours of deliberations, a verdict was reached. Hands clasped before him, Cohen bowed his head when the decision was read. The Los Angeles gang boss was found guilty of eight counts of income tax evasion. He told reporters, "They convicted me because I am Mickey Cohen. They thought they had to."

At the sentencing Judge Boldt made this statement:

> The record in this case shows that since 1955, he has followed a fantas- tically extravagant way of living without paying any income tax and without producing employment or visible means of self-support.
>
> Within a very short time of release [from his 1951 tax conviction] Mr. Cohen was in full flight on a profligate style of living financed by many fraudulent or extorted so-called loans in a very large aggregate amount. The fact that the defendant ingratiates himself into, at least a speaking acquaintance, with a number of prominent and respectable people and that he used them and their names in effecting his frauds does not minimize his misconduct, in which neither religion, patriotism, friendship, sorrow, or fear were excepted by Mr. Cohen as a means toward his unprincipled ends.

Sentenced to a staggering fifteen years in the 1961 verdict, his time was to be served in Alcatraz. Outstripping the unprecedented twelve years Al Capone received in 1931 for tax evasion, Mickey Cohen received the longest penalty ever handed out for tax violations. The veteran of countless courtroom dramas continued to work the system: motions and appeals started immediately. Control of the rackets had already been placed in the hands of others.

Friends, attorneys, and civil libertarians argued it was cruel and unusual punishment to be incarcerated in Alcatraz for a white-collar crime. The most vilified and notorious maximum-security prison in the nation, Alcatraz was reserved for violent hard cases exclusively, "real desperadoes," as Cohen would describe them; the only other tax offender ever placed there had been Alphonse Capone.

Cohen loudly claimed that his civil rights had been abused — and that the extraordinary punishment was a special present from Attorney General Robert F. Kennedy.

Set on a rocky island in the middle of San Francisco Bay, ancient Alcatraz was cold, filthy, dark, damp, and decrepit. Literally falling apart from a half-century of saltwater erosion, the appalling conditions were inhumane. There were no educational or rehabilitation classes and few activities or basic conveniences. Known as the "land of forgotten men," it was hell for every prisoner, let alone Hollywood's most pampered obsessive-compulsive.

"No newspapers, no magazines, no commissary, no nothing . . . In the middle of the ocean. And clammy wet all the time," Mickey railed.

When attorney Melvin Belli complained after visiting his high-profile client, the warden told him, "We don't rehabilitate them. We just warehouse them!"

Legendary criminals were among the sixty-seven inmates still held in the facility that once housed four times that number. Cohen's prison mates included Frankie Carbo, Harlem boss Bumpy Johnson, and Alvin "Creepy" Karpis, one of Hoover's infamous "Public Enemies," as well as a violent young punk, James "Whitey" Bulger, who later became notorious as Boston's answer to Mickey Cohen.

Eighty-two days after his arrival, Mickey Cohen became the first prisoner ever bailed out of Alcatraz. Pending appeal, his $100,000 bond was put up by Paoli's, an exclusive restaurant in San Francisco, and signed by Associate Justice of the U.S. Supreme Court William O. Douglas. A graduate of Yale and the former head of the Securities and Exchange Commission, the Chicago-born attorney was a believer in liberal causes and, particularly, First Amendment rights. Mickey professed that Drew Pearson, the prominent Washington political columnist, had championed his plight to Justice Douglas. Upon his release, the mobster told the press he planned to take five showers and send the esteemed jurist a "thank-you" card.

Eight years later, headed by Representative (and future president) Gerald Ford, a movement began to remove Justice Douglas from the Supreme Court. It was precipitated by dubious business connections that spoke directly to underworld ties, namely the lifetime seat Douglas held on the board of the controversial Albert S. Parvin Foundation.

*Mickey hides from cameras
as he heads back to Alcatraz
for another tax evasion
conviction. 1962.*

Parvin-Dohrmann Inc., which provided the visible source of funding for the charitable foundation, appeared to be a straitlaced corporation dealing in hotel supplies and furnishings. But there were claims it was also a front, holding the controlling shares of Bugsy Siegel's Flamingo Hotel for hidden interests. Old and notorious names associated with Parvin-Dorhrmann cropped up. When the Flamingo was sold to Miami Beach hotelier Morris Landsburgh in 1960, it was Meyer Lansky who received a tidy $200,000 (nearly $1.5 million today) finder's fee. When an investigation was launched into the foundation's suspicious ties, Justice Douglas was pulled into the scandal.

With Mickey free, the FBI began sending memos to other branches of government and police departments stating, "COHEN HAS KILLED IN THE PAST AND SHOULD BE CONSIDERED ARMED AND DANGEROUS," and that the "Top Hoodlum" might flee the country.

For Cohen, it was back to L.A. and the program.

On March 2, 1962, *Time* reported:

> Less than 24 hours after he was sprung from jail on $100,000 bail, pending appeal of a 15-year tax-dodging rap, California Gambling Ganglord Mickey Cohen, 50, was accused of clobbering a Teamsters' picket with

*Sandy Hagen and a placid Mickey Cohen at the Jack Whalen murder trial.
He was not convicted of the crime. 1962.*

his own signboard. The donnybrook, which the short-fused mobster attributed to an anti-Semitic slur, was blamed by his foe on Cohen's unprovoked truculence (sample printable quote: 'I own this local, and you are out!'). This time Mickey only had to drop a niggling $1,050 bond to return to the suburban Van Nuys bungalow he shares with Showgirl Sandy Hagen, 22, an arrangement, Cohen assures his stirred-up bourgeois neighbors, "has been okayed by her parents and my parents."

At the time of his release, a grand jury convened to reexamine the Jack Whalen murder case. With new evidence, Mickey Cohen and four of his men, including Sam LoCigno, were indicted for murder and conspiracy to commit murder.

The *Los Angeles Times* covered Mickey's appeal for bond: "Ever the personification of sartorial splendor, Cohen was nattily dressed for his court appearance but Phillips [bondsman Abe Phillips] carried a set of 'old clothes.'

"'It's just a complete roust,' lamented Cohen about the indictment. 'I'm getting tired of being the whipping boy around here.'"

Denied bail in the Whalen case, he changed his clothes. Continuing his spiel on the way to the booking office, Cohen's last comment was to bondsman Phillips: "Take good care of my hat."

In the spring of 1962, Mickey went on trial in the Jack Whalen murder case. The jury deadlocked. Superior Court Judge Lewis Drucker dismissed all charges, stating there was insufficient evidence to pursue a second indictment. In a footnote, LoCigno would be tried again. Found guilty of manslaughter in a third trial, he served a short prison term for his role in the Whalen homicide.

Having exhausted a final appeal to the United States Supreme Court in the tax case, Mickey Cohen was imprisoned again, at Alcatraz, on May 15, 1962. His full-term release date was December 13, 1976. The first date for a parole eligibility hearing was December 1966. He would be fifty-three.

24

RELIC

*"See, I have been blown up
in the Hollywood way."*
MICKEY COHEN

A ttorney General Robert Kennedy closed Alcatraz in March 1963. Mickey Cohen spent less than a year there and had been transferred to the federal penitentiary at Atlanta the month before. In October 1962, at Alcatraz, the mobster gave a confidential statement to Richard Rogan, a representative from California Governor Edmund "Pat" Brown's office. In it, he made allegations of an association with former Vice President Richard M. Nixon, dating back to the 1940s, and he claimed to have met the politician and raised funds for his early campaigns

Early in Cohen's stay at Atlanta, Bobby Kennedy visited the prison. There were several official versions as to what happened between the bitter adversaries. Mickey claimed that Kennedy confronted him in the shower and made a seductive offer that things would be good — if he cooperated. The LAPD was informed that Kennedy and Cohen had a talk that lasted more than thirty minutes. The FBI's investigation stated that Cohen approached Kennedy as he circulated through the prison and only exchanged a few passing words.

The Feds had recently flipped another Atlanta prisoner with an OC jacket. While serving a long sentence for narcotics trafficking, New York boss Vito Genovese had been running his family from the Atlanta pen. Joe Valachi, a low-echelon soldier also incarcerated there, was suspected of becoming an informant. Genovese issued a contract on him. In June 1962, Valachi, armed with a lead pipe, killed the man he thought to be his assassin. Facing a murder conviction, Valachi put himself in the arms of the law. The first insider willing to speak of the inner workings of the Mafia, he began preparing for a starring role in the latest installment of Senator McClelland's ongoing investigation into organized crime. Guarded by some two hundred federal marshals, Valachi was scheduled to testify before the televised senate committee. To charge the spectacle further, the senators would have readily welcomed a name with Mickey Cohen's star power.

But conjecture was soon put to rest. In a cataclysmic turn of fortune, on August 14, 1963, Mickey Cohen's life lay in limbo. Wielding a three-foot iron pipe, fellow convict Burl Estes McDonald bludgeoned Mickey in the head. Hit multiple times from behind, Cohen sustained a six-inch-long by three-inch-wide wound to the back of his head that was one and a half inches deep. X-rays of the depressed fracture showed skull bone had been driven into his brain. Neurosurgery was performed, saving his life. He remained in a coma for two weeks and was given a spinal tap. In another surgery, a steel plate was placed inside his skull.

Surviving the brutal beating with his mental faculties intact, the man who had long dominated the Los Angeles underworld with a daunting combination of chutzpah and muscle would be crippled for life.

The events surrounding the murder attempt seemed eerily reminiscent of Valachi's convict killing. With reports that Mickey Cohen was near death, speculation spread of underworld reprisals against him, among them payback from Fred Whalen for the murder of his son, Jack. Unsure as to the true circumstances surrounding the attempt on Cohen's life, authorities moved him from Atlanta and segregated him in protective lockup at the federal prison's medical facility at Springfield, Missouri. He would remain in isolation there for the next four years.

On November 22, 1963, the nation went into shock with the assassination of President John F. Kennedy in Dallas. Two days later, Jack Ruby — a well-known local strip club owner with law enforcement and press contacts, as well as underworld alliances — shot and killed Lee Harvey Oswald, the president's alleged assassin, while television cameras rolled.

The killing of the president was a case of many roads that led to L.A. JFK had spent much time in the city, where he engaged in reckless, sex-fueled parties at a Santa Monica beach house used by his brother-in-law Peter Lawford. Frank Sinatra, Marilyn Monroe, and a bevy of discreet party girls at Mickey Cohen's beck and call often attended the gatherings. Cohen recalled, "They were all starlets I kept company with. They weren't prostitutes, wouldn't go to bed with any Tom, Dick, or Harry . . . Some of them discussed with me what was going on at . . . [the beach] house."

And that wasn't all. A contemporary of Cohen's, Chicago-born Jack Ruby lived in that city while Mickey resided there and frequented the Kit Howard gymnasium with champion boxer Barney Ross, whom Cohen knew. Ruby lived in California during the 1940s. Later, in Dallas, he was an intimate friend of Candy Barr's. Candy and Ruby had been in close contact since her release from prison the past April, and FBI agents interviewed her about their relationship just hours after Ruby executed Oswald.

Mickey's friend and attorney Melvin Belli made headlines when he took on Ruby's defense. Johnny Rosselli, a staple of the L.A. underworld, was rumored to have been involved in a conspiracy to kill President Kennedy. And it went deeper. Some claimed Rosselli was Kennedy's true assassin.

As the nation mourned the death of the glamorous president, partially paralyzed Mickey Cohen continued his slow, difficult recovery and conferred with legal experts in the Missouri prison. The IRS auctioned off forty-three pieces of his jewelry in December. The most valuable item was LaVonne's enormous diamond ring. Other items included a heavy gold key chain, a gold house key, a gold pen set, sapphire and gold cuff links, a tie tack with two gold dice studded in diamonds and rubies, and assorted expensive watches. A novelty — the only piece of costume jewelry in the selection — was Candy Barr's engagement ring. The collection fetched $20,000 (about $140,000 today).

In February 1964, using the Torts Claim Act, a new law that granted prisoners the right to sue the federal government, a team of lawyers filed a landmark $10 million suit: Meyer Harris Cohen vs. the United States. The suit charged the prison had failed to protect him from a psychotic assailant, which resulted in the assault that caused brain damage and irreversible paralysis.

The next month, the civil liberties attorney A.L. Wirin requested that Mickey be released on a medical parole. In a handwritten twelve-page document the gangster described his humble beginnings and lack of education, and expounded on sundry unfortunate circumstances that led to a life of crime. Signatures from 305 respectable citizens supported the document. Copies were sent to the Department of Justice and forwarded to the new president, Lyndon B. Johnson. The request was denied.

In February 1965, Mickey Cohen, age fifty-one, was flown to Los Angeles. The IRS had filed suit to collect nearly $350,000 (approximately $3.5 million today) plus fines and interest from the years 1945 through 1950. The *Los Angeles Times* noted, "His arrival at the AiResearch Corporation pad at International Airport was as closely guarded as if he were a high government official on a secret mission."

Avoiding curious press, and the possibility of the infliction of additional bodily harm, the government carefully protected the prisoner. Severely debilitated, Cohen was transported to the jail facility at County General Hospital, where he remained under heavy guard. Since his transfer to Springfield, nearly eighteen months before, it was the first time he had been in open air. Hobbling into the courtroom with the aid of a three-prong metal cane, white-haired Mickey Cohen watched as Jack Dahlstrum argued for dismissal. The motion was denied. Proceeds from the jewelry auction amounting to $15,000 were credited to his tax bill, and the convict was sent back to Springfield Penitentiary's medical facility.

He was in an Atlanta courtroom on the last day of January 1966. Meyer Harris Cohen vs. the United States was heard without a jury before federal judge Sidney O. Smith Jr. Informed of the grievous and extensive injuries that Mickey had sustained, Judge Smith listened intently to his testimony.

His attacker, Burl Estes McDonald, originally sentenced to ten years for forgery and mail obstruction, had a history of psychotic behavior and was involved in a series of assaults while at Leavenworth Penitentiary. In 1962 McDonald drew another ten years for assault with intent to commit murder. At Atlanta, he was confined to an isolated structure for dangerous inmates. However, McDonald had inexplicably managed to make his way from the maximum-security facility, scale a fence, and travel into a building that housed the prison's general population to kill Mickey Cohen.

Ruling in favor of the mobster, Judge Smith awarded Cohen a judgment of $110,000. The IRS immediately garnisheed the entire award.

As Mickey Cohen sat in a wheelchair in prison, the dynamics and mores of the country changed radically. Deeply entrenched in a wildly unpopular conflict in Vietnam, antiwar riots began ripping the nation apart. The Beatles, followed by scores of other British bands, had successfully invaded America; everyone was dancing to a brand-new tune. Responding to the youth quake, films, music, magazines, fashion, and advertising geared up to cater to the massive baby-boomer market. While the film business diminished, the record business, now nearly entirely based in L.A., mushroomed. Long-haired guys and mini-skirted girls revolutionized the legendary Sunset Strip. Mickey's old stomping ground became the epicenter of a new movement, the domain of thousands of teenagers who went there nightly to hear the greatest rock music in the world.

As the crowds on the Strip grew larger, the boys' hair grew longer. The names of the old clubs changed, and so did the acts. Once glamorous Ciro's was now called It's Boss. A singing duo, Sonny and Cher, who now reigned at the top of the music charts, were featured there. The omnipresent talent promoter Joe DeCarlo, who once represented Candy Barr, managed the couple. The Crescendo became The Trip, where top L.A. groups the Byrds and Love played. Formerly a bar, the Sea Witch featured a local band called The Doors. London Fog; Ben Frank's, the all-night diner; the Eating Affair; and ice cream parlor Fred C. Dobbs were packed. Another teen club, Pandora's Box, was the scene of the infamous Sunset Strip curfew riot, where sheriff's deputies tear-gassed hundreds of kids. *Chelsea Girls*, Andy Warhol's underground movie featuring perverse attitudes, casual nudity, and overt drug play, ran for months at the Cinematheque. The miniscule art-movie house was located in the alley behind where Cohen's shops once stood.

Along the Strip, previously empty sidewalks were jammed night and day with teenagers. Both sexes were resplendent in flowing chiffon, feathers, leathers, fur, flowers, and beads; their radios blaring "Purple Haze," cars clogged the street.

The celebrated thoroughfare may have seemed shockingly different, but in one way it hadn't changed. The fevered activity and open drug use fueled the underworld. Constantly morphing, the Hollywood mob met the demands of the times. Much of the action was monitored from Sneaky Pete's. Dense with flashy wise guys and aging ladies of the night, the pitch-black old-school steak joint was punctuated with glowing red lights. It looked like the mouth of hell to the teenyboppers of the Whiskey a Go Go next door.

But one thing was certain: Hollywood's acid-soaked kids had no memories of the gangland capers that had gone down in their Sunset wonderland. And none of them had ever heard of Mickey Cohen.

L.A.'s old-time mobsters were now dead or troubled. Captain Guy McAfee, gone in 1960 at age seventy-one, was fondly remembered as one of Las Vegas's most important citizens. Jimmy Utley died while incarcerated at Folsom, in 1962. He was buried in a potter's field. Joe Sica and Frankie Carbo were in prison. Johnny Rosselli and Allen Smiley, now in their sixties, were indicted with several others in a long-running card cheating scheme that targeted stars and wealthy businessmen at the members-only Beverly Hills Friars Club. Rosselli also faced immigration charges, and talk continued about his allegiance with the CIA and involvement in President Kennedy's assassination. He would eventually serve time for the Friars Club scheme.

Mickey's mortal enemy, LAPD Chief William H. Parker, passed away in 1966. His top aid, Captain James Hamilton, died the same year. A powerful eminence and keeper of countless confidential secrets, LAPD robbery-homicide Captain Jack Donahoe was the man in charge of the Black Dahlia investigation and hundreds of other cases that etched their way into the dark history of the city. Mickey remembered Big Jack Donahoe as a "tough son of a bitch," who in the early days arrested him thirty-two times on robbery charges and warned LaVonne about him. Later, according to Mickey, Donahoe became his "very, very closest of friends." In 1966

Donahoe took his secrets with him into death.

After twenty-six years as the sheriff of Los Angeles County, Eugene Biscailuz retired in 1958. Bestselling mystery writer Erle Stanley Gardner, creator of Perry Mason, called Biscailuz "[an] aristocrat to his finger tips, a competent executive, a courageous law enforcement officer, knows every inch of his empire, Los Angeles County, and is the connecting link between the picturesque pueblo of the past and the great, sprawling industrial center of the present."

Mickey Cohen respected the man, too. Sheriff Biscailuz passed away in 1969, at age eighty-six.

In June 1968, Bobby Kennedy was assassinated in Los Angeles. The Democratic Party's leading presidential candidate, he was celebrating a crucial primary win in the crowded ballroom of the Ambassador Hotel when he was shot and killed.

Palestinian-born Sirhan Sirhan, twenty-four, confessed to his murder. Theories ranged from Sirhan being a programmed "Manchurian candidate" to the existence of a second shooter who was the true assassin. Conspiracy theorists connected crippled prisoner Mickey Cohen with RFK's assassination. They noted the assassination occurred in Los Angeles, at the Ambassador Hotel, once an acknowledged Cohen stronghold, and that Sirhan had worked as a stable boy at Santa Anita racetrack, another center of Cohen activity. Lawyers representing Sirhan, A.L. Wirin and Russell E. Parsons, had also represented the mobster. Prominent attorney Grant Cooper, who later took on the Sirhan case, had represented Lila Leeds in the Robert Mitchum marijuana case and was currently the counsel of one of the gamblers involved in the Friars Club case.

There were many provocative connections, but there was no substantive evidence of a direct Mickey Cohen link in RFK's assassination.

Before the 1968 presidential election, Washington columnist Drew Pearson released Cohen's statement, made at Alcatraz in October 1962, where he described financing the early congressional campaigns of current presidential candidate Richard M. Nixon.

Mickey Cohen's statement:

I am presently serving a sentence in the federal prison in Alcatraz. At my request, I asked for a meeting with a state law enforcement officer, and on October 9, 1962, Richard R. Rogan met with me in the visitor's room at Alcatraz. I informed Mr. Rogan that I wanted to discuss with him a question concerning the influence of persons engaged in gambling and bookmaking on the early political career of Richard Nixon. I first met Richard Nixon at a luncheon in the Goodfellow's Fisherman's Grotto on South Main Street in 1948. The meeting was arranged by Murray Chotiner, who asked me to meet Mr. Nixon, who was about to start his first campaign as a representative in Congress that year. I was asked by Nixon and Chotiner to raise some money for Nixon's campaign. In either 1948 during Nixon's second race for Congress or 1950 in his campaign for the seat, I was again asked by Murray Chotiner to raise funds for Nixon's campaign. During that time I was running most of the gambling and bookmaking in Los Angeles County. I reserved the Banquet Room in the Hollywood Knickerbocker Hotel in Ivar Street in Hollywood for a dinner meeting to which I invited approximately 250 guests who were working with me in the gambling fraternity. Among those who were present, whose names are well known by the law enforcement officers, were Joe and Fred Sica, Jack Dragna, and George Capri. Also present were Hy Goldbaum, who is one of the pit bosses at the Stardust Hotel in Las Vegas, who also served a term of imprisonment at the federal prison at McNeil Island. Capri was one of the owners of the Flamingo Hotel in Las Vegas. Murray Chotiner told me I should have a quota of $25,000 for the campaign. During the course of the evening Nixon spoke for approximately 10 minutes. Chotiner spoke for half an hour. At this meeting my group pledged between $17,000 and $19,000 but this did not meet the quota set by Nixon and Chotiner and the group was informed they would have to stay until the quota was met. In addition to helping Mr. Nixon financially, I made arrangements to rent a headquarters for Nixon in the Pacific Finance Building at Eighth and Olive Streets in Los Angeles, which was the same building occupied by Attorney Sam Rummel. We posted Nixon signs and literature, and I paid for the headquarters for three to four weeks in that building. During the period that I ran the Nixon Headquarters, I contacted most of the gambling fraternity who started him off with $25,000. There have been no promises made to me of any kind or nature and the above statement has been given by me freely and voluntarily.

Drew Pearson wrote in summary: "What the gamblers got in return is spelled out in the records of the Los Angeles County court between 1949 and 1952, which show that Nixon's campaign manager, Murray Chotiner, and his brother [attorney Albert Jack Chotiner] acted as attorney in 221 bookmaking and underworld cases. In almost all instances their clients got off with light fines or suspended sentences."

In August 1969, events spun out of control: L.A. went into lockdown after two sets of unimaginably gruesome murders. In Benedict Canyon, beautiful starlet Sharon Tate, eight-months pregnant with director Roman Polanski's child, and four others were viciously butchered. The next night, eight miles east, in the quiet, affluent Los Felix neighborhood, Rosemary and Leno LaBianca were slaughtered in their home. The heinous ritualistic killings were masterminded by Charles Manson, a psychotic megalomaniac with grandiose Hollywood dreams, and executed by members of the Family, his drug-crazed cult.

In January 1972, Mickey Cohen, fifty-eight, returned to Los Angeles after serving more than ten years of his sentence for tax evasion.

"Dapper, loquacious and free spending in his days as the clown prince of the Los Angeles underworld," the *Los Angeles Times* noted of Cohen in an article that spotlighted his homecoming and recapped his long, violent career. The crippled mobster told reporters, "I don't want nothing — no publicity, no notoriety," as he gamely struggled up the daunting steps of downtown's federal courthouse accompanied by James Smith, his constant companion and physical therapist. There for his first probation hearing, Cohen was told he would remain under the supervision of a parole officer until late 1976.

Richard Nixon was now president. The Vietnam conflict entered its eleventh year. Eight years into society's seismic shift, the Sunset Strip had finally begun to cool down. The music was still there, but the days of the exalted, unending street party had waned. The great music stars were either dead — like Hendrix, Joplin, and Morrison — or playing huge stadiums. The teenagers from the years before had moved on.

The bright and cheery Partridge family may have played on TV, but the tone on Sunset was now dark and intense. The music and drugs were hard: Zeppelin, glitter rock, cocaine, and heroin. Frequenting the scene were baby-faced nymphets and big-haired rockers wearing theatrically streaked black makeup, spandex, and sequins. The Largo strip club had been reinvented as the Roxy, a prime music venue. The latest stars of music and movies held court at On the Rox, the ultra-exclusive private club upstairs. It was once the stripper's dressing room, and Mickey Cohen had appeared there nightly a mere decade before.

Backgammon, a board game first played in ancient Persia, by the early 1970s had become the passion of countless gilt-edged Angelenos. Servicing the gambling fad, Pips' quickly became the hottest club in town. Private and located on South Robertson Boulevard in the county territory of Beverly Hills, the scene was scorching. Pips' owners included *Playboy* founder Hugh Hefner, high-end realtor Stan Herman, and financier Bernie Cornfeld. Cornfeld would soon become internationally notorious when his offshore mutual fund, Investors Overseas Limited (IOS), imploded. A brazen Ponzi scheme, the mutual fund was heavily invested in casinos. The gambling club's fourth partner, ubiquitous talent manager Joe DeCarlo, made his presence felt.

Holed up in his modest West L.A. digs at 1014 Westgate, Apartment 316, Mickey Cohen still carried a thick bankroll and traveled, often to San Francisco and Monterey. Members of his old gang and legitimate businessmen remained indebted to him. He opened charge accounts that went unpaid and received a $25,000 start-up gift from Frank Sinatra. Evangelist Jim Vaus, his former wiretapper, gave Cohen money and made the talk show rounds with him.

There was talk Mickey retained major bookmaking action and owned pieces of restaurants. He carefully avoided any situation that might end his parole and send him back to prison. A new law, a federal anti-racketeering statute, commonly called RICO, had caught his attention. It had been

If looks could kill, the photographer would be dead. Disabled Mickey Cohen seeks privacy at his brother Harry's funeral. 1973.

instituted to ensnare characters precisely like him. His giant debt to the government, dating back to 1946, was still on the IRS's books. Bankroll or not, the fact he was forced to live a diminished lifestyle infuriated him.

The year Mickey returned was surprisingly fortuitous. Suddenly fedora-wearing mobsters were as fashionable as Bowie and backgammon after interest in vintage gangland was piqued by the monumental success of *The Godfather* movie. A book deal was consummated for Mickey to tell the story of the bad old days.

But his return was not seamless. Mickey's brother, seventy-year-old Harry Cohen, who had been his main contact during his years in the penitentiary and a fixture in his post-prison life, was killed in January 1973. The papers reported he was run over by a mysterious black vehicle near his Oxford Avenue home. An all-points bulletin went out for the hit-and-run vehicle, but they never found the car or driver.

From the Meyer Harris Cohen FBI file:

—— stated that COHEN took the death of his brother, HARRY, hard, but philosophically since he feels COHEN has been around so much death, that he is hardened even when death strikes his own brother. —— said COHEN wanted to carry a gun since COHEN believes some young hood might try to "hit him" to build up their reputation.

Mickey liked an occasional drink now. He would periodically visit the West Side Room, Hefner's Playboy Club on the Strip, and the Etc. bar. He purportedly became a hidden owner of Gatsby's, a fashionable new restaurant in Brentwood, which was rumored to offer gambling action. He dined there often, and at La Famiglia, another trendy restaurant that had recently opened in Beverly Hills.

As in the past, Mickey Cohen continued to escort gorgeous women. Actress Lita Baron, the ex-wife of film star Rory Calhoun, was seen on his arm. He also squired Edy Williams, the bodacious leading lady of *Beyond the Valley of the Dolls*, the most outrageous picture to ever come out of the studio system. Another unbridled publicity hound, the starlet was going through an acrimonious divorce from her director husband, soft-core schlockmeister Russ Meyer. The thirty-three-year-old brunette purred of her escort Mickey, "He's my Sir Galahad. He's incredibly strong: I only hope some of his strength rubs off on me."

The frenzied pace of his past days had slowed dramatically, but Mickey Cohen still loved the press. But now the man who said "All I need to do is spit out the window to get a story" had to make a special effort to get attention. Somewhat reconciled with his new existence, the once-feared underworld boss declared, "My heyday is long past." The *Los Angeles Times* observed, "That heyday was a study in violence."

Merv Griffin had him on his talk show; Mickey repeated his trademark lines. Appearing on local programs whenever he could, he often added color commentary to prizefights and was seen as a talking head on a documentary about the underworld.

At the Greater Los Angeles Press Club luncheon held in his honor, he sat on the dais repeatedly wiping his hands with a wet napkin that he dipped into a glass of water. The aging mobster observed, "I just can't get used to seeing what I am seeing. The crime scene is saturated with 'freaks.'" Blaming the "drug scene" for most of the problems, he unabashedly claimed

Mickey Cohen, ready for his close-up. The press came, but the photo and story never ran. 1975.

to have — just recently — encountered his first marijuana cigarette. "What's lacking in society today, I think, is nobody has any shame whatsoever, no respect whatsoever, no pride."

In October 1974, major coverage came again when he attached himself to a story that had been dominating the headlines for months. Patricia Hearst, twenty, granddaughter of the late newspaper tycoon William Randolph Hearst, had been kidnapped the past February by the Symbionese Liberation Army (SLA), a homegrown terrorist group. The SLA was exactly the kind of "freaks" who offended Mickey Cohen.

By April, suffering from Stockholm syndrome, the young heiress had assumed the nom de guerre Tania and pledged herself to the SLA. Captured by security cameras, Patty Hearst made the FBI's "most wanted" list when she was identified as the woman wielding an M1 carbine and shouting orders to captives while members of the SLA robbed a San Francisco bank and killed a hostage.

Her father, Randolph Hearst, offered a $50,000 reward for information leading to his daughter's recovery. Never missing an opportunity, Mickey Cohen "volunteered" his services to the desperate parents. Personally meeting with Randolph and Catherine Hearst at Gatsby's, the former headline-maker for the Hearst chain discussed a plan to locate the young woman. Much chatter followed. But that was all. Mickey got some heavy press coverage, but nothing substantial happened. Some papers alleged that before taking the "assignment," he touched the Hearsts for a $20,000 down payment.

In the fall of 1975, after intense negotiations with the IRS about dispersal of monetary payments, the latest incarnation of the retired mobster's long gestating autobiography was slated to appear. The bestseller lists were topped by mobster revelations. Lucky Luciano had been working with a writer about his life, while negotiating a deal with Hollywood producers, when he succumbed to an apparent heart attack in 1962. The literary collaboration *The Last Testament of Lucky Luciano*, was finally released, to great fanfare, in 1975.

With the death of Frank Costello in 1972, Meyer Lansky was the last living member of the gang that had created organized crime. Speaking to Israeli journalists about his gangster life, the Lansky book, *Mogul of the Mob*, would prove to be another hit. In it he sent a love note to Cohen, giving him credit for making the Teamsters connection. The Mickey Cohen saga seemed like a natural, and publisher McGraw-Hill made plans for the gangster to do what he did best: publicize *Mickey Cohen: In My Own Words*.

But finally the fates caught up with him.

He put on a brave front, but perhaps Mickey Cohen no longer had the energy to seduce and sell. The fire and drive that made him run may finally have waned. Diagnosed with terminal cancer, part of his stomach was removed in October 1975.

The next month he was in New York. Crippled and now dying, the man who plundered Los Angeles in a decades-long crime wave passed through the great marble corridor of the luxurious Pierre Hotel. He knew it was his last hurrah.

Looking older than his sixty-two years by at least a decade, the tiny, frail figure sat in an opulent suite, a clean white sheet draped over his armchair. Locked in his own version of *Sunset Boulevard*, the memories, secrets, and faces of ten thousand bloody midnights flashed through his

Mickey Cohen, sixty-two, the violent and complicated little Angeleno who captivated, corrupted and terrorized Los Angeles for more than a generation, faces the last round-up. 1976.

brain. The show went on: Mickey Cohen met the press.

Recalling only the biggest, most newsworthy names, he hawked away for the final time: recently "disappeared" Jimmy Hoffa, Reverend Billy Graham, Bugsy Siegel, Patricia Hearst. Of President Nixon, disgraced and forced to resign the presidency after the Watergate scandal the year before, Mickey said, "He was a big help to me in my operation in Orange County . . . but if you ever told me he would have been president, I would have died laughing."

Giving his all, he did not disappoint, playing it like a netherworld version of P.T. Barnum.

But his self-serving book, long, rambling, and dense, would not be a hit.

The ultimate survivor died peacefully in his sleep after midnight on July 29, 1976. The cause of death was listed as complications of stomach cancer. His death generated the major press coverage he lived for. The Hollywood dream had never died for Michael Mickey Cohen, the newsboy and kid fighter from East L.A. A dangerous man, full of bluster, violence, charm, greed, grandiosity, obsession, deception, chutzpah, and occasionally self-realization — he understood his time and place. Mickey Cohen was about Los Angeles.

As he reflected in his autobiography, "See, I have been blown up in the Hollywood way . . . in Chicago, Philadelphia, Boston, or New York, I would have been . . . lost in the shuffle, an ordinary high-rolling gambler.

"It's a different situation out here."

The remains of Meyer Harris Cohen were placed in the Alcove of Love at Hillside Cemetery in Culver City, the resting place of many celebrities. Situated in crypt A-217, in the second drawer from the bottom in a massive wall, his plaque reads, "Our Beloved Brother, Meyer H. Cohen, Mickey, 1914–1976."

Approximately 150 mourners attended the private service.

FADE TO BLACK

Cast of Characters

Allen, Brenda Hollywood's madam-to-the-stars after World War II, she allegedly operated in partnership with highly ranked members of LAPD vice squad, archenemies of Mickey Cohen. A major scandal involving Allen and officers was triggered by Cohen, and sullied important police and political figures.

Annenberg, Moses (Moe) As Hearst newspapers' "circulation chief" early in the twentieth century, under his management fighting newsboys and mob-style tactics were used to place the tabloids. Later he bought the *Daily Racing Form* and two major newspapers, and acquired enormous wealth with a monopolistic news wire service that, in an arm's length association with the underworld, legally supplied the instant racing data necessary to control illegal gambling on a national scale. He pleaded guilty to income tax evasion in 1939. The patriarch of legendary philanthropists.

Barr, Candy (born Juanita Slusher) Fiery exotic dancer from Texas. At fifteen, the stunning, bodacious blonde starred in a legendary hard-core porno, *Smart Alec*. In 1959, she was briefly Mickey Cohen's fiancée. She was close to Jack Ruby, assassin of the alleged assassin of President John F. Kennedy.

Belli, Melvin (King of Torts) Famous attorney who first received major publicity in the late 1950s, as Mickey Cohen's counsel.

Biscailuz, Eugene Sheriff of Los Angeles County, 1932–1958. A colorful and powerful man from a prominent California family, the rise of Mickey Cohen occurred during his term.

Bulger, James (Whitey) Violent young hoodlum who served time in Alcatraz with Mickey Cohen. After his release from prison, Bulger became the Mickey Cohen of Boston. A legendary fugitive, he was captured while living in Santa Monica, California, in 2011.

Capone, Al (The Big Fella; Scarface) Murderous, showboating Chicago mob boss who, during Prohibition, became the most famous underworld figure in the world. Like Cohen, he was born in Brownsville, Brooklyn, and was later imprisoned in Alcatraz for tax evasion. Brain-damaged from syphilis, Capone died in 1947. He was the idol and role model of Mickey Cohen.

Carbo, Paul John (Frankie; Mr. Gray) Codefendant with his friend Bugsy Siegel in L.A.'s first eastern syndicate murder (of Harry Greenberg), he was rumored to be the executioner in the unsolved assassination of Siegel in 1947. He became the underworld's "boxing czar" after Siegel's death, reputedly involved in televised boxing and the careers of fighters Primo Carnero, Jake LaMotta, and Sonny Liston, among others.

Chandler, Raymond L.A.'s premier noir novelist, also a screenwriter. In each of his seven novels, dark Angeleno color is beautifully detailed. Chandler changed names to protect the "innocent" (as well as the names of vividly described locations). Protagonist PI Philip Marlowe visits a gambling ship in *Farewell, My Lovely* (1940), and in his 1949 novel, *The Little Sister*, Sunny Moe Stein was inspired by Bugsy Siegel and Weepy Moyer/Steelgrave by Mickey Cohen. As "in life," *The Little Sister* features beautiful but dangerous starlets. The private house down a wooded lane in the novel's denouement is a fine replication of Cohen's so-called Mystery House, an illegal casino that ran on Hazen Drive in

Beverly Hills. The casino that Lauren Bacall's character visits in *The Big Sleep* (1946), a film adapted from Chandler's 1939 novel, is the cinematic representation of the same location.

Cohen, LaVonne (Simone King; Lani Butler; LaVonne Weaver) Mrs. Mickey Cohen from 1940 to 1958, the well-mannered, all-American beauty added a wholesome quality to his public image.

Combination, The Ignoring Mafia traditions, a revolutionary and highly successful underworld order where groups of disparate lineage and religions worked together for financial gain. The Combination was a concept instituted by New York mob legend Lucky Luciano, who had Jews and non-Sicilians as primary partners.

Contreras, George (The Ironman) A captain in the L.A. County Sheriff's Department who was reputed to oversee all illegal action in the territory. Originally the mortal enemy of Mickey Cohen, later, according to Cohen, "the fiery little Mexican sheriff became my very best friend." Contreras's death in 1945 caused problems for Cohen.

Cornero, Tony (The Hat) Powerful, independent L.A. mobster who was a major rumrunner during Prohibition. When squeezed out by the politically connected local syndicate, he inventively took his gaming operations offshore, beginning the era of L.A.'s gambling ships. Among the entertainment onboard was a teenage flamenco dancer, future screen goddess Rita Hayworth. Cornero was forced out of L.A. after Mickey Cohen's rise.

Costello, Frank (born Francesco Castiglia; The Prime Minister) Immensely powerful New York mob boss and the original partner of Lucky Luciano, Meyer Lansky, and Bugsy Siegel. Known for his superb political connections, after Lucky Luciano's imprisonment, Costello headed Luciano's Mafia family (later Genovese family), as well as the syndicate's national commission. He was married to a Jewish woman, Loretta "Bobbie" Geigerman, for more than fifty years, and inspired the impeccably tailored character Don Barzini in *The Godfather*. He was among Mickey Cohen's most influential sponsors.

Crane, Cheryl Daughter of movie legend Lana Turner. At fourteen, Crane became the central figure in Hollywood's most notorious whodunit: the stabbing death of her mother's lover, Cohen associate, Johnny Stompanato.

Crawford, Charlie (The Grey Fox) L.A.'s politically entrenched racket king of the Roaring Twenties. Never officially considered a gangster, Crawford's ties were to City Hall and the police, not the eastern syndicate. Sponsor and lover of Lee Francis, Hollywood's most prominent madam. Assassinated in 1931.

Dandolos, Nick (The Greek) Legendary professional gambler, who was a student of philosophy. He was a father figure to Mickey Cohen.

David, Dee (DaLonne Cooper) Hollywood beauty who was friendly with Mickey Cohen, and wounded during an attempt on his life in 1949. She later married and divorced Cohen's state assigned bodyguard, Special Agent Harry Cooper, and shot and wounded mobster Joe Sica during a business dispute.

di Frasso, Countess Dorothy Taylor American heiress (her brother was a governor of the NYSE) and flamboyant society figure celebrated for her fabulous wealth, glamorous and powerful friends, and extravagant lifestyle. Although she had affairs with movie stars Gary Cooper and Clark Gable, the great love of her life was Bugsy Siegel.

Douglas, William O. Former head of the Securities and Exchange Commission; as a U.S. Supreme Court judge, Douglas signed the bond to release Mickey Cohen from Alcatraz, making Cohen the first and only prisoner ever bailed out of the infamous prison.

Dragna, Jack (Ignacio Rizzotti) Ineffectual, old-school head of the L.A. Mafia. A relative of top New York boss, Tommy "Three Finger Brown" Lucchese, Dragna warred with Mickey Cohen. Unsuccessful in all of his eight attempts to assassinate Cohen, he never gained control of the territory.

Francis, Lee Legendary Hollywood madam who catered exclusively to prominent politicians, Hollywood stars and moguls, and international society figures, from 1921 to 1939. In 1940, she was arrested on the Sunset Strip with "Simone King," the future Mrs. Mickey Cohen.

Frattiano, Jimmy "The Weasel" Violent and ambitious Mafia hit man originally from Cleveland. A noted double crosser and informant, he played central roles in several Mickey Cohen plots.

Gangster Squad Small, secret LAPD Intelligence Unit, with a no-holds-barred policy, formed in late 1946 with the mandate: stop Mickey Cohen.

Giesler, Jerry (The Magnificent Mouthpiece) Los Angeles's most prominent criminal lawyer and fixer who represented the city's most illustrious and wealthiest figures, from mobsters to movies stars to business tycoons.

Graham, Reverend Billy Celebrated and widely respected Christian evangelist who prayed with presidents. Early in his career, he was unusually interested in the religious conversion of headline-making mobster Mickey Cohen.

Guarantee Finance Company A front for a huge illegal gambling empire that operated in L.A. County in the 1940s. Although never proven, it was alleged to be a Mickey Cohen operation.

Guasti, Al Captain in L.A. County Sheriff's Department. In 1945, he was reputedly selected by a "committee," which included Mickey Cohen, to handle corrupt activities in L.A. County. He served a prison sentence for his involvement in the Guarantee Finance case.

Guzik, Jake (Greasy Thumb; Jack) Former pimp and Capone's accountant, this plump, bland man was the titular head of Chicago outfit until his death in 1956. He was reputed to be a Mickey Cohen supporter.

Hagen, Sandy (born Claretta Hashagen) Young, blonde fiancée of Mickey Cohen who was present with him at the murder scene of his rival, Jack "The Enforcer" Whalen, in 1959.

Hearst, Patricia (Patty) Granddaughter of press magnate William Randolph Hearst, she was kidnapped in 1974 by the SLA, a domestic terrorist group. Brainwashed by the group, the young heiress soon became a criminal, appearing on the FBI's most wanted list. With the consent of the Hearst family, Mickey Cohen became involved in her case.

Hecht, Ben Academy Award–winning screenwriter, prominent journalist, and erstwhile Cohen biographer, Hecht brought Cohen to exclusive Hollywood parties and into international politics during the formation of the state of Israel.

Herbert, Edward (Neddie) Bodyguard and lieutenant of Mickey Cohen murdered in 1949 during an attempt on Cohen's life, at Sherry's restaurant on the Sunset Strip.

Hoffa, Jimmy Notorious president of the Teamsters union, who funded a massive mob building spree in Las Vegas, through the union's pension funds. Hoffa disappeared in 1975.

Hollywood Nite Life Movie business scandal sheet and shakedown vehicle that devastated Hollywood stars in the late 1940s; it was secretly financed by Mickey Cohen.

Howard, Mike (Meyer Horowitz) Tough, older "business manager" for Cohen, and buyer for Michael's, Cohen's exclusive Sunset Strip men's shop. Howard was a father figure to Cohen.

Howser, Frederick N. Former L.A. County DA who, as attorney general of California, assigned a special state agent to be Mickey Cohen's bodyguard.

Irgun Zvai Leumi A radical Zionist terrorist organization, active during the formation of the state of Israel in the 1940s. Mickey Cohen became involved with the group.

Jackson, E.V. (Elmer) LAPD vice officer and an alleged partner in Brenda Allen's call girl ring. An enemy of Cohen.

Kefauver, Estes U.S. senator (D-Tennessee) who headed Senate hearings into organized crime during 1950 and 1951. His committee publicly unveiled the workings and leading figures of the underworld, in most cases, for the first time. Later sessions of the Kefauver hearings were televised live and garnered astronomical ratings. In November 1950, Mickey Cohen was a star witness (before the hearings were televised).

Kennedy, Robert F. (Bobby; RFK) A member of the wealthy and legendary political family, who under his brother President John F. Kennedy was appointed attorney general of the United States. Among his greatest enemies was Mickey Cohen (along with Jimmy Hoffa and Carlos Marcello). RFK was assassinated in L.A., during his 1968 bid for the presidency.

Kleinman, Morris A former boxer, he was reputedly the member of Cleveland's "silent syndicate" who sponsored Cohen's early career as a professional boxer. In the mid-1930s, Kleinman served prison time for tax evasion. Beginning in the late 1940s, the Cleveland group developed the most valuable portfolio of holdings in Las Vegas.

Korshak, Sidney (Mr. Silk Stocking) Secretive and powerful labor lawyer and fixer, Korshak allegedly used high echelon fronts to promote lucrative business activities for the Chicago outfit in Los Angeles. He was a sought-after guest on the exclusive Beverly Hills–Bel-Air–Holmby Hills party circuit, and he was reportedly a special friend of 1960s movie actresses Jill St. John, a Bond girl, and Stella Stevens.

Lansky, Meyer (The Little Guy) An original partner of Lucky Luciano, Bugsy Siegel, and Frank Costello, and a criminal mastermind. For decades, he was arguably the most powerful man in the underworld, his reach dotting the world. Lansky was fictionalized as Hyman Roth in *The Godfather II*. In *Mogul of the Mob*, a 1979 biography of him in which he participated, he saluted Mickey Cohen for making the Teamsters' connection.

Leeds, Lila Notorious young starlet arrested in 1948 for marijuana possession with film star Robert Mitchum. After serving a short jail stint, she testified before a grand jury investigating a blackmail ring alleged to involve Mickey Cohen. She's notable as the beautiful receptionist in the 1946 film adaptation of Raymond Chandler's *Lady in the Lake*.

Lucchese, Tommy (Three Finger Brown) The popular head of one of New York's five Mafia families, he was related to L.A. Mafia boss Jack Dragna.

Luciano, Lucky (born Salvatore Lucania; Charlie Lucky; Mr. Charles Ross) Iconic, Sicilian-born New Yorker considered the most important leader in the underworld for decades. He innovatively syndicated and organized crime on a national basis, and brazenly ignored Mafia standards by partnering with Jewish mobsters, most notably Meyer Lansky and Bugsy Siegel, as well as Calabrian Frank Costello. Sentenced in 1936 to fifty years of prison time on a prostitution charge, he was deported permanently to Italy in 1947, where he continued to be involved in American rackets. After Siegel's execution, he approved Mickey Cohen as boss of L.A. He died of an apparent heart attack in 1962 while pursuing a cinematic version of his life story with Dean Martin touted for the lead.

Marcello, Carlos New Orleans Mafia boss with ties to Mickey Cohen. Along with Cohen and Jimmy Hoffa, he was a major enemy of U.S. Attorney General Robert F. Kennedy.

Mayfield Road Gang In a premiere example of the Combination, Cleveland's dominating Mafiosi — Anthony and Frank Milano, Alfred Polizzi, the Licavoli clan, and the Angersola (King) brothers — allied with the city's mainly Jewish "silent syndicate." They were entrenched with the wire service, as well as countless prime and diverse operations that extended throughout the Midwest, Canada, Las Vegas, Kentucky, Arizona, Colorado, Mexico, Miami, Cuba, and — through Mickey Cohen — the lucrative L.A. territory. The Mayfield Road Gang inspired the fictional Lakeville Road Boys in *The Godfather II*, mentioned by the Lansky-inspired character Hyman Roth. Top echelon mentors of Mickey Cohen from his teenage years.

McAfee, Guy (The Captain; The Whistler) Captain of the LAPD vice squad until 1924 when he officially became L.A. racket king Charlie Crawford's second in command. Reputed to be behind the execution of Crawford in 1931. With Crawford's death, McAfee became L.A.'s leading racketeer. Operating in partnership with local politicians and police, after a corruption scandal in 1938 brought down the mayor and LAPD brass, he moved to Las Vegas. One of Las Vegas's earliest and most prominent citizens, the Golden Nugget was among his holdings. He was alleged to maintain control of certain L.A. rackets. Second wife was starlet June Brewster. Prototype for Raymond Chandler's character Eddie Mars.

McDonald, Burl Estes A small time offender who, while incarcerated at the Atlanta penitentiary, attempted to assassinate fellow prisoner Mickey Cohen in August 1963.

McGee, Elihu (Black Dot) Dapper African-American businessman and racketeer who partnered with Mickey Cohen in L.A.'s South Central ghetto.

Meltzer, Harold (Happy) Convicted drug trafficker and mobster who played a central role in critical Mickey Cohen scenarios.

Milano, Anthony Top echelon leader from Cleveland's powerful Mayfield Road Gang. Starting in Cohen's teenage years, he became a lifelong father figure and prominent mentor to Mickey. From the 1940s, Milano and his family resided mainly in Los Angeles.

Muir, Florabel Highly regarded veteran journalist and broadcaster who became one of Mickey Cohen's closest and most influential confidants. The middle-aged woman was slightly wounded during one of the many attempts on Cohen's life.

Nealis, Eddie Handsome gambler who reputedly controlled rackets in L.A. County during the late 1930s and early 1940s, while fronting for Guy McAfee and Farmer Page. He battled with Cohen, as Bugsy Siegel began his drive to control the Los Angeles underworld. Producer of *Johnny O'Clock* (1947), a motion picture set in the gambling world.

Nixon, Richard M. Served as vice-president under President Dwight D. Eisenhower, 1953–1961. In 1969, he became the thirty-seventh president of the United States; he resigned in 1974 after the Watergate scandal. Mickey Cohen swore, under oath, of his personal and financial involvement in Nixon's early political campaigns in California.

O'Mara, Jack Original member of the LAPD's Gangster Squad; he infiltrated Mickey Cohen's home and serviced the illegal wiretap.

Page, Milton "Farmer" Prominent L.A. racketeer during the 1920s and '30s, who was partnered with former police captain Guy McAfee. Reputedly their rackets continued, headed by fronts, after they were forced to move to Las Vegas in 1938.

Parker, William H. Chief of the LAPD from 1950 to 1966. *Star Trek* creator Gene Roddenberry, once an LAPD officer who wrote speeches for Parker, was said to have based the Mr. Spock character on him. A prime enemy and irritant to Mickey Cohen.

Patriarca Sr., Raymond Providence-based boss of the New England underworld until his death in 1984. Alleged to have been both a secret owner of the Dunes Hotel, Las Vegas, and a Mickey Cohen supporter.

Renay, Liz Blonde bombshell associated with major New York underworld characters; she was publicly promoted as one of Cohen's girlfriends. Became involved in a "loan" scheme involving Cohen that had dire implications for both parties.

Richardson, James H. (Jim) Colorful editor of Hearst's *Los Angeles Examiner*, who was privy to the secrets of the city. Beginning in Cohen's newsboy days, Richardson was friendly with Mickey.

Robinson, Curly Prominent, well-connected L.A. figure who ran lucrative legitimate businesses in the gaming machines industry, which was legal under California law until the early 1950s. When Bugsy Siegel assigned Mickey Cohen to take over L.A. in the late 1930s, Robinson allegedly ran the L.A. County rackets with partner Eddie Nealis. According to Mickey Cohen, he became one of his hidden partners.

Rosselli, Johnny Mafioso who represented the Chicago outfit and wire service in Los Angeles from the late 1920s onwards. Strategist for L.A.'s Dragna family. The smooth womanizer was a close friend of studio head Harry Cohn, and was briefly married to beautiful actress June Lang. He was reputedly linked to the assassination of JFK.

Rothkopf, Lou (Lou Rhodi) According to authorities, one of the main partners in the Cleveland syndicate. Rothkopf was a top echelon mentor of Cohen and spent much time in Los Angeles. Found dead at his Cleveland-area farm in 1956; his death was ruled a suicide.

Rothman, Harry (Hooky) Mickey Cohen lieutenant, who was killed during an attempt on Cohen's life in 1948 at the Sunset Strip men's shop.

Ruditsky, Barney During Prohibition, he was a detective with the NYPD, working from a Manhattan precinct. He came west when Bugsy Siegel moved to L.A., becoming the top PI for the Hollywood set, and allegedly a conduit between mobsters and law enforcement. Present before authorities arrived at the Siegel murder scene, Ruditsky managed Cohen hangout, Sherry's restaurant. He was also present at the scene of a deadly massacre there, during a 1949 attempt on Cohen's life. He appeared in films as an extra, and a TV series, *The Lawless Years* (1959–1960), was based in his exploits as a police detective.

Rummel, Sam Top Los Angeles mob lawyer and fixer, who was alleged to be a high echelon partner of Mickey Cohen. He was executed in December 1950 in Laurel Canyon. The case remains unsolved.

Samish, Arthur Prominent, flamboyant California lobbyist who boasted that he manipulated and controlled state politics. He represented high-profile corporate clients and successfully mentored many high-level elected officials. A man Mickey Cohen honored and respected.

Seven Dwarfs Cohen associates Frank Niccoli, Neddie Herbert, Jim Rist, Lou Schwartz, Harold Meltzer, Dave Ogul, and Eli Lubin. In 1949, while acting as muscle, these men were unexpectedly arrested (for a traffic violation) in the midst of an operation alleged to be part of a major, politically linked conspiracy. The headline-making scandal precipitated by their arrest spun out of control, nearly ruining Mickey "Snow White" Cohen.

Sica, Fred The younger of two notorious brothers from New Jersey who were reputedly top members of Cohen's outfit. According to Treasury Department information from 1960, Sica was a "bookmaker and extortionist who acts as a 'muscle.'" The Sicas was indicted in a major narcotics case in 1949, but the murder of the chief prosecution witness stopped the case. Fred Sica worked out of the Savoy Shirt Shoppe on tony Melrose Avenue, and later Capitol Shoe Company, a shoe jobber, on La Cienega Boulevard.

Sica, Joe With brother Fred, reputed to be a top member of Cohen's outfit. According to Treasury Department information from 1960, he employed "strong arm methods and extreme violence." He worked out the Savoy Shirt Shoppe, and later, Sir Sica, a restaurant in the San Fernando Valley. In his 1975 autobiography, Mickey Cohen noted of Joe and Fred Sica, "Two of my very best friends . . . We've been together all these years."

Siegel, Benjamin (born Berish Siegel; Bugsy; Baby Blue Eyes) Volatile, handsome and charismatic New York–born mobster. Criminally and sexually precocious from age ten, by adolescence he was partnered with Lucky Luciano (who called him "his little brother"),

Meyer Lansky, and Frank Costello. During his twenties, he reputedly was personally involved in, or orchestrated, strategic executions of Mafia bosses, as well as victims of less prominence. Siegel moved to Los Angeles in 1935 where he began organizing the rich territory for the eastern Combination. With Mickey Cohen as muscle, he became the boss of L.A. A married man but a relentless womanizer, during this period, the stylish and charming Siegel became a Hollywood socialite. While expanding the rackets, he moved into major "gray" businesses like the wire service, and pioneered Las Vegas. In 1947 he was executed in a Beverly Hills mansion at age forty-one. Mickey Cohen was his heir.

Smiley, Allen (born Aaron Smehoff) Handsome, prematurely white-haired lieutenant and constant companion of Bugsy Siegel in Hollywood. He was safely but precariously seated on the same sofa as Siegel, when Siegel was executed in 1947. Another connoisseur of Hollywood beauties, Smiley married Lucille Casey, a former model, Copacabana showgirl, and movie extra. He began his gambling career with neophyte bookie Mickey Cohen around 1940.

Stompanato, Johnny (John Valentine; John Steele) Young, handsome, and mysterious former Marine who arrived in Hollywood in 1948, and immediately became a close associate of Mickey Cohen. Never convicted for a crime, Stompanato was a renowned lover, and his duties for Cohen usually involved beautiful women and, allegedly, big money blackmail. Found dead from a knife wound in the bedroom of screen goddess Lana Turner in 1958.

Sunset Strip The 1.7-mile-long section, between Hollywood and Beverly Hills, of the major Los Angeles thoroughfare Sunset Boulevard. Winding next to a hill, the location was strategic for dominance of the underworld. Located near the studios and wealthy neighborhoods, the Strip was an island of L.A. County, inside the city of Los Angeles, and under the aegis of the then notoriously pliable Sheriff's Department, rather than the LAPD. In the late 1920s, it was sparsely developed (with a bridle path running through the center) but already the location of the luxurious Garden of Allah and the Chateau Marmont hotels, with the Sunset Tower Hotel in planning stage. By the early 1940s, it had developed into the world-famous playground of Hollywood's elite, top mobsters, and society figures. After Bugsy Siegel's death, the Strip became home to Mickey Cohen's exclusive clubs and businesses.

Tarantino, Jimmy A member of Sinatra's "Varsity," the singer's early group of gofers and hanger-ons. Putting his insider connections to work in the late 1940s, Tarantino was the force behind *Hollywood Nite Life*, the Cohen-backed movie industry scandal sheet/extortion vehicle that terrorized the film community.

Triscaro, Louis (Babe) Teamsters executive and confidant of Jimmy Hoffa, the union's president. Associate of Mickey Cohen's since their teenage years in Cleveland.

Turner, Lana Iconic blonde film star, once one of the most famous women in the world. At the heart of what is arguably still Hollywood's most controversial and notorious whodunit: Johnny Stompanato, her lover and Mickey Cohen's associate, was found dead in her bedroom.

Utley, Jimmy (Squeaky Voice; The Little Giant) A former carnival worker who became a major Los Angeles underworld figure. He was a known informant involved with corrupt police as well as Mafia boss Jack Dragna, and ran lucrative rackets of all types. He held a large piece of Venice Beach's hugely profitable legal gambling (bingo games). An archenemy of Mickey Cohen.

Vaus Jr., James Arthur (Jim) Electronic experts who first worked for the police, then became Mickey Cohen's wiretapper. "Saved" by Reverend Billy Graham, in 1950 Vaus became a religious figure himself; touring the country giving sermons combining electronics, Mickey Cohen, and fire-and-brimstone. Friendly with Mickey Cohen until the mobster's death.

Wellpott, Rudy In the late 1940s Lieutenant Wellpott was the head of LAPD's administrative vice. He became involved in a long-running war with Mickey Cohen.

Whalen, John F. (Jack; The Enforcer; Jack O'Hara) A freelance bookie and debt collector with a major Hollywood following. In late 1959, Jack Whalen, an enemy to Mickey Cohen, was found dead in a restaurant where Cohen was dining.

Wooters, Jerry One of the original members of LAPD's Gangster Squad, by 1959 Wooters had reputedly gone rogue and become associated with prominent bookie and Cohen enemy Jack "The Enforcer" Whalen.

Notes on the Text

Aside from the many interviews Mickey Cohen gave in his later years, the information on Mickey Cohen's early life comes from three invaluable sources: *Mickey Cohen: In My Own Words* (Cohen and Nugent); the drafts and voluminous notes from the unfinished Mickey Cohen biography by eminent screenwriter and author Ben Hecht, now held at the Newberry Library, Chicago, in the Ben Hecht Collection (Box 7, file 226-227); and from "The Incomplete Life of Mickey Cohen," a 1970 *Scanlon's* magazine article, based on the unpublished Ben Hecht material in the Newberry Library.

The FBI files of Meyer Harris Cohen (Mickey Cohen), Benjamin (Bugsy) Siegel, Charles Lucania (Lucky Luciano), Meyer Lansky, Morris B. Dalitz (Moe Dalitz), Abner Zwillman (Longie Zwillman), Lana Turner, Sidney Korshak, and many others have been essential sources, as have the reports of the Assembly of the State of California, Subcommittee on Rackets, Organized Crime in California (California Crime Commission), 1949–1950 and 1957–1959, and the 1961 United States Treasury Department, Bureau of Narcotics file on organized crime.

Mickey Cohen's deposition from the Kefauver senate committee in November 1950 provided insights into how the mobster presented himself and his businesses to authorities; others' testimony before the same committee has also been essential in creating a factual picture. Hundreds of contemporary books, magazines (particularly the in-depth four-part biographical series from *The Saturday Evening Post*, 1958), and newspaper articles on multiple personages have been invaluable.

Interviews with scores of witnesses have provided essential color; unfortunately not every story had a place in the big picture. I particularly wish to thank Rosaline George for her observations and the great Budd Schulberg, creator of Sammy Glick and iconic movies, who was a source and supporter from the beginning of this long undertaking until weeks before his death. Thanks to Brian Hamilton, Anita Keys, Mr. Black, Susan Pile, Anne Horne, Mary Jane Strickland, James Bacon, Bob Spivack, Raeanne Rubenstein, Tommy L., the late Art Aragon and Charles Conaway. DT for your astute recollections and making the connection with that special gentleman, a true sport. This could not have been done without the commitment of my agent, James Fitzgerald.

In a special class by themselves are precious hope and the mighty blue king. You both can never be thanked enough for your support and encouragement, and for being the personification of love, brilliance, and the best of everything.

This is an L.A. story and takes place in the buildings and streets that are as much a part of my life as they were of Mickey Cohen's. My environment permeates and informs this book. As the story unwound, creating access to the properties from the book became a mission for me. I can say that I have been inside the Linden Drive house and stood in the spot where Bugsy Siegel was assassinated. I have been a guest in the house he built in Holmby Hills. I've sat on the bed at Countess di Frasso's while the room still maintained the original Elsie de Wolfe decor. Many years ago I attended a party in the house that Billy Wilkerson built, and where he hosted Lana Turner's third wedding. With my parents, I dined at famous L.A. restaurants that no longer exist, and I've been in the majority of the hotels, restaurants, and clubs that play roles in this story, sometimes in several incarnations. My first apartment was behind what had been Cohen's La Brea Social Club decades before. I once visited what had been Sam Rummel's home, years before I knew the nearly abandoned palazzo was the scene of a famous unsolved murder that I would one day write about. It proved that friends lived a few doors down from what I learned was the Cohen's 1944 "party house." And I lived off the Sunset Strip, the ground zero of Cohen's empire, for seven years.

I would never have been able to write this story without the experiences that a lifetime in Los Angeles has given me.

Prologue: A Dangerous Place

Florabel Muir recounts this evening's events in detail in her book *Headline Happy*, pages 202–216.

1   **It was well after** Temple Black, *Child Star*, 430. | **"Pulling to the curb . . ."** Ibid.
2   **Resplendent in an impeccably** "The Lucky Clay Pigeon of the Sunset Strip," *Time*, August 8, 1949. | **"Not as long as . . ."** Muir, *Headline Happy*, 204. | **Seeing the lawmen at** Ibid., 208.

Chapter 1: Boyle Heights Boychik

7   **Max Cohen "was in . . ."** Cohen and Nugent, *Mickey Cohen: In My Own Words*, 2. | **"According to the rest . . ."** Hecht, unpublished Cohen manuscript and notes, unpaginated.
8   **Boyle Heights was Fanny** Ibid. | **The established gentry of** Gabler, *An Empire of Their Own*, 271–276. | **Mickey remembered his widowed** Cohen and Nugent, *Mickey Cohen: In My Own Words*, 2. | **Settling into rented rooms** Hecht, unpublished Cohen manuscript and notes, unpaginated. | **Mickey's earliest memory was** Ibid. | **Mickey remembered himself as** Ibid.
10   **Harry took the child** Cohen and Nugent, *Mickey Cohen: In My Own Words*, 5. | **Rarely in class, Mickey** Ibid. | **Racking balls for pool** Hecht, unpublished Cohen manuscript and notes, unpaginated. | **He would later boast** Cohen and Nugent, *Mickey Cohen: In My Own Words*, 5. | **His brother Sam was** Ibid., 5. | **Armed with a baseball** Feinman, *Hollywood Confidential*, 86
11   **He later boasted, "I . . ."** Hecht, unpublished Cohen manuscript and notes, unpaginated. | **Spending day and night** Cohen and Nugent, *Mickey Cohen: In My Own Words*, 6. | **Mickey often slept in** Ibid., 7. | **In exchange for the** Ibid. | **It wasn't until later** Ibid.
12   **Mickey remember the Hunts** Ibid., 9.
13   **Thinking he "must have . . ."** Hecht, unpublished Cohen manuscript and notes, unpaginated. | **If there was a** Cohen and Nugent, *Mickey Cohen: In My Own Words*, 8. | **Young Mickey Cohen's credo** Ibid.

Chapter 2: School of Hard Knocks

14   **He hitchhiked and rode** Hecht, unpublished Cohen manuscript and notes, 5.
15   **By this time four** Morris B. Dalitz FBI file. | **The Italian element of** Messick, *The Silent Syndicate*, 47. | **An inside look at** Ibid., 84.

16   Morris Kleinman, once a Ibid., 31, 52. | Mickey observed the mob Cohen and
      Nugent, *Mickey Cohen: In My Own Words*, 12. | Located up a flight Garfield,
      "Stillman's Gym: The Center of the Boxing Universe," EastSideBoxing.com,
      January 13, 2004.

17   Introducing him to prominent Meyer Harris Cohen FBI file. | He would later
      describe Cohen and Nugent, *Mickey Cohen: In My Own Words*, 12. | But the
      experience had Ibid., 14. | A hardened armed robber Ibid., 16.

18   He later described his Ibid., 16. | He later recalled the Hecht, unpublished
      Cohen manuscript and notes, unpaginated. | He confided years later Ibid. |
      One member of his Ibid.

19   He remembered the underworld Ibid. | Standing before the Mafia Ibid. |
      Anthony Milano, FBI #433240 *Mafia: The Government's Secret File on Organized
      Crime*, 47.

20   "Pleasure lay only in . . ." Hecht, "The Incomplete Life of Mickey Cohen," 68. |
      "I must have been . . ." Ibid, 66.

21   A 1961 document titled Meyer Harris Cohen FBI file.

22   "He had a fighting . . ." Muir, *Headline Happy*, 222.

23   Needing someone to identify Hecht, unpublished Cohen manuscript and
      notes, unpaginated.

24   "The case was pushed . . ." Hecht, "The Incomplete Life of Mickey Cohen,"
      69–70. | He was placed with Cohen and Nugent, *Mickey Cohen: In My Own
      Words*, 19.

25   Meyer Lansky revealed to Eisenberg, Dan, and Landau, *Meyer Lansky: Mogul
      of the Mob*, 93. | He said with great Hecht, unpublished Cohen manuscript
      and notes, unpaginated. | Working as protection for Ibid. | Mickey recalled a
      confrontation Ibid.

26   He admitted years later Ibid. | During much of his Cohen and Nugent,
      Mickey Cohen: In His Own Words, 14–15.

27   "It was suggested to . . ." Hecht, unpublished Cohen manuscript and notes,
      unpaginated. | Again at the center Ibid. | Years later he related the Ibid.

28   Mickey was later circumspect Ibid. | He was instructed to Cohen and
      Nugent, *Mickey Cohen: In His Own Words*, 34.

Chapter 3: The Coasters

29   In his hometown, "gambling . . ." Cohen and Nugent, *Mickey Cohen: In His
      Own Words*, 41. | "On Spring [Street] are . . ." Woon, *Incredible Land*, 44. |
      Hearst editor James H. Richardson Richardson, *For the Life of Me*, 213.

30   He first rose to Henstall, *Sunshine and Wealth*, 45–49. | With the election of
      Ibid., 50.

31   The rival, Guy McAfee Rayner, *A Bright and Guilty Place*, 157–160. | In 1933,
      Frank L. Shaw Ibid., 206 | LAPD Chief James E. Davis Ibid., 85, 95; Hull and
      Duxman, *Family Secret*, 73–77.

32   A millionaire by the Henstall, *Sunshine and Wealth*, 61, 66, 71; Newton, *Justice
      For All*, 106, 107.

33   Born Ignaucio Rizzotti in Hecht, unpublished Cohen manuscript and notes,
      unpaginated; Reid, *The Grim Reapers*, 163–165. | A relative of Tommy Hecht,
      unpublished Cohen manuscript and notes, unpaginated. | Involved in criminal

activities Gosch and Hammer, *The Last Testament of Lucky Luciano*, 26;
Eisenberg, Dan, and Landau, *Meyer Lansky: Mogul of the Mob*, 54.

34   "Siegel . . . part and parcel . . ." Hecht, unpublished Cohen manuscript and
notes, unpaginated.

35   "Joe Sica was close . . ." Ibid.

36   "Work . . . that's what . . ." Cohen and Nugent, *Mickey Cohen: In My Own
Words*, 36. | Told that it was Hecht, unpublished Cohen manuscript and notes,
83, 84.

37   Ushered into the steam Ibid. | For an instant, a Ibid. | Immediately shown
who was Ibid.

38   "Siegel's second in command . . ." Ibid. | "'You little son of . . ." Ibid., 85.

Chapter 4: Fields of Manna

39   Sponsored by, and the Francis, *Ladies on Call*, 88. | Recounting details of her
Ibid., 49.

40   Madam Francis's luxurious parlors Ibid., 99. | Guests were entertained by
Ibid. | Mickey Cohen remembered raiding Cohen and Nugent, *Mickey Cohen:
In My Own Words*, 46.

41   The Schulbergs were enormous Phone interview with Budd Schulberg,
October 9, 2000. | "I liked him," Budd Ibid.

42   An American, born Dorothy Stern, *No Innocence Abroad*, 235–253; "What on
Land (or Sea) Will Dorothy Do Next?" *San Antonio Express*, February 26, 1939;
Jennings, *We Only Kill Each Other*, 39–41.

43   When talking to his Eisenberg, Dan, and Landau, *Meyer Lansky: Mogul of the
Mob*, 177. | Gossip columnist Hedda Hopper Jennings, *We Only Kill Each Other*,
65. | The Hollywood royals were Ibid., 40. Footage of the party is included in
Rogue's Gallery: Bugsy Siegel. | Living like a member Muir, *Headline Happy*, 162.

44   "Ben — no one called . . ." Collins, "The Man Who Kept Secrets," *Vanity Fair*,
April 2001, 287–288. | He said, "I found . . ." Hecht, unpublished Cohen
manuscript and notes, unpaginated. | L.A. racket boss Farmer Quotation
from letter by Patricia A. Nealis (daughter of Eddie Nealis, and the niece
of Milton "Farmer" Page) included in Pfeffer, "The Wonderful Nightclubs,"
TheOldMovieMaven.com/TheWonderfulNightclubs.doc.

46   Biscailuz became an iconic Fowler, *Reporters*, 210. | Chandler's sheriff is a
Chandler, *The Long Goodbye*, 218–219.

47   Cohen recalled, "Nealis was . . ." Hecht, unpublished Cohen manuscript and
notes, unpaginated. | According to Mickey, Curly Ibid. | Mickey confirmed
that "Siegel . . ." Ibid.

48   Mickey disclosed years later Ibid. | Mickey affirmed, "Jimmy Fox . . ." Ibid.
| Mickey piously revealed, "Cops . . ." Ibid. | He recalled powerful Captain
Ibid. | Mickey didn't relent: "I . . ." Ibid. | "I laid a perfect . . ." Ibid.

49   In a move that Ibid. | The rough road smoothly Muir, *Headline Happy*, 164,
186–189. | Industrial shakedowns were a Munn, *The Hollywood Connection*,
117–132; interview with Sidney Zion, *Rogue's Gallery: Bugsy Siegel*; Muir,
Headline Happy, 164. | Always looking for a Collins, "The Man Who Kept
Secrets," *Vanity Fair*, April 2001; Muir, *Headline Happy*, 223–224.

Chapter 5: Young Blood

51   **Journalist Florabel Muir would** Muir, *Headline Happy*, 223–224.

52   **Mickey bragged to a** Confidential interview, November 9, 2000. | **But, so the story** Reid, *Mickey Cohen: Mobster*, 79. | **"I'd never seen anyone . . ."** Prager and Craft, *Hoodlums: Los Angeles*, 197. | **Mickey claimed years later** Hecht, unpublished Cohen manuscript and notes, unpaginated.

53   **The "work" was to** Turkis and Feder, *Murder Inc.*, 274–279. | **"He . . . says to me . . ."** Hecht, unpublished Cohen manuscript and notes, unpaginated. | **He confided to writer** Hecht, "The Incomplete Life of Mickey Cohen," 64.

54   **The Greek, he remembered** Hecht, unpublished Cohen manuscript and notes, unpaginated. | **Taking bets a few** Ibid.

55   **Cohen's next foray was** Ibid.; Meyer Harris Cohen FBI file. | **"We had five phones . . ."** Hecht, unpublished Cohen manuscript and notes, unpaginated. | **Lauren Bacall recalled her** Bacall, *Lauren Bacall by Myself*, 165. | **A novel concept for** Cohen and Nugent, *Mickey Cohen: In My Own Words*, 59. | **But the sizzling talent** Ibid.

56   **He dined, surrounded by** Segal, *They Called Him Champ*, 264. | **Mickey's handler, Champ Segal** Ibid., 230–233. | **Budd Schulberg described** Vine Schulberg, *What Makes Sammy Run?*, 238.

57   **Starting out as a** Webb, *The Badge*, 150, 151. | **A convicted morphine peddler** *Los Angeles Times*, October 31, 1962; Stoker, *Thicker'N Thieves*, 4. | **One day at lunchtime** Cohen and Nugent, *Mickey Cohen: In My Own Words*, 63. | **After two years of** Hecht, unpublished Cohen manuscript and notes, unpaginated.

58   **Mickey later admitted he** Ibid., 9, 10. | **"I've never regretted marrying . . ."** Muir, *Headline Happy*, 224. | **A Boyle Heights address** Meyer Harris Cohen FBI file. | **Cohen registered for Selective** Ibid.

Chapter 6: Picked From the Chorus

60   **"I had my sights . . ."** Hecht, unpublished Cohen manuscript and notes, unpaginated. | **"A very beautiful place . . ."** Cohen and Nugent, *Mickey Cohen: In My Own Words*, 73.

61   **Distinguished law enforcer Blayney** Ibid. | **Jack Dineen, a retired** Ibid. | **With Mickey Cohen using** Phone interview with Mary Jane Strickland, July 14, 2007; Lieberman, "Tales from the Gangster Squad," *Los Angeles Times*, October 26, 2008, A21.

62   **"Siegel would throw me . . ."** Hecht, unpublished Cohen manuscript and notes, unpaginated. | **Cohen was circumspect when** Ibid. | **The former boxer eventually** Ibid.

63   **By the mid-1930s, Nationwide** Ogden, *Legacy: A Biography of Moses Annenberg*, 105.

64   **In Chicago, James Ragen** Ibid. | **In July 1942, with** Redston and Crossen, *Conspiracy of Death*, 71. | **A week later,** Cohen Meyer Harris Cohen FBI file. | **Months later, Siegel had** Report of the California Crime Commission, 1949–1950.

65   **Upon his return to** Hecht, unpublished Cohen manuscript and notes, unpaginated. | **He began to change** Ibid. | **Curly Robinson was a** Hecht,

unpublished Cohen manuscript and notes, 1–5. | **At Robinson's behest, Mickey** Ibid. | **The "Furious Forties of . . ."** Stone, *The Wrong Side of the Wall*, 49. | **In the manner of** State of California, Subcommittee on Rackets, Organized Crime in California. Assembly Interim Committee Reports, 1957–59, 108.

66   **For Cohen, McGee also** Stone, *The Wrong Side of the Wall*, 43, 44. | **He expanded into Orange** Cohen and Nugent, *Mickey Cohen: In My Own Words*, 233, 234. | **"Although we started with . . ."** Hecht, unpublished Cohen manuscript and notes, unpaginated. | **Opening a commission betting** Meyer Harris Cohen FBI file.

67   **"At the peak of . . ."** Hecht, unpublished Cohen manuscript and notes, unpaginated. | **He once confided in** Jennings, "The Private Life of a Hood," *Saturday Evening Post*, October 4, 1958, 84. | **Mickey confirmed, "The money . . ."** Hecht, unpublished Cohen manuscript and notes, unpaginated. | **For eight months in** Ibid. | **"There was never an . . ."** Ibid.

68   **Cohen later sniffed that** Ibid. | **Mickey explained, "At the . . ."** Ibid. | **Wartime shortages proved profitable** Meyer Harris Cohen FBI file. | **And he recalled, "As . . ."** Hecht, unpublished Cohen manuscript and notes, unpaginated.

69   **The previous year, after** Muir, *Headline Happy*, 88, 193–199; Prager and Craft, *Hoodlums: Los Angeles*, 88, 90. | **Reporter Florabel Muir mused** Muir, *Headline Happy*, 193.

70   **"The only thing they . . ."** Hecht, unpublished Cohen manuscript and notes, unpaginated. | **Mickey acknowledged they were** Cohen and Nugent, *Mickey Cohen: In My Own Words*, 71–73. | **Impressed by Mickey Cohen's** Meyer Harris Cohen FBI file.

71   **Mickey recalled, "Although the . . ."** Hecht, unpublished Cohen manuscript and notes, unpaginated. | **"As shy as a . . ."** Muir, *Headline Happy*, 187.

Chapter 7: Hollywood Byzantine

73   **According to FBI reports** Abner (Longie) Zwillman FBI file. | **A team of prominent** Hecht, unpublished Cohen manuscript and notes, unpaginated.

74   **Beverly Hills Police Chief** Anderson, *Beverly Hills Is My Beat*, 137, 138. | **A predator alleged to** Reid, *Mickey Cohen: Mobster*, 188, 189. | **Cohen recalled, "Utley . . . had . . ."** Hecht, unpublished Cohen manuscript and notes, unpaginated.

75   **Governor Earl Warren, Cornero's** Wolf and Mader, *Fallen Angels*, 184. | **He recalled, "My vote . . ."** Hecht, unpublished Cohen manuscript and notes, unpaginated. | **In front of scores** Prager and Craft, *Hoodlums: Los Angeles*, 124. | **After the beating, Mickey** Meyer Harris Cohen FBI file.

76   **Originally the exclusive gambling** Wilkerson III, *The Man Who Invented Las Vegas*, 73–79, 109; Muir, *Headline Happy*, 189–193. | **Soon after ground was** Benjamin (Bugs) Siegel FBI file.

77   **On July 14, 1946, Walter** Ibid. | **When Hoover became aware** Ibid.

78   **Battling to clear his** Ibid. | **They told him that** Eisenberg, Dan, and Landau, *Mogul of the Mob*, 236.

79   **Mickey later said, "I . . ."** Cohen and Nugent, *Mickey Cohen: In My Own Words*,

80, 81. | **The three singing Andrews** Benjamin (Bugs) Siegel FBI file. | **Thanks to Mickey Cohen's** Kefauver, *Crime in America*, 44.

80   James Ragen, the head Muir, *Headline Happy*, 190–193. | **Arthur "Mickey" McBride, a** Kefauver, *Crime in America*, 44. | **Everyone seemed content with** Ibid. | **Cash-strapped and desperate, Siegel** Rappleye and Becker, *All-American Mafioso*, 223. | **Ushered to the seat** Muir, *Headline Happy*, 196–199; Benjamin (Bugs) Siegel FBI file.

Chapter 8: Puttin' on the Dog

84   After Benjamin Siegel proved Cohen and Nugent, *Mickey Cohen: In My Own Words*, 80, 81. | **But he was the** Ibid., 81. | **Years later, he would** Ibid. | **Ensconced in a sprawling** Beverly Hills phone directory, 1944.

85   A firm believer in Redston and Crossen, *The Conspiracy of Death*, 75.

86   In the top tier Meyer Harris Cohen FBI file; Hecht, unpublished Cohen manuscript and notes, 6, 7.

88   Slickly handsome and superbly Crane, *Detour*, 202–204 | **Maintaining pretense, the Cohen** Interview with Jerry Leiber, July 3, 2005. | **Mickey said that his** Hecht, unpublished Cohen manuscript and notes, unpaginated. | **To keep his boys** Ibid. | **Mickey teamed Rummel with** Cohen and Nugent, *Mickey Cohen: In My Own Words*, 149, 150; *Los Angeles Times*, June 25, 1951. | **Mickey was a master** Redston and Crossen, *The Conspiracy of Death*, 87.

89   The heady image of Jennings, "The Private Life of a Hood," *Saturday Evening Post*, October 11, 1958, 114; Prager and Craft, *Hoodlum: Los Angeles*, 95. | **He began utilizing a** Ibid., 73, 88. | **A prominent bookmaker mused** Redston and Crossen, *The Conspiracy of Death*, 87. | **But there were other** Hecht, unpublished Cohen manuscript and notes, unpaginated.

92   He scrubbed his hands Ibid. | **In the course of** Meyer Harris Cohen FBI file.

94   Mickey later stated that Hecht, unpublished Cohen manuscript and notes, unpaginated. | **For years, Rosselli's great** Rappleye and Becker, *All-American Mafioso*, 58, 130–131. | **Rosselli demurred, informing his** Ibid., 130, 131.

95   Rosselli complained to a Ibid., 125.

96   At a small downtown Ibid., 124. | **Violent and ruthless, the** Demaris, *The Last Mafioso*, 131, 132. | **"At first Jimmy had** Ibid. | **Mickey even took care** Muir, *Headline Happy*, 212. | **"Twice a week . . ."** Rappleye and Becker, *All-American Mafioso*, 125.

97   In late 1946, the Lieberman, "Tales from the Gangster Squad," *Los Angeles Times*, October 26, 2008.

98   Posing as a technician Interview with Jack O'Mara, *Rogue's Gallery: Mickey Cohen*. | **On February 9, 1948** *Los Angeles Times*, February 10, 1948, 1. | **Claiming that he wasn't** Ibid. | **Just as Johnny Rosselli** Rappleye and Becker, *All-American Mafioso*, 116, 117, 122, 123.

99   On Wednesday evening, August Demaris, *The Last Mafioso*, 30, 31. | **Frattiano realized that by** Ibid.

Chapter 9: A Thousand Hinky Plays

101   Syndicated-columnist Hedda Hopper Server, *Robert Mitchum: Baby, I Don't*

Care, 177, 178. | "**We met at mid-stairway . . .**" Temple Black, *Child Star*, 429, 430.

102   "**When Ruditsky recognized how** Ibid., 430. | **He had recently learned** Server, *Robert Mitchum: Baby, I Don't Care*, 150–152. | **Although he decided not** Ibid. | **Accompanied by Cohen's new** Crane, *Detour*, 202. | **Arrested at a Hollywood** *Humboldt Standard*, April 17, 1958, 18.

103   **Cohen's taste on situations** Cohen and Nugent, *Mickey Cohen: In My Own Words*, 42. | **A former stringer for** Kelley, *His Way: The Unauthorized Biography of Frank Sinatra*, 75, 78, 158, 161. | **Even Sinatra was preyed** Ibid. | **Whenever Judy Garland had** Cohen and Nugent, *Mickey Cohen: In My Own Words*, 109.

104   **Tarantino finally met his** Ibid. | **Painfully self-conscious about** Ibid., 134.

105   "**Mickey picks them up . . .**" Muir, *Headline Happy*, 219, 222. | "**No," he answered, "not . . .**" Ibid., 220. | **He subscribed to the** Zion, "On Ben Hecht," *Scanlon's*, 56, 57.

106   **According to journalist Sidney** Ibid., 57. | **Although the majority of** Gabler, *An Empire of Their Own*, 290, 350. | **When first approached Mickey** Cohen and Nugent, *Mickey Cohen: In My Own Words*, 89–93.

107   **Hecht wrote: "I can't . . .**" Hecht, *A Child of the Century*, 610–613. | **Mickey decided to lend** Interview with Jerry Leiber, December 21, 2006. | **Inspired by Jews fighting** Cohen and Nugent, *Mickey Cohen: In My Own Words*, 89–93. | **He said, "There were . . .**" Ibid. | **There were allegations, never** Demaris, *The Last Mafioso*, 28, 29.

108   **He snorted, "I was . . .**" Cohen and Nugent, *Mickey Cohen: In My Own Words*, 92, 93. | **Attorneys Rummel and Ferguson** Ibid.

Chapter 10: High Jingo

109   "**Mickey knew I intended . . .**" Jennings, "The Private Life of a Hood," *Saturday Evening Post*, September 20, 1958, 85.

110   **A sergeant in LAPD's** Stoker, *Thicker'N Thieves*, 96–98. | **A typical example of** Ibid. | **Cabbies on the Westside** Henstell, "How the Sex Queen of Hollywood Brought Down City Hall," *Los Angeles*, June 1978, 70–84. | **After dialing the confidential** Stoker, *Thicker'N Thieves*, 96, 98.

112   **Entering the private office** Vaus, *Why I Quit Syndicate Crime*, 27, 28. | **With relief, the electronics** Ibid. | **After thirteen months the** Ibid. | **Vaus continued to monitor** Ibid.

113   **Trying to reclaim the** Hecht, unpublished Cohen manuscript and notes, unpaginated. | "**We got some of . . .**" Ibid. | **Cohen admitted to a** Ibid.

114   **Recovering there for months** Demaris, *The Last Mafioso*, 33, 34.

115   **The mobster asserted years** Cohen and Nugent, *Mickey Cohen: In My Own Words*, 94. | **Captain Lorenson met Mickey** Ibid., 95, 99. | **The situation with the** Ibid., 95.

116   **One phone call later** Muir, *Headline Happy*, 227–233.

117   **Mickey later claimed he** Cohen and Nugent, *Mickey Cohen: In My Own Words*, 99. | **Positioned on a hill** Hecht, unpublished Cohen manuscript and notes, unpaginated. | **Mickey recalled, "The lieutenant . . .**" Ibid.

118   **Mickey recalled, "For weeks . . .**" Ibid. | "**Mick," Richardson suggested, "I . . .**" Jennings, "The Private Life of a Hood," *Saturday Evening Post*, October 2,

1958, 122.

119   He lavishly praised Cohen's Ibid.; Reid, *Mickey Cohen: Mobster*, 169–171.

Chapter 11: Smog Alert

122   **"We will prove by . . ."** Stoker, *Thicker'N Thieves*, 198–203.

123   **Rummel brought to the** Ibid., 198.

124   **In light of the** Prager and Craft, *Hoodlums: Los Angeles*, 113, 114. | **Allen swore that she** Ibid., 115.

125   **Gangland's prime minister now** Interview with Jim Smith, *Rogue's Gallery: Mickey Cohen.* | **Wielding power from a** Samish and Thomas, *The Secret Boss of California*, 134. | **With a dossier on** Velie, "The Secret Boss of California," *Collier's*, August 1949, 21. | **When Governor Earl Warren** Newton, *Justice for All*, 230. | **Samish's long list of** Russo, *Supermob*, 36.

126   **One of Samish's most** Samish and Thomas, *The Secret Boss of California*, 124, 126. | **In July 1949, Howser** Cohen and Nugent, *Mickey Cohen: In My Own Words*, 125.

128   **When sheriff's deputies finally** Muir, *Headline Happy*, 206–209.

130   **While Cohen rehabilitated his** Prager and Craft, *Hoodlums: Los Angeles*, 116. | **When critics noted more** Ibid., 117. | **A federal grand jury** Ibid.; Meyer Harris Cohen FBI file.

131   **Attorneys Sam Rummel and** "Details of Cohen's Big Deals Recorded," *Los Angeles Times*, August 16 and 22, 1949. | **In a hushed call** Ibid. | **After his dog tore** Ibid. | **And in a domestic** Muir, *Headline Happy*, 233–236.

132   **On August 30 at** Ibid.

133   **"Well then go fuck . . ."** Hecht, unpublished Cohen manuscript and notes, unpaginated. | **His counsel, the distinguished** "Atty. Vernon L. Ferguson, Partner of Rummel Dies," *Los Angeles Times*, June 25, 1951. | **Years later Mickey admitted** Hecht, unpublished Cohen manuscript and notes, unpaginated.

134   **And, in another small-world** "Cohen's 50,000 Year Job Offer to 'Bug' Man Told," *Los Angeles Times*, September 2, 1949. | **According to Mason, Tarantino** Ibid. | **Mason testified Tarantino derided** Ibid. | **After Mason rejected Cohen's** Ibid. | **Out on bail and** "Dead Man Stymies Quiz on Vice Ring," *Los Angeles Times*, October 6, 1949. | **Admitting to the grand** "Hollywood Extortion Racket Took in Vast Sums," *Los Angeles Times*, September 21, 1949.

135   **Spinning a lurid** Ibid.; "Hollywood Expose for Revenge Hinted," *Los Angeles Times*, September 27, 1949. | **Seven beautiful young women** "Police Arrest Toni Hughes in Extortion Case," *Los Angeles Times*, October 13, 1949. | **When told of Behrmann's** "Hollywood Extortion Racket Took in Vast Sums," *Los Angeles Times*, September 21, 1949. | **When the DA heard** "Extortion Inquiry Takes New Turn," *Los Angeles Times*, September 24, 1949.

Chapter 12: Star-Crossed

137   **On Labor Day weekend** Demaris, *The Last Mafioso*, 23–25.

138   **Harold Meltzer, the man** Ibid., 39. | **Opportunistic "sightings" of** Ogul "Missing Actress Cohen Pals Seen in Texas," *Los Angeles Times*, March 22, 1950.

139   **Lansky's activities were clearly** Lacey, *Little Man: Meyer Lansky and the Gangster Life*, 175–177.

140 "Hollywood is like Egypt . . ." Hecht, *A Child of the Century*, 467. | In a show of Cohen and Nugent, *Mickey Cohen: In My Own Words*, 85.

Chapter 13: Bum-Steered and Bum-Rapped

141 *Time* labeled him "Clay Pigeon," *Time*, August 1, 1949. | His notoriety had even Muir, *Headline Happy*, 235; Vaus, *Why I Quit Syndicated Crime*, 34. | "Puff Graham" were the "God's Billy Pulpit," *Time*, November 15, 1993; Cohen and Nugent, *Mickey Cohen: In My Own Words*, 107.

142 Vaus had worked for Vaus, *Why I Quit Syndicated Crime*, 52–55. | Before meeting Mickey, he Ibid., 42, 47, 48. | He recalled their initial Cohen and Nugent, *Mickey Cohen: In My Own Words*, 105, 106.

143 Joseph McCarthy, Republican from Lacey, *Little Man: Meyer Lansky and the Gangster Life*, 190.

144 He fancied pretty ladies Ibid. | In light of recent Kefauver, *Crime in America*, 5. | Personally packed by Tom Demaris, *The Last Mafioso*, 40. | Mickey later revealed, "I . . ." Cohen and Nugent, *Mickey Cohen: In My Own Words*, 133.

145 Broadcasting from Cohen's den Muir, *Headline Happy*, 238.

146 They pleaded, "The presence . . ." Ibid., 123.

147 Pressure was put on Ibid., 125.

148 Charging false arrest, the Muir, *Headline Happy*, 241. | In his heavy Sicilian Ibid., 242. | Full use of force Manchester, *American Caesar*, 694, 695.

149 "In fact, 'Kefauveritis,' that . . ." Kefauver, *Crime in America*, 11.

Chapter 14: Tsuris

150 By 1950, trumpeting that Prager and Craft, *Hoodlums: Los Angeles*, 127. | The crooner insisted on Cohen and Nugent, *Mickey Cohen: In My Own Words*, 85.

151 Irritated by what Sinatra Ibid. | The flat-bottomed automobile had Ibid., 123.

152 Society woman Agnes Albro Webb, *The Badge*, 251. | The day began badly Cohen and Nugent, *Mickey Cohen: In My Own Words*, 148. | A buttoned-down Yalie, Kefauver Kefauver, *Crime in America*, 249, 250.

153–160 Testimony of Mickey Cohen, November 17, 1950. Kefauver, Investigation of Organized Crime in Interstate Commerce: Hearings Before the Special Committee to Investigate Organized Crime in Interstate Commerce. United States Senate, eighty-first congress, second session, and eighty-second congress, first session.

161 After the session concluded Kefauver, *Crime in America*, 249.

Chapter 15: Death and Taxes

162 Fresno drug dealer Abraham "Key Witness in Dope Case Murdered," *Los Angeles Times*, March 1, 1950. | Stunning blonde starlet Barbara "Barbara Payton Backs Story of Accused Man," *Los Angeles Times*, November 30, 1950. | An ongoing investigation into Kefauver, *Crime in America*, 242, 243; "Rummel Links to Payoff Hinted in Officer's Testimony," *Los Angeles Times*, December 14, 1950.

163 When asked at an Prager and Craft, *Hoodlums: Los Angeles*, 193. | "I didn't care if . . ." Cohen and Nugent, *Mickey Cohen: In My Own Words*, 95–96. | Gangster

Flippy Sherer was Lait and Mortimer, *U.S.A. Confidential*, 118. | **Now publicly involved with** Webb, *The Badge*, 256. | **Years later, Cohen frostily** Cohen and Nugent, *Mickey Cohen: In My Own Words*, 93. | **Less than a month** Kefauver, *Crime in America*, 241–243; "Two Officers Suspended in Rummel Quiz," *Los Angeles Times*, December 12, 1950.

164 **Norma Rummel expressed great** "Gang Roundup Opens Rummel Killer Hunt," *Los Angeles Times*, December 12, 1950; "Rummel Mansion Scene of Confusion," *Los Angeles Times*, December 12, 1950.

165 **Cohen said, "My accountant . . ."** Hecht, unpublished Cohen manuscript and notes, unpaginated. | **On April 15, 1951** Meyer Harris Cohen FBI file. | **From an FBI memo** Ibid.

166 **Donning his showman hat** Lewis, *Hollywood's Celebrity Gangster*, 172.

167 **Potential bidders and the** Prager and Craft, *Hoodlums: Los Angeles*, 202, 203. | **Roused from his mahogany** Ibid.

168 **After a thorough investigation** "Harry Sackman, Cohen Tax Aide, Dies Suddenly," *Los Angeles Times*, June 1, 1951. | **"It's a pleasure walking . . ."** Prager and Craft, *Hoodlums: Los Angeles*, 203.

169 **A vivid cast of** "Cohen Profits Told as Tax Case Opens," *Los Angeles Times*, June 5, 1951. | **An Italian cobbler told** Hecht, unpublished Cohen manuscript and notes, unpaginated.

170 **When Mickey saw them** Prager and Craft, *Hoodlums: Los Angeles*, 205. | **Calling Mickey a "hard-luck . . ."** "Mickey Cohen Gets 5 Years, $10,000 Fine," *Los Angeles Times*, July 10, 1951.

171 **Comparing the case to** Prager and Craft, *Hoodlums: Los Angeles*, 204, 205.

Chapter 16: Judas and Iago

172 **If Bugsy Siegel had** Hecht, unpublished Cohen manuscript and notes, unpaginated. | **Cohen later asserted that** Ibid. | **"The Siegel drug conspiracy . . ."** Valentine, *The Strength of the Wolf*, 70–73.

173 **Later Siegel and Hill** Ibid. | **In 1944, Meyer Lansky** Ibid., 71. | **Harold Meltzer's operation prospered** Ibid., 71, 72. | **"Happy" Harold began smoking** McCoy, *The Politics of Heroin*, 41–44. | **In a plan to** Ibid. | **"Even an appeal to . . ."** Ibid.; State of California, Subcommittee on Rackets, Organized Crime in California. Assembly Interim Committee Reports, 1957–59, 78–79.

174 **Heard on wiretaps planted** Stoker, *Thicker'N Thieves*, 150; Prager and Craft, *Hoodlums: Los Angeles*, 126. | **When Siegel was alive** Hecht, unpublished Cohen manuscript and notes, unpaginated. | **The Judas of the** Ibid. | **Mickey later revealed, "The . . ."** Ibid. | **For this supreme act** Ibid. | **Cohen recalled, "My refusal . . ."** Ibid.

175 **During 1950, Price Spivey** Valentine, *The Strength of the Wolf*, 95. | **He recovered, and by** "Federal Agents Seek 18 of 21 Opium Indictees," *Long Beach Press Telegram*, March 6, 1951. | **Among the unindicted co-conspirators** Valentine, *The Strength of the Wolf*, 95.

Chapter 17: Shifting Winds

180 **Comic Redd Foxx cooked** Cohen and Nugent, *Mickey Cohen: In My Own Words*,

155. | **He claimed to immediately** Ibid., 156–160. | **He ate whatever he** Meyer Harris Cohen FBI file.

181 **"Working" for the federal** Cohen and Nugent, *Mickey Cohen: In My Own Words*, 155.

182 **"They saw to it . . ."** Webb, *The Badge*, 147.

183 **"The few big books . . ."** Lait and Mortimer, *U.S.A. Confidential*, 157. | **Many gamblers get their** Ibid., 155, 156. | **Cecilia Potts . . . is the** Ibid., 157 | **In late 1952, Joe** "Sica Brothers and Three Others Begin Jail Term," *Los Angeles Times*, September 18, 1952. | **Mickey's bodyguard, Sam Farkas** Ibid.; "Sam Farkas, Ex-Guard of Cohen Beats Charge," *Los Angeles Times*, September 18, 1952. | **"But before that happy . . ."** Webb, *The Badge*, 147. | **"The episode [the Two . . ."** Demaris, *The Last Mafioso*, 60.

184 **In early 1954, Frattiano** Webb, *The Badge*, 150. | **The LAPD Intelligence Squad** Ibid., 150–154.

185 **In August 1955, elusive** "Jimmy Utley Jailed in Illegal Operation Raid," *Los Angeles Times*, September 2, 1956. | **Perhaps as a prelude** "Gang-Style Attempt to Kill Bingo King," *Los Angeles Times*, September 16, 1955. | **He was also busy** Stern, *No Innocence Abroad*, 40. | **Charlie Lucky shopped a** Ibid.

Chapter 18: Brave New World

188 **As he told Ben Hecht** Hecht, "The Incomplete Life of Mickey Cohen," 75, 76. | **"He was very miserable,"** Prager and Craft, *Hoodlums: Los Angeles*, 196.

191 **She would later admit** Jennings, "The Private Life of a Hood," *Saturday Evening Post*, September 27, 1958. | **In July 1956, he** Beckler, "Reformed Mickey Cohen, in Plant Business," Associated Press, July 4, 1956.

192 **On July 24, 1956** Reid, *Mickey Cohen: Mobster*, 189, 190. | **Ben Tue Wong, alias** Ibid., 190. | **Cohen's close associates Joe** "Two Sica Brothers Cleared of Burglary Assault," *Los Angeles Times*, February 8, 1957.

193 **Twenty-four-hour guards** Ibid.; "Sica Trial Interrupted By Spectator's Actions," *Los Angeles Times*, January 19, 1957. | **On August 16, federal** Reid, *Mickey Cohen: Mobster*, 190, 191.

194 **His old mainstay, the** Meyer Harris Cohen FBI file. | **His old fight managers** State of California, Subcommittee on Rackets, Organized Crime in California. Assembly Interim Committee Reports, 1957–59, 99. | **A chain letter, alleged** Meyer Harris Cohen FBI file. | **Miller, who had a** Reid, *Mickey Cohen: Mobster*, 191.

Chapter 19: Sacrificial Lamb

196 **The state's case was** "Sica Trial Interrupted by Spectator's Actions," *Los Angeles Times*, January 19, 1957.

197 **She also testified that** Ibid. | **The *Los Angeles Times*** Ibid.

198 **Hoping to annex his** Reid, *Mickey Cohen: Mobster*, 113–115. | **Mickey informed them: "I . . ."** Lyle and David, "Mickey Cohen and Billy Graham Pray and Read Bible Together," *New York Herald Tribune*, May 18, 1957; "Mickey Cohen See Billy Graham, Talks on Religion," *Los Angeles Times*, April 2, 1957. | **Reverend Vaus declared, "Michael . . ."** Ibid.

199 **When Wallace brought up** "Ex-Gangster Cohen Puts Foot in Mouth," *The*

Charleston Gazette, May 21, 1957. | **A female viewer called** "Mickey Cohen Asks Police Help," *Oakland Tribune,* May 20, 1957.

200   **In a patented move** Ibid. | **Immediately after the program** "Cohen's Blast Touches Off Study of FCC Regulations," *Cedar Rapids Gazette,* May 20, 1957. | **The news services reported** Ibid. | **Graham responded to the** "Ex-Gangster Cohen Puts Foot in Mouth," *The Charleston Gazette,* May 21, 1957.

202   **Before flying out of** "Will Sue Chief, Says Cohen," *Oakland Tribune,* May 23, 1957. | **He growled, "I didn't . . ."** "Gambler Cohen Pushes Fued Against L.A. Police," *Florence Morning News,* May 27, 1957. | **A lawyer representing him** "Cohen Aims New Salvo, Calls Chief 'A Totalitarian,'" *Long Beach Independent,* May 27, 1957. | **Cohen contended the LAPD** "Will Sue Chief, Says Cohen," *Oakland Tribune,* May 23, 1957. | **Coached by his coterie** "Cohen Aims New Salvo, Calls Chief 'A Totalitarian,'" *Long Beach Independent,* May 27, 1957.

203   **Claiming Parker was "a . . ."** Ibid. | **Parker told the United** "Will Sue Chief, Says Cohen," *Oakland Tribune,* May 23, 1957. | **He said that ABC** "Cohen Aims New Salvo, Calls Chief 'A Totalitarian,'" *Long Beach Independent,* May 27, 1957. | **"Any retractions by those . . ."** "Gambler Cohen Pushes Feud Against L.A. Police," *Florence Morning News,* May 27, 1957. | **Years later he said** Cohen and Nugent, *Mickey Cohen: In My Own Words,* 172.

204   **A product of the corrupt** Carter, *LAPD's Rogue Cops,* 74, 75. | **Immediately after becoming chief** Webb, *The Badge,* 253, 256. | **Chief Parker's techniques were** Gates, *Chief: My Life in the LAPD,* 71, 78, 79, 80, 81.

205   **Gates later remembered those** Ibid., 32. | **As to the degenerate** Cohen and Nugent, *Mickey Cohen: In My Own Words,* 172.

Chapter 20: Ink Junky

207   **But law enforcement agencies** Meyer Harris Cohen FBI file. | **Mickey had the inside** Aronowitz, "The Gift," TheBlackListedJournalist.com/column7a.html, March 1, 1996.

208   **It was easy for Mickey** Ibid. | **Syndicated columnist Walter Winchell** Meyer Harris Cohen FBI file; Reid, *Mickey Cohen Mobster,* 198.

209   **Fred Sica donned a** Hecht, "The Incomplete Life of Mickey Cohen," 63. | **Cohen would reward Sica** Reid, *Mickey Cohen: Mobster,* 202. | **Phil Packard, aka Philip** Jennings, "The Private Life of a Hood," *Saturday Evening Post,* September 27, 1958, 112. | **Wholesale appliance dealer George** Ibid. | **Under the name "Mr. Jones"** Ibid., 41, 110.

210   **"It was extraordinary. I . . ."** Interview with Dean Tavoularis, November 17, 2006. | **Long-suffering Lavonne, whose** Jennings, "The Private Life of a Hood," *Saturday Evening Post,* September 27, 1958, 112.

211   **"I was living in . . ."** Interview with Barbara Bain, December 19, 2004. | **In the eyes of** Jennings, "The Private Life of a Hood, *Saturday Evening Post,* October 8, 1958, 122. | **The young lawyer had** Ibid.

212   **The waiter hit back** Jennings, "The Private Life of a Hood," *Saturday Evening Post,* September 28, 1958, 114. | **The FBI followed Cohen** Meyer Harris Cohen FBI file.

214   **Mickey later claimed the** Cohen and Nugent, *Mickey Cohen: In My Own Words,* 174.

Chapter 21: The Oscar

215   At the strict all-male Crane, *Detour*, 201.

216   Stompanato once claimed to Turner, *Lana*, 204. | **Mickey's boys were "panicked . . ."** Cohen and Nugent, *Mickey Cohen: In My Own Words*, 196. | **Although often incorrectly described** Ibid., 185. | **Involved with legions of** Ibid., 186. | **The next month, he** "Hair Pulling Charged in Tone Custody Battle," *Los Angeles Times*, December 9, 1950.

217   **His criminal record was** State of California, Subcommittee on Rackets, Organized Crime in California. Assembly Interim Committee Reports, 1957–59, 98. | **According to the John** Document from John Stompanato's FBI file, included in Lana Turner FBI file (9-12601).

218   **Reportedly one of the boss's** Reid, *Mickey Cohen: Mobster*, 190. | **A United Press article** "Police Dig into Background of Lana's Slain Boyfriend," *Humboldt Standard*, April 17, 1958; "Stompanato Owed $80,000 in 'Loans,'" *Long Beach Independent*, April 17, 1958. | **"Handsome Johnny was one . . ."** Anderson, *Beverly Hills Is My Beat*, 69. | **In his syndicated "New . . ."** Meyer Harris Cohen FBI file. | **In divorce court Miss** "Cohen Takes Stand in His Own Defense," *Los Angeles Times*, June 19, 1957. | **At divorce proceedings she** Ibid. | **The actress testified he** Ibid.

219   **The theory was based** "Police Dig into Background of Lana's Slain Boyfriend," *Humboldt Standard*, April 17, 1958. | **By 1955, at age** Interview with Rosaline George, April 21, 2008. | **"Nice and polite, if . . ."** George, "I Remember Johnny!" unpublished article, 2. | **Assortments of women were** Interview with Rosaline George, April 21, 2008. | **One frequent visitor was** Ibid. | **A dignified widow, Mrs.** "Stompanato Owed $80,000 in 'Loans,'" *Long Beach Independent*, April 17, 1958. | **Several married tenants, and** Interview with Rosaline George, April 21, 2008.

220   **"But one day all . . ."** Ibid. | **When she was ten** Turner, *Lana*, 18, 19. | **She was sipping a** Ibid., 26, 27.

221   **A mysterious young man** Crane, *Detour*, 52–57. | **"A great dancer,"** Turner Ibid., 56. | **When stories of a** Phone interview with James Bacon, August 22, 2008. | **MGM's Louis B. Mayer** Crane, *Detour*, 56.

222   **Hollywood columnist Hedda Hopper** Ibid., 70 | **In 1946, he was** Ibid., 89, 90; Lana Turner FBI file. | **By 1948, Crane was** Crane, *Detour*, 89, 90, 106, 107. | **Daughter Cheryl Crane noted** Ibid., 128, 129. | **The reception, for sixty** Ibid., 102, 103. | **Topping told** *Life* **magazine** Ibid., 102.

223   **The servant circle that** Ibid., 149. | **When Cheryl told her** Ibid., 182, 183. | **Turner recalled in her** Turner, *Lana*, 200. | **When she asked Stompanato** Ibid., 200. | **Mickey recalled that she** Cohen and Nugent, *Mickey Cohen: In My Own Words*, 187.

224   **Occasionally Mickey would join** Crane, *Detour*, 226. | **Complaining about his own** Cohen and Nugent, *Mickey Cohen: In My Own Words*, 287, 288. | **George noted, "One Sunday . . ."** George, "I Remember Johnny!" unpublished article, 3, 4. | **Associated Press's Hollywood correspondent** Phone interview with James Bacon, August 22, 2008. | **Stompanato complained to actress** Calvet, *Has Corinne Been A Good Girl?*, 299–301.

225   **In a heated encounter** Phone interview with James Bacon, August 22, 2008;

Crane, *Detour*, 207–209. | **They stayed in the** Turner, *Lana*, 210, 218, 219, 228–233; Crane, *Detour*, 213. | **Impressed by her nomination** Turner, *Lana*, 221.

226 **"I received a telephone call . . ."** Anderson, *Beverly Hills Is My Beat*, 70. | **Simultaneously, Johnny's apartment was** Lana Turner FBI file; Anderson, *Beverly Hills Is My Beat*, 72. | **Beverly Hills Police Chief** Anderson, *Beverly Hills Is My Beat*, 72.

227 **The missing container reputedly** Ibid., 74–75. | **Mickey did his best** Crane, *Detour*, 243. | **He delivered Lana's love** Ibid., 243.

230 **Lana's feckless raptures became** Ibid., 243. | **Cheryl Crane wrote, "Mickey . . ."** Ibid., 238.

231 **"I saw them come . . ."** Testimony of Lana Turner at Los Angeles County coroner's inquest into the death of John Stompanato Jr., April 11, 1958.

Chapter 22: Bombshells and Bobby

233 **Shedding light on the** "Mickey Cohen Divorced as Bad Tempered," *Los Angeles Times*, June 18, 1958. | **Mickey's former sister-in-law supported** Ibid. | **"My lawyer says there's . . ."** Jennings, "Private Life of a Hood," *Saturday Evening Post*, September 20, 1958, 86.

235 **"She married a bookmaker . . ."** Confidential interview, April 10, 2003. | **"Cohen always liked to . . ."** Redston and Crossen, *The Conspiracy of Death*, 115. | **His much-publicized female** Cohen and Nugent, *Mickey Cohen: In My Own Words*, 176.

236 **On the periphery of** Renay, *My Face for the World to See*, 94–97. | **Her boyfriend was Anthony** Ibid., 97. | **Renay spent her first** Ibid., 240. | **While their relationship grew** Ibid., 153. | **The stunning blonde observed** of Ibid., 155.

237 **In her memoir, My** Ibid., 154. | **He told Renay that** Ibid. | **While working on Mickey's** Hecht, "The Incomplete Life of Mickey Cohen," 67. | **"He would kiss his . . ."** Confidential interview, November 10, 2001.

238 **From Renay, it was** Renay, *My Face for the World to See*, 176–180. | **As the first installment** Meyer Harris Cohen FBI file. | **Living up to the** Jennings, "The Private Life of a Hood," *Saturday Evening Post*, October 4, 1958, 30. | **But now it is** Jennings, "The Private Life of a Hood," *Saturday Evening Post*, October 11, 1958, 36. | **On taxes, he declared** Jennings, "The Private Life of a Hood," *Saturday Evening Post*, September 20, 1958, 86.

239 **On Chief Parker** Ibid. | **On his California Highway** Jennings, "The Private Life of a Hood," *Saturday Evening Post*, October 4, 1958, 121, 122. | **And he boldly talked** Jennings, "The Private Life of a Hood," *Saturday Evening Post*, October 11, 1958, 118. | **"Mickey, anxious for publicity . . ."** Zion, "On Ben Hecht," *Scanlon's*, 57.

240 **His father, Joseph P. Kennedy** Ogden, *Legacy*, 374. | **In the late 1920s** Swanson, *Swanson on Swanson*, 357, 404–407. | **Left in extreme financial** Ibid., 404–407. | **Mobster Frank Costello was** Russo, *Supermob*, 52, 97, 221, 221*n*. | **Bobby Kennedy, now in** "Gangs Used Union, Quiz Figure Says," *Los Angeles Times*, March 22, 1959.

243 **Khrushchev arose and with** Carlson, "Khrushchev in Hollywood," *Smithsonian*,

July 2009. | **In a final effort** Gates, *Chief*, 77, 78. | **"By then, the Feds . . ."** Ibid. | **Cohen's friends and associates** Renay, *My Face for the World to See*, 229.

244   **Born Juanita Dale Slusher** "Candy Barr Obituary," *Los Angeles Times*, January 3, 2006.

245   **Using the stage name Candy** Cartwright, "Candy," *Texas Monthly*, July 1978. | **"A victim . . . vulnerable, bright . . ."** Interview with Nino Tempo, August 10, 2008. | **Mickey gallantly stepped in** Cohen and Nugent, *Mickey Cohen: In My Own Words*, 176, 178.

246   **No well-mannered LaVonne** Ibid., 177. | **In June 1959, the** Meyer Harris Cohen FBI file. | **The Los Angeles County** Summers, *Goddess*, 235n. | **He had already announced** Cohen and Nugent, *Mickey Cohen: In My Own Words*, 178.

Chapter 23: End Games

248   **Private Eye Fred Otash** Otach, *Investigation Hollywood!*, 99. | **Fred Whalen, his father** Lieberman, "Tales from the Gangster Squad," *Los Angeles Times*, October 30, 2008.

249   **He quickly gained a** Redston and Crossen, *The Conspiracy of Death*, 111. | **Behind the bluster was** Ibid., 110–113; Lieberman, "Tales from the Gangster Squad," *Los Angeles Times*, October 29–30, 2008. | **Soon after the incident** Redston and Crossen, *The Conspiracy of Death*, 118. | **Rumors began circulating about** Meyer Harris Cohen FBI file; Redston and Crossen, *The Conspiracy of Death*, 112–118.

250   **It was imperative to** Redston and Crossen, *The Conspiracy of Death*, 118. | **The FBI noted in** Meyer Harris Cohen FBI file. | **The FBI believed that** Ibid. | **The Mafia boss of** Reid, *The Grim Reapers*, 64. | **Mickey raised a war** Redston and Crossen, *The Conspiracy of Death*, 119. | **LAPD Officer Gary Wean** Summers, *Goddess*, 234. | **On December 2, 1959** "Mickey Cohen Jailed in Murder of Bookie," *Los Angeles Times*, December 4, 1958.

252   **Walking into Chief Parker's** "Slayer of Bookmaker Surrenders to Police," *Los Angeles Times*, December 9, 1959.

253   **In March 1960, LoCigno** "LoCigno Found Guilty, Gets Life for Murder," *Los Angeles Times*, March 30, 1960. | **Recanting to the prison** Redston and Crossen, *The Conspiracy of Death*, 128–129. | **There he met with** Ibid. | **He never named the** Meyer Harris Cohen FBI file. | **The proprietor of the** Redston and Crossen, *The Conspiracy of Death*, 129. | **In hushed tones, he** Ibid.

254   **The mobster could be** Meyer Harris Cohen FBI file. | **Newspapers reported a car** "Mickey Buries His Bulldog," *Kingsport Times*, June 30, 1960. | **Cohen was seen outside** Meyer Harris Cohen FBI file.

256   **Special assistants from his** Ibid. | **Half of the Los** Ibid. | **"Paper evidence seemed to . . ."** Reid, *Mickey Cohen: Mobster*, 99. | **They were shown examples** Meyer Harris Cohen FBI file. | **Dr. Leonard Krause, a** Reid, *Mickey Cohen Mobster*, 104.

257   **Lewis kibitzed with Skelton** Lewis, *Hollywood's Celebrity Gangster*, 274. | **Charles Schneider, a tree** Reid, *Mickey Cohen Mobster*, 107. | **When the spectacle ended** "Mickey Cohen Tax Case Put in Jury's Hand," *Los Angeles Times*, June 29, 1961.

258   **Control of the rackets** Cohen and Nugent, *Mickey Cohen: In My Own Words*,

NOTES ON THE TEXT 311

205.

259 "No newspapers, no magazines . . ." Meagher, "Mickey Cohen Saddened by State of Society, Crime World," *Los Angeles Times*, February 15, 1974. | **When attorney Melvin Belli** "To the Editors," *Time*, July 21, 1975. | **Eighty-two days after his** Cohen and Nugent, *Mickey Cohen: In My Own Words*, 206. | **Eight years later, headed** Russo, *Supermob*, 343, 344, 344, 359. | **It was precipitated by** Ibid.

262 **Superior Court Judge Lewis** "Mickey Cohen, 3 Aides Cleared in L.A. Murder," *Eureka-Humboldt Standard*, April 19, 1962.

Chapter 24: Relic

263 **Mickey claimed that Kennedy** Cohen and Nugent, *Mickey Cohen: In My Own Words*, 214. | **The LAPD was informed** Meyer Harris Cohen FBI file.

264 **Wielding a three-foot iron** "Mickey Cohen Beaten by Fellow Prisoner," *Los Angeles Times*, August 15, 1963. | **Hit multiple times from** Meyer Harris Cohen FBI file. | **Neurosurgery was performed, saving** Ibid. | **Unsure as to the** Ibid.

265 **Cohen recalled, "They were . . ."** Cohen and Nugent, *Mickey Cohen: In My Own Words*, 236; Summers, *Goddess*, 244–252. | **Candy and Ruby had** "Candy Barr Obituary," *Los Angeles Times*, January 3, 2006. | **Some claimed Rosselli was** Collins, "The Man Who Kept Secrets," *Vanity Fair*, April 2001, 102; Bonanno, *Bound by Honor*, 301, 312.

271 **"Dapper, loquacious and free . . ."** Hertel and Martinez, " Mickey Cohen Will Be Released Today," *Los Angeles Times*, January 7, 1972. | **The crippled mobster told** "Mickey Cohen in First Visit to L.A. Parole Office," *Los Angeles Times*, January 25, 1972.

272 **Pips' owners included** *Playboy* Delugach, "Hefner Testifies About DiCarlo at N.J. Hearing," *Los Angeles Times*, January 13, 1982.

273 **Mickey's brother, seventy-year-old Harry** "Auto Kills Brother of Mickey Cohen," *Los Angeles Times*, January 17, 1973. | **From the Meyer Harris** Meyer Harris Cohen FBI file.

274 **Mickey liked an occasional** Ibid. | **Actress Lita Baron, the** Lewis, *Hollywood's Celebrity Gangster*, 321. | **The thirty-three-year-old brunette** "People," *Time*, September 1, 1975. | **Somewhat reconciled with his** "Mickey Cohen in First Visit to L.A. Parole Office," *Los Angeles Times*, January 25, 1972. | **At the Greater Los** Meagher, "Mickey Cohen Saddened by State of Society, Crime World," *Los Angeles Times*, February 15, 1974.

275 **In October 1974, major** Hazlett, "Mickey Cohen Aids Hearsts in Search for Daughter," *Los Angeles Times*, October 24, 1974; "Mickey Cohen Is Bizarre Sleuth in the Search for Patty Hearst," *Newsweek*, November 11, 1974.

277 **Of President Nixon, disgraced** Lewis, *Hollywood's Celebrity Gangster*, 323–324.

278 **As he reflected in** Cohen and Nugent, *Mickey Cohen: In My Own Words*, 82.

Selected Bibliography

Anderson, Clifton H. *Beverly Hills Is My Beat*. Englewood Cliffs, NJ: Prentice Hall, 1960.

Anderson, Jack and Fred Blumenthal. *The Kefauver Story*. New York: The Dial Press, 1956.

Anger, Kenneth. *Hollywood Babylon*. New York: Dell Publishing, 1975.

———. *Hollywood Babylon II*. New York: E.P. Dutton, 1984.

Bacall, Lauren. *Lauren Bacall by Myself*. New York: Ballantine Books, 1978.

Bacon, James. *Made in Hollywood*. Chicago: Contemporary Books, 1977.

Balsamo, William and George Carpozi Jr. *Crime Incorporated*. Far Hills, NJ: New Horizon Press, 1991.

Banham, Rayner. *Los Angeles: The Architecture of Four Ecologies*. London: Penguin, 1971.

Berman, Susan. *Easy Street*. New York: G.P. Putnam's Sons, 1981.

———. *Lady Las Vegas*. New York: T.V. Books, 1996.

Black, Shirley Temple. *Child Star*. New York: Ballantine Books, 1988.

Bonanno, Bill. *Bound by Honor*. New York: St. Martin's Press, 2000.

Bonelli, William G. *Billion Dollar Blackjack*. Beverly Hills: Civic Research Press, 1954.

Calvet, Corrine. *Has Corrine Been a Good Girl?* New York: St. Martin's Press, 1983.

Capozi Jr., George. *Bugsy*. New York: Pinnacle Books, 1973.

Carter, Vincent A. *LAPD's Rogue Cops*. Lucerne Valley, CA: Desert View Books, 1993.

Cassini, Oleg. *In My Own Fashion*. New York: Simon & Schuster, 1987.

Chandler, Raymond. *The Long Goodbye*. New York: Ballantine Books, 1953.

Cohen, Mickey, as told to John Peer Nugent. *Mickey Cohen: In My Own Words*. Englewood Cliffs, NJ: Prentice-Hall, 1975.

Colby, Robert. *The California Crime Book*. New York: Pyramid Books, 1971.

Connelly, Michael. *The Closers*. New York: Little, Brown, 2005.

Conrad, Harold. *Dear Muffo: 35 Years in the Fast Lane*. New York: Stein & Day, 1982.

Cox, Bette Yarborough. *Central Avenue: Its Rise and Fall.* Los Angeles: BEEM Press, 1996.

Crane, Cheryl with Cliff Jahr. *Detour: A Hollywood Story.* New York: Arbor House/ William Morrow, 1988.

Davies, Marion. *The Times We Had.* New York: Ballantine Books, 1975.

Demaris, Ovid and Ed Reid. *The Green Felt Jungle.* New York: Pocket Books, 1964.

———. *The Last Mafioso.* New York: Times Books, 1981.

Denton, Sally and Roger Morris. *The Money and the Power.* New York: Alfred A. Knopf, 2001.

Dunne, Dominick. *The Way We Lived Then.* New York: Crown, 1999.

Eig, Jonathan. *Get Capone.* New York: Simon & Schuster, 2010.

Eisenberg, Dennis, Uri Dan, and Eli Landau. *Meyer Lansky: Mogul of the Mob.* New York: Paddington Press, 1979.

English, T.J. *Havana Nocturne.* New York: William Morrow, 2008.

Fleming, E.J. *The Fixers.* Jefferson, NC: McFarland & Company, Inc., 2005.

Fowler, Will. *Reporters: Memoirs of a Young Newspaperman.* Malibu, CA: Roundtable Publishing, Inc., 1991.

Francis, Lee. *Ladies on Call.* Los Angeles: Holloway House Publishing, 1965.

Fried, Albert. *The Rise and Fall of the Jewish Gangster in America.* New York: Columbia University Press, 1993.

Friedrich, Otto. *City of Nets: A Portrait of Hollywood in the 1940s.* New York: Harper & Row, 1986.

Gabler, Neil. *An Empire of Their Own: How the Jews Invented Hollywood.* New York: Crown Publishers, 1988.

———. *Winchell.* New York: Alfred A. Knopf, 1994.

Gates, Daryl F. with Diane K. Shah. *Chief: My Life in the LAPD.* New York: Pantheon Books, 1992.

Giesler, Jerry and Peter Martin. *The Jerry Giesler Story.* New York: Simon & Schuster, 1960.

Goodman, Ezra. *The Fifty-Year Decline and Fall of Hollywood.* New York: Simon & Schuster, 1961.

Goodwin, Betty. *Chasen's: Where Hollywood Dined, Recipes and Memories.* Los Angeles: Angel City Press, 1996.

Gosch, Martin A. and Richard Hammer. *The Last Testament of Lucky Luciano.* Boston: Little, Brown, 1974.

Granlund, Nils T. *Blondes, Brunettes, and Bullets.* New York: David McKay, 1957.

Hanna, David. *Bugsy Siegel: The Man Who Invented Murder Inc.* New York: Belmont Tower Books, 1974.

Hecht, Ben. *A Child of the Century.* New York: Primus, 1954.

Heinmann, Jim. *Sins of the City.* San Francisco: Chronicle Books, 1999.

Henstall, Bruce. *Sunshine and Wealth: Los Angeles in the Twenties and Thirties.* San Francisco: Chronicle Books, 1984.

Hodel, Steve. *Black Dahlia Avenger.* New York: Arcade, 2003.

Hopper, Hedda and James Brough. *The Whole Truth and Nothing But.* Garden City, NY: Doubleday, 1963.

Horne, Gerald. *Class Struggles in Hollywood: 1930–1950.* Austin, TX: The University of Texas Press, 2001.

Howard, Jean. *Jean Howard's Hollywood*. New York: Harry Abrams, 1988.

Hull, Warren Robert with Michael B. Druxman. *Family Secret*. Tucson, AZ: Hats Off Books, 2004.

Jennings, Dean. *We Only Kill Each Other*. Englewood Cliffs, NJ: Prentice-Hall, 1967.

Kagenhoff, Benjamin C. *Dictionary of Jewish Names and Their History*. New York: Schocken Books, 1977.

Kanin, Garson. *Hollywood*. New York: Viking Press, 1974.

Katcher, Leo. *The Big Bankroll: The Life & Times of Arnold Rothstein*. New York: Da Capo Press, 1958.

Katz, Leonard. *Uncle Frank: The Biography of Frank Costello*. New York: Drake, 1973.

Kefauver, Estes. *Crime in America*. Garden City, NY: Doubleday, 1951.

Kelley, Kitty. *His Way: The Unauthorized Biography of Frank Sinatra*. New York: Bantam Books, 1986.

Lacey, Robert. *Little Man: Meyer Lansky and the Gangster Life*. Boston: Little, Brown, 1991.

Lait, Jack and Lee Mortimer. *U.S.A. Confidential*. New York: Crown Publishers, 1952.

Lambert, Gavin. *Nazimova*. New York: Alfred A. Knopf, 1997.

Lamparski, Richard. *Lamparski's Hidden Hollywood*. New York: Simon and Schuster, 1981.

Leaming, Barbara. *Orson Welles: A Biography*. New York: Viking, 1985.

Levinson, Peter J. *Tommy Dorsey: Livin' in a Great Big Way*. Cambridge, MA: Da Capo Press, 2005.

Lewis, Brad. *Hollywood's Celebrity Gangster: The Incredible Life and Times of Mickey Cohen*. New York: Enigma Books, 2007.

Lombard, Rav and Alexander Yochanan. *The Kohen's Handbook*. Jerusalem: Jerusalem Publications, 2005.

Manchester, William. *American Caesar*. New York: Little, Brown, 1978.

Mann, William J. *Behind the Screen*. New York: Viking, 2001.

McCoy, Alfred W. *The Politics of Heroin: CIA Complicity in the Global Drug Trade*. Brooklyn: Lawrence Hill Books, 1991.

McDougal, Dennis. *The Last Mogul: Lew Wasserman, MCA and Hidden Hollywood*. New York: Crown, 1998.

Messick, Hank. *The Beauties and the Beasts: The Mob in Show Business*. New York: David McKay, 1973.

———. *Lansky*. New York: G.P. Putnam's Sons, 1971.

———. *The Silent Syndicate*. New York: Macmillan, 1967.

Morella, Joe and Edward Z. Epstein. *Lana: The Public and Private Lives of Miss Turner*. New York: Citadel, 1971.

Muir, Florabel. *Headline Happy*. New York: Holt, Rinehart, Winston, 1951.

Munn, Michael. *The Hollywood Connection*. London: Robson Books, 1993.

Newman, Peter C. *The Bronfman Dynasty: The Rothschilds of the New World*. Toronto: McClelland & Stewart, 1978.

Newton, Jim. *Justice for All*. New York: Riverhead Books, 2006.

Niklas, Kurt with Larry Cortez Hamm. *The Corner Table*. Los Angeles: Tuxedo Press, 2000.

Otash, Fred. *Investigation Hollywood*. Chicago: H. Regnery, 1976.

Pestos, Spero. *Pin-up: The Tragedy of Betty Grable*. New York: G.P. Putnam's Sons, 1986.

Pitt, Leonard and Dale Pitt. *Los Angeles: A to Z*. Los Angeles: University of California Press, 1997.

Powdermaker, Hortense. *Hollywood, the Dream Factory: An Anthropologist Looks at the Movie Makers*. Boston: Little, Brown, 1950.

Prager, Ted and Larry Craft. *Hoodlums: Los Angeles*. New York: Retail Distributors, 1959.

Prall, Robert H. and Norton Mockridge. *This Is Costello*. New York: Gold Medal Books, 1951.

Pye, Michael. *Moguls: Inside the Business of Show Business*. New York: Holt, Rinehart & Winston, 1979.

Quigley, Martin. *International Motion Picture Almanac*. New York: Quigley Publishing, 1936–75.

Rappleye, Charles and Ed Becker. *All-American Mafioso: The Johnny Rosselli Story*. New York: Doubleday, 1991.

Rayner, Richard. *A Bright and Guilty Place*. New York: Doubleday, 2009.

Redston, George with Kendall C. Crossen. *The Conspiracy of Death*. Indianapolis, IN: The Bobbs-Merril Company, 1965.

Reid, Ed. *The Grim Reapers*. New York: Bantam Books, 1970.

———. *Mickey Cohen: Mobster*. New York: Pinnacle Books, 1973.

Renay, Liz. *My Face for the World to See*. New York: Lyle Stuart, Inc., 1971.

Richardson, James H. *For the Life of Me: Memoirs of a City Editor*. New York: G.P. Putnam's Sons, 1954.

Riva, Maria. *Marlene Dietrich*. New York: Alfred A. Knopf, 1993.

Rose, Frank. *The Agency: William Morris and the Hidden History of Show Business*. New York: HarperCollins, 1995.

Rosenstein, Jack. *Hollywood Leg Man*. Los Angeles: Madison Press, 1950.

Rothmiller, Mike and Ivan G. Goldman. *L.A.'s Secret Police*. New York: Pocket Books, 1992.

Russo, Gus. *Supermob*. New York: Bloomsbury USA, 2006.

Samish, Arthur H. and Bob Thomas. *The Secret Boss of California: The Life and High Times of Art Samish*. New York: Crown, 1971.

Sarlot, Raymond and Fred E. Basten. *Life at the Marmont*. Santa Monica, CA: Roundtable, 1987.

Schulberg, Budd. *Moving Pictures: Memories of a Hollywood Prince*. New York: Stein and Day, 1983.

———. *What Makes Sammy Run?* New York: Vintage, Random House, 1941.

Server, Lee. *Robert Mitchum: Baby, I Don't Care*. New York: St. Martin's Press, 2001.

Sharp, Katherine. *Mr. and Mrs. Hollywood*. New York: Carroll & Graf, 2003.

Smith, John L. *The Animal in Hollywood*. New York: Barricade Book, 1998.

Starr, Kevin. *Americans and the California Dream: 1850–1915*. New York: Oxford University Press, 1973.

———. *The Dream Endures*. New York: Oxford University Press, 1997.

———. *Inventing the Dream*. New York: Oxford University Press, 1985.

———. *Material Dreams*. New York: Oxford University Press, 1990.

Stern, Michael. *No Innocents Abroad*. New York: Viking, 1953.

Stevens, Steve and Craig Lockwood. *King of the Sunset Strip*. Nashville, TN: Cumberland House, 2006.

Stoker, Charles. *Thicker'N Thieves*. Santa Monica, CA: Sidereal, 1951.

Stone, Eric. *The Wrong Side of the Wall*. Guilford, CT: The Lyons Press, 2004.

Stuart, Mark A. *Gangster: The Story of Longie Zwillman*. London: W.H. Allen, 1986.

Summers, Anthony. *The Arrogance of Power*. New York: Penguin, 2000.

———. *Goddess: The Secret Life of Marilyn Monroe*. New York: Macmillan, 1985.

———. *Official and Confidential: The Secret Life of J. Edgar Hoover*. New York: G.P. Putnam's Sons, 1993.

Swanson, Gloria. *Swanson on Swanson*. New York: Random House, 1980.

Thomas, Bob. *Clown Prince of Hollywood: The Antic Life & Times of Jack L. Warner*. New York: McGraw-Hill, 1990.

———. *King Cohn: The Life and Times of Harry Cohn*. New York: G.P. Putnam's Sons, 1967.

Tosches, Nick. *Dino: Living High in the Dirty Business of Dreams*. New York: Doubleday, 1992.

———. *King of the Jews*. New York: Ecco, 2005.

Turkus, Burton and Sid Feder. *Murder, Inc.* New York: Farrar, Strauss & Young, 1951.

Turner, Lana. *Lana: The Lady, the Legend, the Truth*. New York: Dutton, 1982.

Underwood, Agness. *Newspaperwoman*. New York: Harper's and Brothers, 1948.

United States Treasury Department, Bureau of Narcotics. *Mafia: The Government's Secret File on Organized Crime*. New York: Collins, 2007.

Valentine, Douglas. *The Strength of the Wolf: The Secret History of America's War on Drugs*. London: Verso, 2004.

Vaus, Jim and D.C. Haskins. *Why I Quit Syndicated Crime*. Wheaton, IL: Van Kampen Press, 1952.

Vaus, Will. *My Father Was a Gangster*. Washington, DC: Believe Books, 2007.

Wanger, Walter. *Beverly Hills: Inside the Golden Ghetto*. New York: Grosset & Dunlap, 1976.

Warner, Jack L. with Dean Jennings. *My First Hundred Years in Hollywood*. New York: Random House, 1965.

Webb, Jack. *The Badge*. New York: Thunder's Mouth Press, 1958.

Weller, Sheila. *Dancing at Ciro's*. New York: St. Martin's Press, 2003.

Wilkerson III, W.R. *The Man Who Invented Las Vegas*. Beverly Hills, CA: Ciro's Books, 2000.

Winters, Shelley. *Shelley*. New York: Ballantine Books, 1980.

Wolf, George with Joseph Di Mona. *Frank Costello: Prime Minister of the Underworld*. New York: Morrow, 1974.

Wolf, Marvin J. and Katherine Mader. *Fallen Angels*. New York: Ballantine Books, 1986.

Wolfe, Donald H. *The Black Dahlia Files*. New York: Regan Books, 2005.

Wolsey, Serge G. *Call House Madam*. San Francisco, CA: The Martin Tudordale Corp., 1954.

Woon, Basil. *Incredible Land*. New York: Liveright Publishing Corporation, 1933.

Young, Paul. *L.A. Exposed*. New York: St. Martin's Press, 2002.

Zevon, Crystal. *I'll Sleep When I'm Dead*. New York: Ecco Press, 2007.

Zion, Sidney. *Loyalty and Betrayal: The Story of the American Mob*. San Francisco, CA: Collins Publishers, 1994.

Photo Credits

Watson Family Photographic Archive: 12, 70, 87, 128, 129, 132, 135, 167, 169, 197, 234 (bottom), 236.

Author's collection: 23 (from FBI file #755912), 35, 120 (from FBI file #755912), 127, 193.

UCLA Charles E. Young Research Library Department of Special Collections, Los Angeles Times Photographic Archives. © Regents of the University of California, UCLA Library: 30, 32, 78, 95, 111, 139, 164, 184, 221, 273, 275, 277.

Courtesy of University of Southern California, on behalf of the USC Specialized Libraries and Archival Collections: 31, 34, 42, 85, 90, 91, 93, 119, 123, 126, 143, 145, 149, 155, 159, 168, 171, 175, 181, 205, 213, 226, 227, 234 (top), 235, 252, 260, 261.

Herald-Examiner Collection/Los Angeles Public Library: 66, 97, 217, 229, 231.

David Mills/ShutterPoint Photography: 189.

Ben Hecht Collection, Newberry Library, *New York Herald Tribune*. April 6, 1957: 201.

AP Photo: 241 (Henry Griffin), 244, 251 (HPM).

Bill Walker/Los Angeles Public Library: 255.

Index